THE SOVIET UNION AND THE PLO

ST ANTONY'S SERIES
General Editors: Alex Pravda (1993–97), Eugene Rogan (1997–), both Fellows of St Antony's College, Oxford

Recent titles include:

Mark Brzezinski
THE STRUGGLE FOR CONSTITUTIONALISM IN POLAND

Peter Carey (*editor*)
BURMA

Stephanie Po-yin Chung
CHINESE BUSINESS GROUPS IN HONG KONG AND POLITICAL
CHANGE IN SOUTH CHINA, 1900–25

Ralf Dahrendorf
AFTER 1989

Alex Danchev
ON SPECIALNESS

Roland Dannreuther
THE SOVIET UNION AND THE PLO

Noreena Hertz
RUSSIAN BUSINESS RELATIONSHIPS IN THE WAKE OF REFORM

Iftikhar H. Malik
STATE AND CIVIL SOCIETY IN PAKISTAN

Steven McGuire
AIRBUS INDUSTRIE

Yossi Shain and Aharon Klieman (*editors*)
DEMOCRACY

William J. Tompson
KHRUSHCHEV

Marguerite Wells
JAPANESE HUMOUR

St Antony's Series
Series Standing Order ISBN 0–333–71109–2
(*outside North America only*)

You can receive future titles in this series as they are published by placing a standing order.
Please contact your bookseller or, in case of difficulty, write to us at the address below with
your name and address, the title of the series and the ISBN quoted above.

Customer Services Department, Macmillan Distribution Ltd
Houndmills, Basingstoke, Hampshire RG21 6XS, England

The Soviet Union and the PLO

Roland Dannreuther
Lecturer, Department of Politics
University of Edinburgh

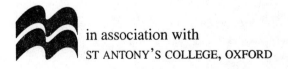

in association with
ST ANTONY'S COLLEGE, OXFORD

First published in Great Britain 1998 by
MACMILLAN PRESS LTD
Houndmills, Basingstoke, Hampshire RG21 6XS and London
Companies and representatives throughout the world

A catalogue record for this book is available from the British Library.

ISBN 0–333–68220–3

First published in the United States of America 1998 by
ST. MARTIN'S PRESS, INC.,
Scholarly and Reference Division,
175 Fifth Avenue, New York, N.Y. 10010

ISBN 0–312–17223–0

Library of Congress Cataloging-in-Publication Data
Dannreuther, Roland.
The Soviet Union and the PLO / Roland Dannreuther.
p.   cm. — (St. Antony's series)
Includes bibliographical references.
ISBN 0–312–17223–0 (cloth)
1. Munaẓẓamat al-Taḥrīr al-Filasṭīnīyah.   2. Soviet Union—Foreign
relations—Middle East.   3. Middle East—Foreign relations—Soviet
Union.   I. Title.   II. Series.
DS119.7.D257 1997
327.47056'09'045—dc21   97–37888
                                                             CIP

This book is printed on paper suitable for recycling and made from fully managed and
sustained forest sources.

10   9   8   7   6   5   4   3   2   1
07   06   05   04   03   02   01   00   99   98

Printed in Great Britain by
The Ipswich Book Company Ltd
Ipswich, Suffolk

To my Mother and Father

Contents

Acknowledgements

My foremost thanks must go to Professor Avi Shlaim who acted as my supervisor for the original dissertation upon which this book is based. Avi provided me with the necessary support and encouragement to pursue research into the seemingly impenetrable and secretive relationship between the Soviet Union and the PLO. I am grateful for Avi's thoughtful advice throughout my postgraduate studies at Oxford, and his diligence and conscientious efforts in guiding me safely through the pitfalls and obstacles of research.

This book is associated with happy memories of a number of places and friends. At St Antony's College, I remember with affection the Middle East Centre and the friends I made there – Maha Azzam, Reem Mikhail, Khaled Fahmy and Tareq Tell. In Moscow, I had the pleasure to be a guest of the Oriental Institute and I would like to thank the friends I made there – Vitalii Naumkin, Irina Zviagelskiaia, Dmitry Makharov and Brian Harvey. In the Middle East, I would like to extend my appreciation to Dr Nabil Haidari at the PLO Research Centre in Cyprus and to Marai' Abd al-Rahman and Sulaymann al-Najjab from the PLO headquarters in Tunis for all the help they gave me in furthering my research. In addition, I wish to express my gratitude for all the help and support my friends have given me, in particular Sonali Wijeyaratne, Julia Hawkings, Laura Monaghan and Agnès Guinebert.

Finally, I would like to thank my parents for all their help and support during my many years of student life.

List of Abbreviations

ALF	Arab Liberation Front
CPSU	Communist Party of the Soviet Union
DFLP	Democratic Front for the Liberation of Palestine
ICP	Israeli Communist Party
INA	Iraqi News Agency
JCP	Jordanian Communist Party
LCP	Lebanese Communist Party
LNM	Lebanese National Movement
KUNA	Kuwaiti News Agency
MEiMO	Mirovaia ekonomika i mezhdunarodnye otnosheniia
MENA	Middle East News Agency
NATO	North Atlantic Treaty Organization
QNA	Qatari News Agency
MFA	Ministry of Foreign Affairs of the USSR
PCP	Palestine Communist Party
PDFLP	Popular Democratic Front for the Liberation of Palestine
PFLP	Popular Front for the Liberation of Palestine
PFLP-GC	Popular Front for the Liberation of Palestine – General Command
PLA	Palestine Liberation Army
PLF	Palestine Liberation Front
PLO	Palestine Liberation Organization
PNC	Palestine National Council
PNF	Palestine National Front
PNSF	Palestine National Salvation Front
PPS	Progressive Socialist Party
PPSF	Palestine People's Struggle Front
PRM	Palestine Resistance Movement
SCP	Syrian Communist Party
SEATO	South East Asia Treaty Organization
SKSSAA	Soviet Afro-Asian Solidarity Committee
UAK	United Arab Kingdom
UNIFIL	United Nations Interim Forces in Lebanon
WAFA	Palestine News Agency
WAKH	Gulf News Agency
WCPD	Weekly Compilation of Presidential Documents

Introduction

In 1988, when I first started to research the subject of this book for my doctoral dissertation, the Soviet–PLO relationship appeared to be in an unusually healthy condition. There was a genuine optimism that the new-found political dynamism of the Soviet Union and the PLO, which was reflected in their bilateral relations, might herald a breakthrough in the Arab–Israeli peace process. Both the Soviet Union and the PLO were enjoying a political renaissance in the region. While Mikhail Gorbachev was breathing new life into Soviet foreign policy through the promotion of his 'new thinking', the foreign policy equivalent to *glasnost* and *perestroika*, the PLO was engaged in a political reform process which culminated in the historic decision in 1988 to recognize Israel. During 1989 the dynamic was maintained as the Soviet foreign minister, Eduard Shevardnadze, embarked on an extensive tour of the Middle East, promoting the virtues of 'new thinking' for the resolution of the region's conflicts and regularly praising the PLO's decision to recognize Israel as an example of such radical new strategic thinking. During this period, the Soviet and PLO leadership clearly believed that it was only a question of time before the United States and Israel would have to accept the logic of the long-standing Soviet demand for a comprehensive peace settlement which would include the participation of the PLO.

In reality, Shevardnadze's 1989 tour proved to be a false dawn. Immediate hopes for a breakthrough subsided as Israel persuaded the United States that the Soviet Union should remain excluded from the peace process. As 1989 progressed, the internal crisis within the Soviet empire increasingly consumed Moscow's energies and, by the end of the year, the Soviet Union effectively ceased to be a major regional actor in the Middle East. As Soviet power waned, so the Soviet–PLO relationship rapidly deteriorated. Relations became increasingly acrimonious and bitter as Gorbachev permitted the large-scale emigration of Soviet Jews into Israel. The dissolution of the Soviet Union in 1991 finally concluded a relationship which was already practically defunct. During this period, the PLO also experienced a crisis almost as severe as that faced by the Soviet Union. After the defeat of Iraq in the Gulf War, the PLO's alliance with the Iraqi dictator exacted a heavy penalty. With the loss of the support of much of the moderate Arab world, in particular the financial support of the Gulf states, the PLO was under a real threat of extinction. It was only through the unprecedented step of seeking a peace directly with Israel that the PLO, through the Oslo Accords in 1993, managed to regain some of its tarnished authority and to ensure it retained its right to be the legitimate representative of the Palestinian people.

Thus, in the short period from 1988 to 1991, the extraordinary pace of events and developments had thoroughly changed the subject matter of my proposed research. The Soviet Union had ceased to exist and the PLO had been fundamentally transformed. More significantly, the Soviet–PLO relationship, which had in 1988 appeared to be of immediate policy relevance, had been reduced to a seemingly anachronistic concern with a strictly limited historical value or interest. In 1991, it was also unavoidable to conclude that the Soviet–PLO relationship was a historical failure. For the Soviet Union, its close relations with the PLO never gained the prize of Soviet participation in a superpower-sponsored international conference which the Soviet leadership had so earnestly sought from the 1970s onwards. For the Palestinians, the PLO's relationship with the Soviet Union followed an unfortunate Palestinian tendency to support the wrong strategic allies. Just as the Palestinians suffered from their leadership's support for Nazi Germany in the Second World War and for Iraq in 1990–1, so the PLO's strategic alliance with the Soviet Union ended ultimately in bitter disappointment.

With such a disappointing and negative conclusion to the Soviet–PLO relationship, there inevitably arises the question of the value of an in-depth historical study of this relationship. The first point in its favour is that, although the Soviet Union has ceased to exist, the Arab–Israeli peace process has continued to be a central feature of Middle East politics. Admittedly, Russia – as the successor state to the Soviet Union – has not played a major role in this process but there are at least some elements of continuity. But, of greater significance is that the legacy of the Soviet contribution to the peace process has remained an issue of contemporary interest and debate. For over twenty years, the Soviet Union was a direct and influential external actor in the Arab–Israeli conflict, whose objectives and goals continue to be a source of controversy. There remain disputes over whether the Soviet Union was, as many analysts contend, an unambiguously negative actor who continually sought the destabilization of the region or whether more positive evaluations of the Soviet contribution might be a more accurate reflection of Soviet ambitions.

This question of assessing the Soviet role in the Arab–Israeli conflict is a central concern of this book. In addressing this question, there are clear benefits in being able to approach the Soviet–PLO relationship as a purely historical rather than a constantly developing and evolving subject. With the collapse of the Soviet Union in 1991, the Soviet–PLO relationship had a clear beginning, middle and end which makes it possible to tell the full and comprehensive story of the relationship. Although the policy relevance of the Soviet–PLO relationship might have been undermined, there is the clear advantage of being able to make a more definitive and, without the ideological tensions of the Cold War, perhaps more objective assessment of what the Soviet Union was seeking to achieve in its policies towards the PLO. It is also possible to locate this relationship within the wider context of a historically delimited Soviet involvement in the Middle East. It is now clear that the Soviet Union had only a brief period of intensive engagement with the Arab world – from about 1955 to 1991 – which was even shorter than Britain's Middle Eastern 'moment', as Elizabeth Monroe famously described Britain's short-lived hegemony of the region.[1]

The Soviet–PLO relationship also provides an excellent prism for understanding this wider context of the overarching Soviet engagement in the Middle East. This is because, as Soviet officials were frequently to complain, the PLO refracted the political and ideological divisions of the Arab world. The unusualness of the PLO as a faction-ridden, ideologically divided non-state actor, which was critically dependent on other Arab states for its existence and sustenance, made it a complex organization for Soviet policy-makers to deal with. Soviet leaders and diplomats had to balance their relations with the PLO on many different levels. There was the need to develop relations with the PLO as a collective body on the one hand, and with the independent factions which constituted the major power blocs within the PLO on the other. On a higher level, there was the necessity of managing relations with the PLO and those Arab states closely aligned to the Soviet Union, such as Egypt (at least in the late 1960s and early 1970s) and Syria with whom the PLO frequently had tense and conflictual relations. In addition, the Soviet Union had to consider its global and superpower interests and seek to ensure that its relationship with the PLO also contributed to the realization of these interests, in particular through securing US recognition of the Soviet Union's right to be an equal partner in any settlement of the Arab–Israeli conflict.

The study of Soviet policy towards the PLO involves an analysis of all these different levels and thus offers insights into a wider policy framework than that normally associated with studies strictly focused on bilateral relations. As such, it provides a number of critical insights into the wider Soviet relations with the Arab world and Moscow's overarching ambitions towards the Arab–Israeli conflict. Thus, to some extent, the seemingly narrow study of the Soviet relationship with the PLO does act as a prism more broadly illuminating some of the most critical features of the 'Soviet moment' in the region.

As well as this broader regional and international perspective, the study of Soviet–PLO relations also offers important insights into the interaction between the Soviet Union's strategic and ideological interests in the Middle East. The Soviet–PLO relationship was always a difficult and uneasy relationship with the PLO regularly enjoying, and regularly losing, favour with Moscow. In part, the warmth of Moscow's embrace of the PLO reflected a *realpolitik* assessment of the relative strategic value of the organization; for example, Moscow's interest in the organization increased when Egypt shifted towards the United States in the mid-1970s. However, such fluctuations in the relationship also reflected changing Soviet perceptions of the ideological soundness and loyalty of the PLO. Soviet officials constantly fretted about the disunity and ideological heterogeneity of the PLO which led to differing views about whether the PLO was an unacceptable reactionary and capitulationist force; or an equally undesirable extremist 'infantile leftist' and terrorist organization; or whether it was an objectively progressive and anti-imperialist national liberation movement. Through an analysis of the strategic and ideological components of Soviet policy towards the PLO, the study of these relations provides insights into the more general role that ideology played in Soviet policy towards the Middle East.

This book, therefore, seeks to provide a comprehensive analysis of Soviet policy towards the Palestinian dimension of the Arab–Israeli conflict. The principal focus of the study is the evolution of the relationship between the Soviet Union and the Palestine Liberation Organization (PLO) from the formation of the organization in 1964 to the dissolution of the Soviet Union in 1991. However, attention is also given to the elements of continuity in Soviet and Russian involvement in the Palestinian question, both looking backwards to earlier Soviet and Tsarist Russian periods and to the more recent developments in post-Soviet Russia's engagement in the Middle East. The book also seeks, through the analysis of the Soviet–PLO relationship, to provide insights into the history of the 'Soviet moment' in the region and to assess the contribution that the Soviet Union made to the resolution of the Arab–Israeli conflict. In addition, the study seeks to offer insights into Soviet policy-making, with particular attention to how ideological factors influenced and constrained Soviet foreign policy.

THE STRUCTURE OF THE BOOK

The structure of the book essentially follows the chronological development of the Soviet relationship with the PLO. For those readers seeking a quick glance of the contents of the book, each chapter starts with a brief summary of the contents and major conclusions of that particular chapter.

1 Framework of Soviet Engagement in the Arab–Israeli Conflict

By the time of the formation of the Palestine Liberation Organization in 1964, the Soviet Union had already been deeply involved in the affairs of the Middle East. Indeed, some of the influences on Soviet policy can been traced back to the Russian Imperial involvement in the affairs of the Ottoman empire, which included an active interest in the region of Palestine. However, the Soviet Union developed its own distinctive set of policies which reflected its specific interests in response to the tumultuous geostrategic changes in the Middle East after the dissolution of the Ottoman Empire. Two developments in Soviet policy-making towards the Middle East and the Palestine question were of particular significance. The first was the decision made by Stalin in 1947 to support the partition of Palestine and subsequently to provide substantial diplomatic and material support to the creation of the state of Israel. The second was the decision by Stalin's successor, Nikita Khrushchev, to sanction the Czechoslovak arms deal with Egypt in 1955, which initiated the Soviet commitment to the radical Arab nationalist regimes in their confrontation with the West and with Israel.

This chapter provides an overview of the reasons for these critical developments in Soviet policy-making prior to the mid-1960s and the emergence of the PLO as an independent actor in the region. It is argued that, in this earlier formative period, there had gradually emerged a reasonably coherent and internally consistent framework for Soviet engagement in the Arab–Israeli conflict, which then set the parameters for its policy towards the Palestine Resistance. This framework also remained substantially intact throughout the duration of the Soviet–PLO relationship up to the demise of the Soviet Union in 1991. The objective of this chapter is to provide the broad outlines of this framework as a background to the more detailed historical analysis of the Soviet–PLO relationship covered in following chapters.

The chapter has four sections. The first section deals with the legacy of Russian Imperial policy towards the Middle East and the elements of continuity with subsequent Soviet policy. The second section provides

7

the background to Stalin's decision to support the creation of the state of Israel and the impact this had on subsequent Soviet policy towards the Arab–Israeli conflict. In particular, attention is focused on how Soviet policy-makers resolved the seeming contradiction between recognition of Israel's right to exist and Soviet ideological hostility towards Zionism. The third section assesses the reasons behind Khrushchev's decision to support radical Arab nationalism in the Middle East and how the Soviet Union sought to manage the reality that many of these regimes remained indifferent or even antagonistic towards communism and tended to be more interested in their own regional inter-Arab disputes.

The final section sets out the broad framework which had emerged by the mid-1960s, defining the parameters of Soviet policy towards the Middle East and the Arab–Israeli conflict. Although much of this framework was driven by a realist determination to assert Soviet national security and Great Power interests, ideology also played a highly significant role – a role which has tended to be ignored or minimized by other analysts. How these inputs to foreign policy were filtered through the foreign policy bureaucracy and institutions which subsequently dealt with the PLO is then assessed.

CONTINUITY AND CHANGE – FROM RUSSIA TO THE SOVIET UNION

Russian linkages with the Middle East can be traced back to the early history of the Russian state when Vladimir, Grand Duke of Kiev, was baptised a Christian by the Byzantines in the tenth century. The fall of Constantinople in 1453 left the Russian church as the principal independent seat of Eastern Orthodoxy and the city of Moscow proclaimed itself as a third Rome and assumed the functions of Constantinople. Although these religious credentials were a vital source of legitimation for Tsarist rule – the title of 'Tsar' being a term traditionally used of the Byzantine Emperors – it was over a century before Russia was in any position to advance its pretensions as the heir of Byzantium. In the intervening period, Russian rulers were engaged in the task of unifying their state and expelling the Tatar invaders. However, in 1570 Russia succeeded in countering an Ottoman invasion of Astrakhan which was to be the forerunner of many subsequent clashes. By the late seventeenth century, Russian forces were regularly in armed conflict with the Turks, fighting seven wars between 1676 and 1812, and forcing a number of concessions from the Sublime Porte.

The growing Russian involvement in the affairs of the Ottoman Empire was driven by a mixture of strategic and religio-ideological interests. The principal strategic objectives were to prevent the encroachment of any hostile powers on its southern borders and to wrest control of the Turkish straits from Ottoman control, so as to secure a free passage for Russian warships from their Black Sea bases to the Mediterranean. This ambition was pursued within the wider geostrategic rivalry between the major European powers – Britain, France and Germany – who continually competed with each other to secure their specific interests and objectives. As a relatively recent and only reluctantly recognized Great Power, Russia was particularly concerned that its voice should be heard in determining the future of the ailing Ottoman empire. However, Russia's key objective of gaining control of the Turkish straits was never realized. Despite fighting three wars over this objective – in 1853, 1876 and 1914 – success was always thwarted by the British determination to leave the straits in Turkish hands and to ensure that Russia did not succeed in becoming a Mediterranean power, thereby threatening Britain's communication route to India.[1]

Russia's religio-ideological, as against its strategic, interests were more prominent in two other concerns that Russia had in the internal affairs of the Ottoman empire. The first was the presence of large numbers of Slavs and Orthodox Christians in the territories under Ottoman control. This was initially a specifically religious interest and in the 1774 Treaty of Küçük Kaynarca Russia gained the right to make representations to the Sublime Porte on behalf of the Orthodox community. In the nineteenth century, this religious interest converged with the militant ideology of Panslavism, which had a broad base of support inside Russia and was in some ways the official ideology of Imperial Russia.[2] The principal objective of this ideology was to secure the liberation of the Slavs under Turkish rule, with attention primarily focused on the European Slavic territories of the Ottoman empire. However, there were also significant strands in Panslavist thought which sought to extend this liberation to the non-Slav but nevertheless Orthodox Christians, such as the Greeks and Arabs. Dostoevskii was a fervent advocate for this more ambitious Panslavist cause, expressing his conviction that 'Constantinople must be ours, even if it should take another century' and that 'the Eastern Question [is] nothing other than the liberation of Orthodox Christianity as a whole and the future unity of the Church'.[3] He also believed that the Second Coming of Christ would occur in a country under the Russian flag, implicitly suggesting that the Arab countries of the Middle East would also be under Russian tutelage.[4]

The second Russian concern was with Palestine and the fact that the Holy Places, particularly Jerusalem, were under Ottoman sovereignty. Despite the severe difficulties involved, Russian pilgrims had continued to make their journey to the Holy Land throughout the centuries. In 1700, after the Treaty of Carlowitz, their passage was made easier when Russian subjects were allowed free access to Palestine and the Holy Places. A large part of Russian interest in Jerusalem involved providing support for these pilgrims which, at their zenith in the year 1900, numbered over 11,000. After the Greek national uprising had led to the granting of Greek autonomy in 1829, Russia promoted its claim to protect Orthodox subjects more forcefully and its involvement in Orthodox affairs in Syria, of which Palestine was then a part, increased. In 1839, a Russian Consulate to Syria and Palestine was established in Beirut which was then followed by the setting up of a Russian mission to Jerusalem in 1857.

The formation of the Imperial Orthodox Palestine Society in 1882 represented the most intensive Imperial Russian engagement in Palestinian affairs. Although the society had important supporters in the Russian religio-political establishment, most notably the arch-reactionary Procurator of the Holy Synod, Konstantin Pobedonostsev, its mission was principally in educational and charitable work and relied heavily on private rather than public donations. Nevertheless, its impact on the Arab Orthodox communities in Palestine and Syria was considerable; the Society managed in 1905 over 77 schools and 9,000 pupils. Also, although the principal objective of the Society was to ensure that Protestant and Catholic missionaries did not expand their activities among the Orthodox communities, Russian officials gave much moral and diplomatic support for the Arab Orthodox subjects to assert their independence from the Greek-dominated religious hierarchy and, indirectly, from Turkish control. By so doing, Russia supported the first flowering of an Arab nationalist sentiment among the Arab Orthodox community, which continued to develop and grow in strength during the period of the British mandate of Palestine. It is perhaps not accidental that the most well-known of the early books on Arab nationalism, *The Arab Awakening*, was written by an Arab Orthodox, George Antonius.[5]

Ironically, it was in the twilight days of Tsarist rule that Imperial Russia appeared to come closest to realizing its principal objectives in the Middle East. Once Turkey joined Germany in the war against the Entente powers in November 1914, Britain and France agreed to Russian claims to 'Constantinople, the left bank of the Bosphorus, the Sea of Marmara and the Dardanelles' in any prospective partition of the Ottoman empire. Although Russia submitted to French claims for Syria and Cilicia, it refused to surrender the Palestinian Holy Places to exclusive French control. A vague compromise on the future of the Holy Places was then agreed between the French and Russians. In the early part of 1915 many in Russia were expecting that the age-old dream of control of the Turkish straits and of Constantinople would finally be realized. Among the more excitable, there were discussions of the possible occupation of Palestine and even of a connecting corridor between Jaffa and the Caucasus.[6]

These dreams were to be dashed in the turbulence of the Russian revolution in 1917. In November 1917, the Bolshevik government in Petrograd publicly denounced the Tsarist agreements over the Near East and published the secret Sykes-Picot agreement which divided the region between Britain and France and provided for an international regime for Palestine. In the period of revolutionary turmoil, Lenin signalled that the new regime had more pressing concerns than the fate of Turkey and that it had no interest, given its self-confessed militantly atheistic ideology, in the future of the Palestinian Holy Places.

However, this seemingly decisive rupture in Soviet policy-making towards the Middle East was only to prove temporary. Like the early rulers of Russia, the new Bolshevik leaders needed first to focus their energies on unifying the Soviet state and repelling the interventions of foreign powers. But, once these objectives had been achieved and the Soviet state had regained most of the territory of the Tsarist imperium, the traditional Russian national security and strategic interests reasserted themselves. As in Tsarist times, the Middle East, being a region directly contiguous to the southern borders of the Soviet Union, was seen as a vital component of the Soviet defence territory and control of the Turkish straits as a critical strategic objective. Indeed, the Soviet Foreign Ministry statement of 16 April 1955 could almost have been written a century earlier, most notably in its assertion that:

> Of course, the Soviet Union cannot remain indifferent to the situation arising in the Near and Middle East ... [which] has a direct bearing on the security of the USSR. The attitude of the Soviet government should be all the more understandable, since the USSR is situated very close to these countries.[7]

Just as Russian strategic interests in the Middle East regained their importance, the role of ideology in determining Soviet interests in the region had striking parallels with the Russian Imperial past. Although the Soviet government jettisoned the religious commitment to Ortho-doxy and to Panslavist ideology, it promoted a secular revolutionary ideology with analogous millenarian ambitions and with a similarly confident expression of Russia's historic destiny. Moreover, the doc-trines of Marxism-Leninism included a specific role for the anti-colonial struggle in Asia, as Lenin emphasized at the Second Comintern Con-gress in 1920 when he predicted that 'the revolutionary proletarians of the capitalist, advanced countries' would be joined in the coming revol-ution by the 'oppressed masses of colonial, Eastern countries'.[8] Thus, the Soviet Union defined a new ideological basis for its involvement in the Middle East and a new set of allies – not the religious adherents of orthodox Christianity but the believers of the new faith of revol-utionary socialism.

There was, thus, a continuity of the form, if not the content, of Russian ideological interests in the Middle East. Imperial Russia's contribution to the Arab nationalist movement, which was subsequently vigorously promoted by the Soviet Union as part of the anti-imperial-ist struggle, was sometimes recognized by Soviet historians. One So-viet writer noted the degree of continuity when he observed that historically 'Russia [had] stood on the side of the liberation movement of the Arab peoples against Turkish slavery. Many Arab revolution-aries welcomed the victory of the Russian army over Turkey, the lib-eration of the Bulgarian people with Russian aid from the many centuries of Turkish slavery. Arab revolutionaries found in Russia a warm wel-come and hospitality.'[9]

The continued existence of the Imperial Orthodox Palestine Society, which in Soviet times was renamed the Russian Palestine Society, also pointed towards a certain degree of continuity. Although the society lost its intimate connection to the fate of Orthodoxy in Palestine, it became a new ideological forum for the communist world's defence of 'the rights of the Palestinian Arabs in their struggle against Zionist aggression'.[10] Just as Palestine, with its possession of the Holy Places, had been a central religious and ideological concern for Russia, so the Palestinian question in the twentieth century emerged as a critical Soviet concern in its ideological support for the national liberation movements of the Third World. As such, ideology and Palestine remained one key linkage from the Russian to the Soviet periods.

STALIN AND THE CREATION OF THE STATE OF ISRAEL

Nevertheless, in the period before the Second World War, the extent to which the Soviet Union could influence developments in the Middle East and in the growing Arab–Jewish conflict was distinctly limited. With the dissolution of the Ottoman empire, Britain and France assumed control of most of the Middle Eastern region and successfully blocked even the most limited Soviet penetration in the region. Constrained from any effective power projection, the Soviet Union could only influence developments through its interventions into the policy-making of local pro-Soviet communist parties.

The Palestine Communist Party (PCP) was established in 1924 and became the principal vehicle for advancing Soviet interests amongst the Jewish and Arab communities in mandate Palestine.[11] Although the PCP was never to gain great popularity, the evolution of the party's policies, and the constraints under which it operated, provide important insights into the difficulties of applying Soviet Marxist-Leninist ideology to the intensifying confrontation between Arabs and Jews. It was also in this period that some of the key features of the Soviet approach to the Palestinian problem were defined, which provide the background to the decision by Stalin to recognize and support the creation of the state of Israel in 1948.

The position of the PCP to the critical question of a Jewish national home was founded on two underlying principles which guided the Soviet approach to this issue. The first was the unambiguous identification of Zionism as a utopian and reactionary ideology and as a bourgeois-imperialist conspiracy directed towards weakening the national liberation movement in the Middle East. At the Second Congress of the Comintern, held in August 1920, an explicitly anti-Zionist clause confirmed this view:

> A glaring example of the deception practised on the working-classes of an oppressed nation by the combined efforts of Entente imperialism and the bourgeoisie of that same nation is offered by the Zionists' Palestine venture (and by Zionism as a whole, which, under the pretence of creating a Jewish state in Palestine in fact surrenders the Arab working people of Palestine, where the Jewish workers form only a small minority, to exploitation by England).[12]

The second principle was based on a distinction between Zionist Jews, who were linked to a chauvinist national bourgeoisie, and progressive anti-Zionist Jews, drawn from the ranks of the Jewish working class. The latter group was accepted as an integral part of the revolutionary anti-imperialist movement and, in Palestine, was deemed to be a progressive force in the struggle for national liberation from British colonialism.

It was on the basis of this latter principle that the Comintern decided to recognize the PCP in 1924, despite the fact that practically all the members of the party were Jewish.[13] But, particularly for a party with a majority Jewish membership, there remained a clear tension between its rigorously anti-Zionist stance and implicit support for the progressive role of the Jewish presence in Palestine. This tension was also a constant irritant in the relations between the party and the Comintern. The Comintern regularly criticized the PCP as focusing too much on the Jewish community and recommended the adoption of a programme of 'arabization'. Furthermore, the Comintern viewed this nationalist over-representation as the cause of the PCP's 'erroneous' interpretation of the August 1929 revolt in Palestine as an anti-Jewish pogrom rather than as a genuine anti-imperialist rebellion.[14]

During the 1930s, the PCP did implement an extensive 'arabization' programme and was successful in encouraging a sizeable number of Arabs to join the party. However, the party's internationalist political programme, and the visible Jewish dominance of the party, were significant obstacles to the development of a wide base of support among the Arab community. Moreover, as the Arab members secured a greater voice within the party, they promoted a more exclusive and implicitly nationalist Arab position, which alienated many members in the Jewish section of the party. The tensions between the Arab and Jewish sections of the party grew even more intense in the context of the Second World War and, in 1943, the party decisively split into its two national components.

The internal problems of the PCP provide the first indication of the difficulty that the Soviet Union would face in defining an ideologically acceptable internationalist critique of the Arab–Jewish conflict which was also attractive to the participants involved. The position of the PCP, like other communist parties elsewhere, also had to adapt to the changing strategic priorities of the Soviet Union. During the 1930s, the Soviet Union had consistently maintained a strong pro-Arab position and had unequivocally condemned the idea of an exclusively Jewish state in Palestine. However, after the German invasion of Soviet territory in mid-1941, there emerged a more nuanced and implicitly more sympathetic attitude to the Yishuv, the Jewish community in Palestine. In 1941, and early in 1942, there were a number of meetings between Soviet representatives and Zionist leaders, who tried to gain Soviet support for Jewish aims in Palestine. In the Summer of 1942, two Soviet diplomats went to Palestine to tour the Yishuv on the occasion of the establishment of a countrywide League for Friendly Relations with the USSR.[15]

The reason for this new Soviet openness to the Yishuv was the Jewish community's involvement in the anti-Nazi war effort, which contrasted with the Palestinian leadership's support for Hitler. The Soviet Union also hoped that a sympathetic reception of the Yishuv's aims would directly influence American Jewry, who would in turn bring pressure to bear on the US administration for the early establishment of a second front in Western Europe. In the latter part of the war, from 1943 onwards, Soviet interest was strengthened by the prospect that Palestine would become an urgent international issue at the end of the war. At Yalta in February 1945, Stalin secretly agreed with Roosevelt and Churchill to the consolidation of the Jewish national home in Palestine and to the opening of that country's doors to Jewish immigration in the immediate future.[16]

Despite this agreement, however, Stalin had still not committed himself to a fixed position on the future of Palestine. With the British decision in late February 1945 not to bring up the Palestine question in an international forum, the Soviet Union returned to a position of studied ambiguity. Most official commentaries adopted a wholehearted pro-Arab stance, such as a book published in 1946, which stated bluntly that Palestine was 'an Arab country' and that Zionism was the 'the propaganda of racist exclusivity and of racial superiority, totalitarianism, and the use of terror, together with social demagoguery'.[17] Yet, at the same time, the Soviet Union took a number of practical steps, which directly aided the Jewish cause. The most notable of these was the aiding and abetting of emigration from Eastern Europe, notably Poland, to the Western Occupation Zones of Austria and Germany, with the full knowledge that the emigrants intended to make their homes in Palestine.

The turning point in Soviet policy occurred in 1947. It was sparked by Britain's decision to refer the question of the Palestine mandate to the United Nations in February 1947. The British expectation was that the United States and the Soviet Union would be unable to adopt a common position, which would result in a UN decision to leave Palestine under British mandatory control.[18] The Soviet Union, however, was determined to forestall such an outcome. To the great surprise of the British government and to most of the rest of the world, on 14 May 1947 the Soviet Deputy Foreign Minister, Andrei Gromyko, indicated

that the Soviet Union would support the establishment of two independent states in Palestine, one Jewish and one Arab. On 13 October,
after many months of Soviet–US co-operation in the United Nations
over the Palestine question, the Soviet Union formally expressed its
approval of partition and the creation of a Jewish state. On 29 November 1947, the Soviet Union voted for UN General Assembly Resolution 181, which provided for the establishment of two independent
states in Palestine.

Gromyko's support for partition in May 1947 initiated an extraordinary period in Soviet–Israeli relations. The Soviet Union became the
most consistent and outspoken supporter for the new Jewish state. The
Israeli Foreign Minister Moshe Shertok frequently expressed his gratitude for the Soviet stance at the UN Security Council, at one time
remarking that Soviet officials acted 'as if they were our emissaries'.[19]
When the state of Israel was proclaimed at midnight on 14 May 1948,
the Soviet Union was the first country to offer *de jure* recognition of
the new country and then consistently pressed for Israel's admission
to the United Nations. In the subsequent invasion of Israel by the Arab
armies, the Soviet Union offered its unconditional support to Israel,
arguing that the Arab states were completely subservient to British
imperialist designs.[20] More significantly, the Soviet Union helped the
Jews with military training and sanctioned the supply of arms from
Czechoslovakia, the first consignment of which arrived in Palestine in
March 1948.[21] It is not an exaggeration to say that, without the un-
swerving support of the Soviet Union, the state of Israel might not
have been created and would probably not have survived the Arab
attack. In this sense, the Soviet Union made possible the fulfilment of
the Zionist dream.

The decision to recognize and support the creation of the state of
Israel was clearly promoted and sanctioned by Stalin. Why he should
have decided on this course of action has been the subject of much
controversy. However, it is highly unlikely that Stalin expected Israel
to become communist, given his rigid 'two camps' vision of international relations. Rather, Stalin's support was driven by more short-
term and opportunistic strategic objectives. First, the Palestine question
provided the Soviet Union with the opportunity to assert its new-found
international power as one of the select group of permanent members
in the UN Security Council. Second, the Soviet Union was determined
to use tactical flexibility in that forum to undermine British imperial
interests in the Middle East and, as an additional bonus, to exacerbate
US–British relations.[22]

Support for Israel in 1947–9 satisfied these wider Soviet ambitions perfectly. In the United Nations, the Soviet Union was shown to be a Great Power, whose point of view had to be respected over a vital international question. In the Middle East, the British lost their position in Palestine and the state of Israel created a wedge in Britain's overall control of the region. At the same time, the problem of Palestine had created tensions within the US–British alliance and in the internal politics of the United States. Moreover, the Soviet Union could, at least partially, conceal its activities in favour of Israel by focusing Arab resentment on US support for Israel and the Zionist enterprise. As Gromyko confidently predicted in his November 1947 speech at the United Nations, 'the time will come when Arabs and the Arab countries will more than once look in the direction of Moscow, expecting assistance from the Soviet Union in their struggle for their legitimate interests, in their striving to free themselves from the remaining strings of foreign dependence.'[23]

However, the Soviet Union could not entirely ignore the problematic question of how its support for Israel might be compatible with its ideological principles. Gromyko had come perilously close at his UN speech on 14 May 1947 to endorsing the fundamental tenets of the Zionist creed such as in the assertion that 'the aspirations of a considerable part of the Jewish people are linked with the problem of Palestine and its future administration.'[24] However, Gromyko and other Soviet officials were always careful, as in the above quotation, to speak of the 'Jewish people', the 'Jewish population' and the 'Jews', but not of 'Zionism' or 'Zionists'. There was never any indication that Zionism itself had become an acceptable creed or that it had ceased to be seen as a negative and reactionary form of national chauvinism.

This dualistic approach to the Jewish national question in Palestine was grounded in the ideological distinction between Zionist Jews and progressive anti-Zionist Jews, which had provided the political foundations of the PCP. But the Soviet position of 1945–7 extended this distinction in a radically new direction. While previously only sections of the Jewish community were seen to be progressive, Stalin now asserted that the whole Jewish community in Palestine had been transformed into a dynamic, progressive, anti-imperialist force. In this new perspective, the Yishuv, through its armed resistance to British rule in Palestine, was acting as an ideal national liberation movement, inflicting decisive blows to British power and imperialism in the Middle East.

This interpretation of the historically progressive role of the Jewish community at this particular historical juncture was to become embedded as part of Soviet orthodox thinking even when, in later years, the Soviet Union supported the Arab nationalist regimes in opposition to Israel. But it was to cause considerable headaches for academic apologists of Soviet involvement in the Middle East. The central problem was how to avoid the implication that, by supporting the partition of Palestine, the Soviet Union did not also indirectly support the creation of a Zionist state. The most common line of argument was that the partition resolution was a just solution but it was thwarted by British support of Arab reaction and American manipulation of Zionist extremism.[25] The less frequent, and far less plausible, line of argument was that there were significant Jewish anti-Zionist forces in Palestine, who could have created a non-Zionist progressive Jewish state, if the imperialist powers had not assured the success of the Zionists.[26]

Despite the difficulties in formulating a coherent ideological justification for Soviet support for the creation of Israel, this episode left a significant historical legacy to later Soviet involvement in the Middle East. The decisions made in 1947–9 did set certain boundaries to the Soviet Union's political and ideological framework for dealing with the Arab–Israeli conflict. First, it reinforced the Soviet Union's internationalist critique of the conflict between Arabs and Jews and the central contention that Jews as well as Arabs could contribute to the struggle for the social transformation of Middle Eastern society. The idea of the Arab–Israeli conflict as a purely nationalist struggle remained, for Soviet thinking, a perverted and illegitimate conception. As a consequence, the Soviet Union never denied Israel's right to be recognized as a legitimate state in the international community. This position remained steadfast, even when the Soviet Union later began to provide support to Arab nationalist regimes who refused to recognize Israel's right to exist.

A corollary of this internationalist critique was an essentially conservative and statist conception of the Middle East political order and the responsibility of the international community to preserve that order. The manner in which the future of Palestine was determined – by a political decision of the Great Powers at the United Nations – continued to be the Soviet Union's preferred forum for the resolution of the Arab–Israeli conflict. The Soviet Union consistently maintained that a political resolution of the dispute was possible, but that it had to be resolved through international and collective efforts, with the Soviet Union's position and rights as a Great Power being respected. The roots of the constant Soviet demand for an international conference to settle the conflict between Israel and the Arab states can be traced to this period of Soviet involvement in the formation of the state of Israel.

There was, however, one factor which qualified the Soviet Union's initial support for the Israeli state and its outwardly moderate political approach to the Arab–Israeli conflict. This was its refusal, even in the halcyon period of the Soviet–Israeli relationship, ever to consider Zionism as a legitimate political doctrine or form of nationalism. Zionism was always defined as a tool of imperialism and as inherently hostile to socialism and progress. This purely negative appraisal acted as a fundamental obstacle to the development of close Soviet–Israeli relations and ultimately led Israel, in the heightened polarization of the Cold War in the early 1950s, to ally itself with the United States. Not unsurprisingly, Israel was unwilling to place its trust in a country, however supportive it might have been in the past, which had an unmitigatedly hostile attitude to the ideological foundations of Jewish nationalism.

Israeli perceptions of the Soviet Union were also to be deeply scarred by the anti-Jewish policies of the last years of Stalin's rule. Stalin appeared to have miscalculated the effect that the creation of the state of Israel might have on the Soviet Jewish population. When Golda Myerson (later Meir) arrived as the Israeli ambassador in Moscow, she was received rapturously by thousands of Soviet Jews. Stalin's response to these unprecedented nationalist demonstrations was characteristically brutal.[27] From the late summer of 1948, hostile references to Zionism began to reappear in the Soviet media. From 1949–53, this developed into a massive anti-Zionist campaign which culminated with the Prague trial of November 1952 and the unmasking of the 'Doctors Plot' of January 1953. Rudolf Slansky and the ten other Jewish defendants of the Prague trial were accused of using communism as a cover to cloak their true role as members of a world-wide anti-communist, imperialist and Zionist conspiracy.[28]

In these last bleak years of Stalin's life, anti-Zionism was not only viewed as the legitimate opposition to a reactionary ideology but also as a barely veiled euphemism for anti-Semitism. This was undoubtedly inspired by Stalin's increasing paranoia over the Jewish presence in Soviet society, with all its international 'cosmopolitan' connections.[29] After his death on 5 March 1953, the anti-Zionist campaign was almost immediately halted. However, the effects of the campaign were to last longer. For Israel, it confirmed and sustained the belief that underlying the official Soviet ideology there continued to exist a virulent anti-semitic strain and a deeply-rooted lack of sympathy for Jewish nationalist objectives. Within the Soviet establishment, the anti-Zionist campaign partially blurred the distinction between reactionary Zionism and progressive Jewish nationalism, which had been the justification for the creation of the PCP and the support for the state of Israel. Instead, there was the effective legitimation for an undifferentiated and monolithic critique of Zionism, widened to include traditional anti-semitic overtones of the diabolical activities of international Jewry and their conspiratorial plottings with imperialism and capitalism.

This conception of Zionism outlasted Stalin's death and became a structural part of Soviet ideological discourse. Periodically, it resur-faced in anti-Zionist campaigns analogous to that in 1949–53. It was not, though, always the dominant discourse and it competed with the more benign Leninist anti-Zionist analysis.[30] But it undoubtedly affected the Soviet perception of Israel and limited the potential for the devel-opment of normal relations with the Zionist state. Henry Kissinger was implicitly pointing to this deep Soviet ambivalence to the Jewish question when he remarked that he had been capable of talking rationally with the Soviet Union on all subjects, including even Vietnam, with the one exception of Israel.

KHRUSHCHEV AND THE SOVIET TURN TO THE ARAB WORLD

The late Stalin period had laid the first key foundations of a frame-work for Soviet involvement in the Middle East. Some of the most distinctive features of the Soviet conception of the Arab–Israeli con-flict find their origin from this period – support for Israel's existence tempered with a deep antagonism to the Zionist enterprise; an inter-nationalist critique of the conflict as a joint struggle of Jews and Arabs against imperialism and reaction, in opposition to the idea of an irrec-oncilable nationalist confrontation; and the assumption of the Soviet Union's legitimate right, as one of the Great Powers, to be involved in the international resolution of the conflict, and its conviction that such an international settlement was both necessary and desirable. How-ever, after the brief but intensive Soviet involvement in the delibera-tions over the future of Palestine, the Soviet Union found its avenues for influence into the Middle East again obstructed as Britain, with the support of the United States, reassumed control of the region.

It was only after Stalin's death, with the new leader Nikita Khrushchev, that the Western monopoly of influence in the Middle East was finally disturbed. The critical turning point was the Soviet decision in 1955 to sanction the Czechoslovak–Egyptian arms agreement. The primary motivation behind the decision was the traditional strategic concern for the security of the Soviet Union's southern borders. In April 1955, Iraq had joined a military alliance with the West, the so-called Baghdad Pact, which was viewed by the United States as an important bridge between the North Atlantic Treaty Organization (NATO) and the South East Asia Treaty Organization (SEATO) in the global containment of Soviet aggression. For its part, the Soviet Union saw the new military alliance as the extension of NATO's capability into the very heart of the Middle East, thereby transforming the region into a potential theatre of war.[31] The arms deal with Egypt was Khrushchev's response to this increased sense of threat. With no avenues for changing the pro-Western stance of the Northern Tier countries, the Soviet Union leapfrogged the containment circle and lent its support to those Arab states which objected to the Baghdad Pact – Egypt and, soon afterwards, Syria.[32]

Khrushchev's decision to support the Arab nationalist regimes of Egypt and Syria represented a significant departure from earlier Soviet and Tsarist Russian involvement in the Middle East. Previously, the principal strategic Russian interests had been in countries contiguous to its territory, most prominently Turkey and Iran. Khrushchev's new strategic orientation was to refocus Soviet priorities towards the traditionally less important southern Arab region, to countries like Egypt which were located at a much greater distance from the Soviet Union's southern borders.

Khrushchev also provided some innovative ideological justifications for this strategic decision. Instead of Stalin's fatalistic expectation of an inevitable confrontation between East and West, Khrushchev relocated the struggle between the capitalist and socialist worlds to the anti-colonial struggles of the Third World. While Khrushchev asserted that 'peaceful coexistence' was now necessary in the nuclear age to avoid the 'the most destructive war in history', he enthusiastically resurrected the Leninist belief that the path to proletarian victory in the West lay in a revolutionary alliance with the liberation movement of the colonial world.[33] As he argued at the 20th Congress of the CPSU on 14 February 1956, the 'new period in world history, predicted by Lenin, when the peoples of the East play an active part in deciding the destinies of the whole world and become a new and mighty factor in international relations, has arrived.'[34]

Khrushchev had, therefore, considerable ideological expectations of the Arab nationalist regimes embraced in the mid-1950s. Egypt and other radical Arab states, like Syria, were promoted as the prototypes of the newly liberated countries which Khrushchev believed to have revolutionary, anti-imperialist potential. However, to justify this ideo-logical revisionism and its associated foreign policy implications, Khrushchev had to overcome the opposition of some powerful detrac-tors in Moscow and convince them of two things. First, he had to demonstrate that these countries would genuinely follow the path of socialist reconstruction. And, second and perhaps more critically, he had to show that these new and unpredictable allies would not under-mine the Soviet Union's other strategic objectives, in particular the higher-order interests of maintaining Soviet prestige and safeguarding peaceful coexistence between East and West.

Gamal Abd al-Nasir's decision to nationalize the Suez canal in July 1956 brought this latter concern to the forefront of Soviet policy-makers. In the early days of the tripartite invasion of Egypt in October, the Soviet Union had almost acceded to the defeat of Nasir. Ironically, it was the United States' decision to support Nasir which saved the Soviet Union from a humiliating retreat. When the United States finally de-cided to oppose the invasion, the Soviet Union realized that the tide had turned in Nasir's favour and that the chances of war had radically diminished. It was only after this US decision, a full nine days after the invasion, that the Soviet Union felt sufficiently confident to adopt a more belligerent stance, sending severely worded messages to Britain, France and Israel, including threats of the use of nuclear weapons. These messages had the advantage of giving the impression of Soviet pressure to enforce the cessation of hostilities and even of US collusion in the invasion.[35]

The end result was that the Soviet Union gained a great deal from the Suez crisis. The nationalist policies of Nasir had undermined Brit-ish power in the region, and the Soviet Union's diplomatic support for Egypt had increased its prestige among most Arabs. Nasir's victory also unleashed powerful nationalist forces throughout the region. From 1956–8, there were a series of crises in Lebanon, Jordan, Syria and Iraq, which the Soviet Union capitalized upon and, to a certain extent, intensified, but always taking care that its actions would not provoke the West to intervene militarily. The overthrow of the pro-British Iraqi government in July 1958 and the demise of the Baghdad Pact appeared to provide a final vindication of Khrushchev's support for the Arab nationalist regimes. It also seemed to demonstrate that such support would reap significant dividends for the Soviet Union in the Third World without materially damaging its strategic relationship with the West.

However, as these new regimes began to consolidate their hold on power, the issue of whether these countries would genuinely embark on the desired path of socialist reconstruction emerged as a critical Soviet concern. Soviet disquiet focused particularly on the role of the Arab communist parties. While the Soviet Union insisted that the communists should be permitted to participate constructively with the ruling elites, the Arab nationalists leaders, most notably Nasir, refused to sanction such participation, perceiving the communists as a destabilizing force and communism as antithetical to the goals of Arab nationalism. The anti-communist direction of Nasir's conception of Arab nationalism became even more apparent with the creation of the United Arab Republic (UAR) in 1958 and Nasir's decision to dismantle all individual parties in Syria, including the Syrian Communist Party. The Soviet Union was thereby faced with the diminution of its influence in Syria through the implementation of the Arab nationalist goal of the unification of the Arab world – a goal moreover which the Soviet Union had previously vigorously supported for its anti-imperialist content.

These contradictions between Soviet doctrine and Arab nationalism reached a crisis point in 1959. In the latter part of that year, there was wide-scale persecution of communists in all the main Arab countries supported by the Soviet Union – Iraq, Syria and Egypt. These developments invigorated the opposition which certain sections of the Soviet bureaucracy had consistently maintained against Khrushchev's opportunistic strategy in the Middle East. In particular, the International Department of the Central Committee of the CPSU, which acted as the official link with foreign communist parties, felt that the position of their clients had been undermined. Boris Ponomarev, the First Secretary of the Department, launched a counter-offensive, calling for communists in countries like Egypt and Iraq 'to remove the remnants of the colonial administration, to seize the power from the nationalist traitors who serve imperialism, and to take the fate of the country in their own hands'.[36]

The critics of Khrushchev's policies were not merely, in Jerry Hough's words, 'petulant defenders of old truths'.[37] They highlighted the considerable contradictions involved in attempting to secure political gains in the Middle East with the limited resources available to the Soviet Union and in a region where the dominant Arab nationalist ideology expressed a deep-seated hostility to communism. Their policy advice was for a Soviet retreat from the region and for leaving the task of the promotion of socialist revolution to the local communist parties.

Although Khrushchev was unable completely to overcome opposition to his policies, which was a contributory factor to his downfall in 1964, the basic outlines of his strategy were eventually accepted. In the end, it was developments within the Arab nationalist regimes themselves which gradually silenced the critics in Moscow. In 1961, Syria seceded from the UAR, and Nasir moved in the direction of domestic socialist reconstruction with wide-scale nationalizations and the creation of more tightly organized vanguard party, the Arab Socialist Union. By late 1963, Syria and Iraq had similarly embarked on socialist economic programmes and relations with the Soviet Union had been enhanced. Some commentators, like Georgii Mirskii, were even confidently predicting that, like Cuba, 'the national liberation movements can immediately break out of the framework of bourgeois democratic revolution and begin the transition to socialist revolution'.[38]

Khrushchev's strategy towards the Third World, and the Middle East in particular, survived his overthrow from power in 1964. His contribution to the question of Soviet involvement in the Middle East had been twofold. First, he had shown that the risks associated with an activist policy were outweighed by the potential benefits, both in reducing Western influence and in encouraging the newly liberated regimes to advance on a socialist path with strong ties of friendship with the Soviet Union. Second, Khrushchev had justified his faith in the Arab nationalist leaders and the concomitant reduction of support for the indigenous Arab communist parties. The new Soviet leadership confirmed this approach, encouraging the Arab communists to work within nationalist parties, thereby avoiding persecution while being in a more favourable position to encourage socialist policies. Once this compromise had been reached, there were no more substantial obstacles to the full Soviet embrace of the Arab nationalist regimes of the Middle East.

THE IDEOLOGICAL AND INSTITUTIONAL FRAMEWORK

By the mid-1960s, the Soviet Union had defined a reasonably stable and internally consistent framework for its involvement in the Arab–Israeli conflict. From the late Stalin period, Soviet recognition of the legitimacy of the state of Israel was confirmed, though qualified by a continuing hostility towards the nationalist objectives of Zionism. The inclusion of the Soviet Union in the deliberations for the UN-sponsored partition of Palestine also established the Soviet conviction that the only legitimate resolution of the Arab–Israeli conflict was through international negotiations, under the auspices of the United Nations, where the interests of the Great Powers, including those of the Soviet Union, must be respected. For his part, Khrushchev's legacy was to initiate the Soviet embrace of the Arab nationalist cause and to give the official Soviet imprimatur to the legitimacy of this struggle as an integral part of the wider liberation struggle of the colonial world against imperialism and capitalism.

This broad policy framework towards the Arab–Israeli conflict represented the pragmatic, if often problematic, marriage between the Soviet Union's strategic and ideological interests and the political realities of the Middle East. This was not something new, as this combination of strategic and ideological interests involved a significant continuity from Tsarist Russian engagement in the region.

However, emphasis on the ideological content of Soviet policy-making diverges from most conventional analyses of Soviet policy-making towards the Middle East. Typically, commentators attribute only a minor role for ideology in the formation of Soviet policy in the region. For example, Robert O. Freedman, who has written the main textbooks on Soviet policy towards the Middle East, gives little operative value to ideology except as consolidating the Soviet Union's 'zero-sum game competition with the United States for influence, where a gain by the United States becomes an equivalent loss for Moscow and vice-versa'.[39] In this simple bifurcated model of Soviet engagement, ideology acts merely as an infinitely flexible tool for justifying Soviet competition with the United States and the Soviet Union's ceaseless drive for power and influence in the region. Other analysts on Soviet relations to the Middle East avoid the extreme reductionism of Freedman's approach but still assert that ideology had only a marginal impact on Soviet decision-making. Galia Golan takes into account ideological factors but stresses that 'strategic interests have taken immediate precedence'.[40] Similarly, Efraim Karsh accords little attention to ideology as a potential factor in influencing Soviet decision-making.[41]

However, if ideology is defined less as a rigid set of doctrines and strategies, connected to the unchanging dogmas of Marxism-Leninism, and more as the particular *Weltanschauung* through which the Soviet foreign policy elite viewed the world, then its central role becomes clearer. Asserting the primacy of ideology is to emphasize the point that, despite the many subtleties and nuances within the inherited Marxist-Leninist framework, it still predisposed the Soviet foreign policy elite to view the outside world within certain relatively simple categories. At its most basic and fundamental level, it predisposed them towards a Manichean view of the world, divided between the forces of progress and reaction. It also provided a determinist vision of the future, whereby the forces of progress would inexorably advance through changes in their favour or, to use Soviet terminology, through the evolution in the correlation of forces. Even if Soviet decision-makers might not individually have believed in these articles of faith, they had to operate within this ideological framework which defined the language and concepts of their discourse and set the parameters of the debate on any given issue.

Inevitably, this had an impact on the decisions which were eventually made. Although strategic and national security interests were obviously central to foreign policy debates, discussions and arguments over policy were filtered through the Marxist-Leninist ideological prism and the consequent 'orthodox' end result was normally the outcome of some degree of compromise. In analysing these compromises, it is not possible simply to separate strategic and ideological reasons and argue that the latter were only a *post hoc* justification for the former. Ideological factors were necessarily tied up with strategic considerations and cannot be cleanly separated from one another.

In addition, it should be remembered that the Soviet ideological framework aided decision-makers by providing a relatively clear and simple explanation of complex social phenomena. Such clarity contributed to the decision-making process. However, as Marx himself first noted, such an ideologically driven approach inevitably involved a distortion of reality and Soviet decision-makers were not immune from following a course of action which might appear subjective or even irrational in relation to the actual facts on the ground. Too often in the literature on Soviet foreign policy, Soviet decision-makers are depicted as perfectly rational actors. It is true that, in the Soviet foreign policy establishment, the Middle Eastern specialists were of a high professional standard, probably more so than their American counterparts. But, they were not immune from the consequences of ideological distortion and even from that most extreme form of ideological perversion – the conspiracy theory.

In understanding Soviet policy towards the Middle East, it is also important to emphasize that the Soviet ideological prism was not cast in stone in certain Marxist-Leninist texts but was continually developed in praxis, through the incorporation of the actual decisions and policies adopted by the Soviet leadership. One example already mentioned is the incorporation into the Soviet ideological canon of the historical justification of the creation of the state of Israel and the illegitimacy of seeking its extinction. To use a legal analogy, Stalin's decision to recognize Israel was a precedent which then became part of the ideological case law establishing the framework of Soviet policy towards the region.

In understanding how Soviet policy-makers approached the question of any prospective relationship with the PLO, it is necessary to assess the mix of both strategic and ideological interests. Clearly, strategic considerations played a central role in determining the nature, timing and the relative warmth of the Soviet embrace of the PLO. The Soviet Union had strategic and Great Power interests in the Arab–Israeli conflict and was engaged in a competitive drive for influence in the region, primarily in opposition to the United States, which influenced the nature of its relationship with the PLO. However, Soviet decision-makers also devoted considerable attention to such questions as the ideological acceptability of the PLO and its constituent factions; the legitimacy of its political programme in relation to Soviet policies; and the progressiveness of its relations with the rest of the Arab and non-Arab world, particularly when the PLO was in conflict with other Soviet Middle Eastern allies. Such issues had a direct and independent influence on Soviet policy towards the PLO, complementing rather than simply providing an artificial legitimation of the more directly strategic considerations.

Such ideological concerns also had a particular prominence since it was the International Department of the Central Committee of the CPSU (through its front organization the Soviet Afro-Asian Solidarity Committee (SKSSAA), the Soviet component of the Afro-Asian Peoples' Solidarity Organization (AAPSO)) which held direct responsibility for the PLO. Since the PLO was a non-state actor, it was not granted a direct relationship with the Ministry of Foreign Affairs (MFA), though the MFA did become increasingly involved as the PLO assumed a central role in the Soviet Middle East peace proposals. It is generally accepted that the International Department was more ideologically inclined than the MFA.[42] Given its role as the mouthpiece of the party, it certainly had a functional responsibility for maintaining the ideological integrity of Soviet foreign policy, which partially distinguished it from the MFA. In relation to the PLO, the International Department was particularly involved in determining Soviet relations with the different factions within the organization, and its preference for the more leftist groups indicated its ideological approach. In addition, officials such as the head of the department, Boris Ponomarev, and Rostislav Ul'ianovskii, the department specialist for national liberation movements and head of SKSSAA, were notable hardliners, who were protégés of the Politburo chief in charge of ideology, Mikhail Suslov.

However, it is too simplistic to make a hard and fast division between an ideological International Department and a moderate Ministry of Foreign Affairs. Andrei Gromyko, the Foreign Minister, was
less engaged in the affairs of the PLO more due to his temperamental
dislike of the Middle East than any particular ideological stance.[43] Certain
officials in the International Department were also notable for having
a more flexible and less ideologically defined approach, such as Vadim
Zagladin, the First Deputy Chief, and Karen Brutents, the Deputy Chief
for Middle Eastern affairs.

In addition, there was considerable flexibility and inter-institutional
co-operation on a variety of issues. For instance, an important figure
in the development of Soviet–PLO relations was Evgenii Pyrlyn, who
was a Deputy Head of the Near East Department of the MFA. But, in
addition to his position in the MFA, he was also a senior member in
the Oriental Institute of the Soviet Academy of Sciences and had close
personal ties with the Middle Eastern section in the International Department. During the 1970s Pyrlyn became a committed advocate for
a greater Soviet involvement in the Palestinian question and with the
PLO. As he emphasized in his doctoral abstract, Soviet researchers,
and by implication Soviet policy-makers, had looked too much at the
Arab struggle against Israel and had not given sufficient attention to
the purely Palestinian part of the problem.[44] This work, and his subsequent publications on the Palestinian question, were sanctioned and
commissioned by the Central Committee and were influential on Soviet
policy.[45]

Pyrlyn's example provides an insight to a fairly small community of
Soviet policy-makers on the Middle East, where the prima facie evidence suggests that institutional affiliation might not be the most significant factor in determining particular policy positions. This proposition
is given added weight by an analysis carried out by George Breslauer,
who argues that it is the particular ideological outlook and belief system of the individual policy-maker which is the principal determinant
of differing policy approaches.[46] Through a rigorous analysis of the
writings of the five main Soviet commentators of the Middle East from
1970–87, Breslauer concludes that all of them submit to a core set of
beliefs about the nature of the Arab–Israeli conflict. These include such
beliefs as the historical inevitability of the US and Israel having to
submit to the underlying reality of the region – most notably that the
Palestinians will eventually have to be granted the right to self-determination. But, beyond these core common beliefs, there was room for
diverging points of view, ranging from a militant and polarized vision

of the struggle between progressive and reactionary forces to a more moderate and pragmatic approach which sought collaboration with the United States and the potential reconciliation of Israel with the Arab world.[47] The interesting discovery made by Breslauer is that the five commentators broadly stood by their individual and distinctive stances throughout the 17 years covered, suggesting that it was their individual convictions and outlook which were the most important factors in defining their approach to Middle Eastern politics.

Breslauer's analysis confirms that the ideologically driven Soviet framework for engagement in the Middle East was the prism through which Soviet decision-makers defined policy towards the region. This framework did, though, permit differing policy prescriptions which reflected the relative rigidity or flexibility with which individuals translated this framework into actual practice. Vigorous and sometimes heated debates took place between the advocates of these differing positions. The evolution of the Soviet response to the PLO was itself part of the outcome of such debates. Although the principle of democratic centralism sought to hide such debates in an impenetrable 'black box', the following chapters seeks to reveal at least some part of these background discussions.

2 Towards a Reluctant Relationship: 1964–70

In the memorable phrase of Malcolm Kerr, the late 1950s and early 1960s was the period of the 'Arab Cold War', when the quest for Arab unity assumed a greater priority to the goal of the liberation of Palestine.[1] However, by the mid-1960s increasing frustration with the Arab states' failure either to unite or effectively to confront the Israeli state forced the nationalist Arab regimes to refocus their energies on the Palestinian question. Nasir's sponsorship of the formation of the Palestine Liberation Organization in 1964 was Egypt's response to defending its self-proclaimed leadership of the radical Arab struggle against Israel. Syria's support for the guerrilla activities of Fatah, the Palestinian faction which remained independent of the PLO until 1968, reflected Syria's competitive resolve to assume the Palestinian mantle against its Egyptian rival. The massive Israeli victories of the June 1967 war only accelerated the process whereby the Arab–Israeli conflict dominated Arab policy-making and the PLO emerged as an independent Palestinian actor in its own right, with Fatah and the other Palestinian guerrilla organizations assuming leadership of the organization.

This chapter argues that the Soviet Union was far from enthusiastic over the increased salience of the Palestine question in the Arab world and the growing authority and independence of the PLO. The first section of the chapter analyses the period up to the 1967 war when the Soviet Union categorically refused to develop any direct relationship with either the PLO or Fatah. Both organizations were considered to be strategically marginal and to be ideologically suspect, given their radical opposition to the Soviet objective of seeking a political, rather than a military, solution to the Arab–Israeli conflict.

The Soviet Union did change its position in the aftermath of the 1967 war. Starting in 1968, a dialogue was initiated with the PLO, now controlled by Fatah and the other Palestinian guerrilla factions, which culminated in February 1970 with the first official visit by a PLO delegation to Moscow. However, the second section of the chapter argues that this shift in the Soviet position was primarily tactical in nature and did not represent any substantive change from the earlier assessment of the PLO as an illegitimate and ideologically unacceptable organization. In the context of the enormous popularity of Palestinian guerrilla activity after the Arab defeat in 1967, the Soviet Union concluded that some evidence of Soviet support for the PLO was critical for maintaining the overall health of Soviet–Arab relations. In addition, the Soviet Union found that public support for the PLO could be a useful device for signalling its opposition to political and military developments which were perceived to undermine the Soviet diplomatic position in the region, particularly when Moscow felt that Israel or the United States were deliberately ignoring Soviet interests.

However, the strictly limited and tactical nature of Soviet support for the PLO became apparent during the Jordanian–Palestinian conflict of 1970–1. The final section of the chapter shows how the Soviet Union's sympathies during the conflict lay more with King Husayn of Jordan than with the Palestinian guerrillas and, far from encouraging the Palestinian revolt, Soviet officials focused their efforts on a speedy resolution of the crisis.

FROM THE FORMATION OF THE PLO TO THE 1967 WAR

The creation of the PLO in May 1964 was an important watershed in the history of the Arab–Israeli conflict. It represented the first attempt for over a decade to give institutional form to a specific Palestinian entity. However, the PLO was not born of independent Palestinian initiative but through the sanction of the Arab states and the personal resolve of Nasir. The PLO was seen as strictly subordinate to Nasir's wider political strategy, which in 1964 was driven by two principal factors. First, Nasir had grown disillusioned with the prospects of an Arab order based upon radical progressive unity, the so-called 'unity of aims', and he embarked on fostering a less ambitious and more moderate Arab alignment through a series of Arab summits from 1964 to 1966, including both radical and conservative regimes.[2] Second, Nasir sought to defuse Arab expectations of a military response to the expected completion during 1964 of the Israeli plans for the diversion of water from Lake Tiberias to central and southern Israel.

The creation of the PLO fulfilled certain important functions in this wider strategy. It was formed to preserve the revolutionary spirit of the struggle for Palestine and to sustain the notion of a Palestinian entity as the concrete expression of Arab claims on the territory of Palestine. More directly, it protected Nasir from criticism that he was not acting forcefully enough to engage Israel in battle and thereby preserved his revolutionary credentials. In general, the Soviet Union reacted favourably to Nasir's new strategy of Arab reconciliation but expressed certain underlying concerns noting that 'Arab communist and revolutionary-democratic leaders realize that this unity can only be based on socialism.'[3] Moreover, when Nasir decided in mid-1966 to conclude the era of summitry and return to the polarization of the Arab world into progressive and reactionary camps, the Soviet Union wholeheartedly approved and indicated that this realignment of political forces was more to its taste.[4]

The Soviet Union also expressed reservations with Nasir's ambition to forge a greater Arab reconciliation based on a more co-ordinated and activist policy against Israel. This can be seen in an unprecedented exchange in the Soviet journal *New Times*. Most unusually, a Moscow-based journalist from the Israeli Communist Party was given permission to respond to an article on the September 1966 Arab Summit in Casablanca by the Soviet commentator, Farid Seiful'-Muliukov.[5] The editors of the journal commented that they had published this reply to give 'our readers a more rounded and objective picture of the Arab–Israeli conflict'. The Israeli commentator's main criticism was that the earlier article had been one-sided and excessively pro-Arab. He argued that it had presented only the Arab side to the problem of the Jordan waters, the Arab decision to break off relations with West Germany and the Arab rejection of the Tunisian suggestion of a reorientation of Arab policy towards Israel, which had been proposed by President Bourguiba. More substantively, he argued that the article had failed to make a distinction between Israel's 'temporary' rulers and the 'forces fighting for a new policy for Israel, a policy of peace and progress'. It had also ignored the fact that the Arab side was not blameless since it 'is openly threatening to use force against Israel'. By so doing, the article had left out 'that the principle of peaceful settlement of disputes applies in full measure to the conflict between Israel and the Arab states' and had 'missed an opportunity to appeal for a peaceful settlement of the Israeli–Arab conflict'.

This Israeli journalist had forcefully reasserted the traditional Soviet position on the Arab–Israeli conflict and the nature of the Israeli state. It is the continuing salience of this Soviet approach to the conflict, which provides the main reasons why the Soviet Union ignored the PLO in the period prior to the June 1967 war. It was certainly not due to lack of application on the part of the PLO's leader, Ahmad Shuqayri. In his memoirs, Shuqayri relates how he had assiduously courted the Soviet embassies of the Arab world:

For two long years I knocked at the gates of Moscow as though I were Henry IV, standing 700 years ago at the gates of Canossa, doing penance before the Pope. . . . I sought a large debt from the Soviet Union which I had accumulated over 15 years. . . . and I came to request the redemption of the debt, even the smallest fraction of it.[6]

Despite these exertions, the Soviet Union refused to give Shuqayri a 'single rouble', so he went to the gates of Peking, where he was received with enormous enthusiasm.[7] The effusive Chinese embrace of Shuqayri did not deflect the Soviet Union from its negative appraisal of the PLO. In later Soviet accounts of the history of the PLO, Shuqayri was presented in the most unfavourable light, as fatally inclined towards 'adventurism, demagoguery, and anti-Sovietism, strengthened by his contacts with Peking'.[8] His denunciations of Israel and his threats to 'drive the Jews into the sea' were presented as contributory factors to the Israeli aggression of June 1967.[9]

The Soviet Union undoubtedly had a similarly dismissive attitude to Shuqayri and his organization prior to the June 1967 war. From the Soviet perspective, the PLO was the embodiment of all the most unacceptable aspects of the Arab opposition to Israel. Its political programme called for the destruction of the State of Israel and it proposed a purely military solution of the Arab–Israeli conflict and rejected any political settlement. Its political stance was nationalist in orientation and, in Soviet eyes, only served to divert the attention of the Arab world away from the tasks of internal socialist construction and towards dangerous and illusory dreams of the liberation of Palestine.

Not only was the PLO's ideological platform unacceptable, the PLO could offer no practical benefits for the Soviet Union. The PLO's subordination to its sponsoring Arab regimes, with which the Soviet Union already had close relations, made any relationship with the PLO strictly superfluous. Even the PLO's ties with China represented no immediate threat, since China was unable to use these relations to disturb the dominant Soviet influence in the region. Overall, the intrinsic weakness of the PLO and its dependence on the Arab states made it of little interest for the Soviet Union. The Soviet Union was content to develop its substantive relations with the Arab states and rigorously ignore the bombastic pretensions of Shuqayri.

The rise to prominence of the Fatah guerrilla organization, which carried out its first act of sabotage in Israel on 31 December 1964, was met with even greater Soviet disdain. From the Soviet perspective, Fatah not only had the same inherent problems of the PLO but also had additional failings. It was antagonistic to Nasir's pan-Arab strategy, being sponsored by Syria contrary to Nasir's wishes; its policies were directed towards immediate military confrontation with Israel; and its ideological stance was narrowly nationalistic in that it emphasized Palestinian independence from the constraints of pan-Arab co-ordination of political and military strategy. For the Soviet leadership this amounted to a reckless adventurism and, in a meeting with the Sneh-Mikunis faction of the Israeli communist party on 19 November 1965, it was emphasized that the Soviet Union opposed all terrorist activities on Israeli territory.[10]

However, the guerrilla raids were less easy to ignore than the rhetorical posturing of Shuqayri's PLO. On the one hand, these raids provoked Israeli military intervention, increasing tension in the region and threatening an escalation of hostilities into all-out war. On the other, Fatah was directly supported by Syria, which was viewed in the Soviet Union as a radical and progressive state, which it could not afford to alienate by demanding too forcefully that Fatah curb its cross-border attacks. The tension between these contradictions became even more apparent after the February 1966 Syrian *coup d'état*. The new Syrian regime promised to improve relations with the Soviet Union, to engage in genuine 'socialist construction' and to involve Syrian communists in a political national front. Yet, at the same time, the regime promoted a 'popular liberation war as the sole way of liberating Palestine', and stressed that guerrilla actions were to be a central part of Syrian strategy.[11]

The Soviet Union's decision to provide full support for the new Syrian regime, whose radical ambitions were matched by a chronic internal instability, only served to accentuate these contradictions. Indeed, Soviet policies towards Syria during 1966–7 directly contributed to the outbreak of war. However, it is difficult to ascertain the precise nature of Soviet decision-making during this critical period. There is evidence that the Soviet Union viewed the destabilization of Syria as part of a wider imperialist counter-offensive, which had in the mid-1960s secured the fall of Sukarno's regime in Indonesia, the overthrow of Nkrumah in Ghana and the American decision to commit troops to Vietnam.[12] Ilana Kass has also convincingly argued, from a close analysis of the Soviet press of the period, that the 'pre-war escalation reflected the temporary predominance of hardliners. . . . [who] advocated throughout 1966–1967 a more forward and aggressive policy in the Middle East'.[13]

The historical parallel of the 1966–7 crisis that the Soviet press most frequently alluded to was the Syrian crisis in 1957.[14] In that earlier crisis, a similarly radical anti-Western regime had secured power in Damascus, had survived external attempts at destabilization and had contributed to the further radicalization of the region, leading to the overthrow of the pro-Western Iraqi regime in the following year. The Soviet Union probably hoped that the 1966–7 crisis might have a similarly beneficial outcome. The sense of imminent gains was captured most clearly in a *Krasnaia zvezda* article immediately preceding the June 1967 war which suggested that 'Israel does not have any chances against the united Egyptian and Syrian armies.'[15]

However, there is no evidence that the Soviet Union had adopted the Arab call for the complete liberation of Palestine or had deviated from its policy of recognition of the right of Israel to exist. Certainly, official Soviet communiqués of the period did accord greater attention to the issue of Palestinian rights, such as the joint Soviet-Syrian communiqué in February 1967 where both sides declared 'their complete support for the struggle of the Palestine Arabs for their inalienable and legitimate rights'.[16] But, when pressed to clarify its position on Palestinian rights, Soviet officials stressed the 'legal' rights of the Palestinian refugees rather than any 'national' right to secession.[17] However, Soviet ambiguity over whether it supported Israel's borders as set out in the 1947 partition plan or as established by the 1949 armistice lines might have emboldened Arab militancy.[18] On this basis, a number of analysts have argued that the ultimate strategic objective of the Soviet escalation of the 1966–7 Arab–Israeli crisis was to change the balance of forces to the advantage of the Arabs so that Israel would be forced to return to its allotted partition borders.[19] Support for this analysis can perhaps be gleaned from an *Izvestiia* article on 31 May 1967 which printed a map of Israel with the legend that 'the map shows the actual frontiers of Israel fixed in violation of the decision of the resolution of the UN General Assembly of . . . November 1947.'

The evidence is, though, far from conclusive and will remain so until further documentary evidence becomes available. But what can be said is that the Soviet Union remained remarkably complacent over the growing crisis in the region. At the outbreak of the war, the top Soviet leadership was on a ceremonial visit to the Soviet fleet in Murmansk. Such complacency can also be seen in the Soviet response to the increasingly destabilizing consequences of the Palestinian guerrilla raids into Israel. There is little reason to believe that the Soviet Union approved or actively encouraged these raids.[20] But the Soviet Union failed to condemn these raids or even officially to admit their existence. The Soviet media depicted the Fatah infiltrations as 'mythical inventions' and as 'organized expressly by well-known services or by agencies of these services for provocative purposes'.[21] In response to Israeli requests for the Moscow to restrain Syria, Israel was told not to exaggerate the terrorist issue and was warned not to be a tool of imperialism and oil monopolists, who wanted to overthrow the leftist Syrian regime.[22]

The crushing Israeli victory in the June 1967 war brutally exposed the extent of Soviet miscalculation in its opportunistic exploitation of Syrian and Palestinian militancy. In the aftermath of the war, Soviet defence analysts conceded a new respect for Israeli military prowess which had been conspicuously absent previously. The Soviet Union was also forced to engage in a comprehensive reassessment of its Middle Eastern strategy, one important element of which was to seek to combine its negative appraisal of the Palestine Resistance with more sustained efforts to curb independent Palestinian military activism.

AFTERMATH OF THE JUNE 1967 WAR

The June 1967 war not only affected Soviet relations in the Middle East. It also had a direct domestic impact with the Israeli victory inspiring many Soviet Jews with a new sense of national pride and increasing the demands for emigration. In response to this internal challenge, Moscow unleashed a barrage of neo-Stalinist anti-Zionist propaganda seeking to demonstrate the parallels of Zionism with Nazism. In Poland, where the proxy defeat of Soviet arms similarly encouraged opposition to the Soviet-backed regimes, the anti-Zionist campaign led to the forceful eviction of the 25,000 Jews still remaining in the country after the Nazi holocaust.

The Soviet decision to break off diplomatic relations with Israel was partly a starting signal to this anti-Zionist frenzy.[23] It was also a symbolic demonstration of Soviet support for its Arab allies. However, in Soviet diplomatic terms, the decision represented an unparalleled move, since the Soviet Union had always recognized the legitimacy of the state of Israel and official Soviet policy upheld diplomatic relations with all internationally recognized states, irrespective of their ideological leanings. The decision was also to have significant long-term implications, since it precluded the possibility of the Soviet Union acting as an impartial mediator in relations between Israel and the Arab states, leading Israel to be tied exclusively to the United States and the West.

However, while Moscow was making these public gestures of its extreme displeasure, the Soviet leadership was also pursuing a more pragmatic diplomatic and political strategy. Immediately after the war, the Soviet government requested the convening of a Special Emergency Session of the General Assembly of the United Nations. During that session, Prime Minister Kosygin also met with US President Lyndon Johnson for summit talks in Glassboro, New Jersey, where two-thirds of the discussion was reportedly centred on the Middle East. The underlying impetus for these Soviet initiatives reflected the old Khrushchevian fears of local wars escalating to world war. Such fears were vividly expressed by Kosygin in his speech at the UN General Assembly, when he stated that 'if a limit is not placed on the dangerous development of events, now taking place in the Near East, . . . there will be a great war in which no state will be able to remain to one side.'[24] It was these concerns of a potential global confrontation which led the Soviet Union to propose that the Arab–Israeli conflict could no longer continue to be the object of US–Soviet competition for influence and that it was now in the interest of both superpowers to combine their efforts to secure a peaceful and just settlement.

To promote this settlement, the Soviet Union engaged in a sustained diplomatic and propaganda attack on the militant slogans of its Arab allies. The urgency of the need for a peaceful settlement was continually stressed and the relatively moderate stance of Nasir's Egypt was held up as an example to the rest of the Arab world.[25] A vigorous campaign was initiated against the slogan of the liquidation of the state of Israel, which was the central tenet of the Arab militant programme.[26] The traditional criticism that the Arabs were making the mistake of seeing the war as a 'nationalist rather than an imperialist war' was used to emphasize the necessity for moderation and the need for the Arabs to align their policies with the Soviet Union.[27]

The PLO and the Palestinian guerrilla organizations were a central focus of Soviet criticism, as they were implacably opposed to any hint of compromise and placed their faith on protracted guerrilla warfare in the absence of any more conventional war-making capability. The fact that China, who felt that their long-term support for the PLO and Fatah was finally bearing fruit, supported this strategy of a 'people's war' only strengthened Soviet opposition.[28] In an attack on China's activities in the Middle East, criticism of the Palestinian guerrillas was only barely veiled:

The Mao Tse Tung gang, which is pursuing its normal splitting tactics . . . is accusing our country of "deals with the imperialists", counting on those *most backward or irresponsible elements* in the Arab world, and it is directed towards undermining the friendship and trust between the Arabs and the peoples of the socialist countries [emphasis added].[29]

The Chinese–Palestinian alliance was condemned explicitly after the resignation of Ahmad Shuqayri from the leadership of the PLO in December 1967, who the Soviet media attacked as an unrepentant extremist and a Chinese stooge.[30]

These attacks on Arab and Palestinian militancy were matched by Soviet diplomatic activity on the international level, which increasingly came into conflict with the Arab consensus of a minimally acceptable resolution of the conflict. During the months of US–Soviet negotiations leading to the 22 November 1967 UN Security Council Resolution 242, the Soviet Union agreed to drop its condemnation of Israel and its demands for refugee compensation from drafts put forward to the Council.[31] Further concessions were made during the two-power and four-power talks in 1969–70. In the Soviet plan presented to the four-power talks on 17 June 1969, the Soviet Union accepted the US demand for a 'package' deal, including a lasting peace agreement, and explicitly specified that the Arabs would have to recognize Israel in its pre-1967 borders.[32] The provisions of this plan were not even acceptable to the veteran Syrian communist, Khalid Bakdash, who Mohamed Heikal recalls 'admitted that there was no Arab communist who could defend the Gromyko plan – and no Arab nationalist who could defend it either.'[33]

Privately, however, Soviet diplomacy went even further, accepting with the United States the principle of direct talks between Egypt and Israel patterned on the Rhodes armistice negotiations in 1949.[34] During the same period, Kissinger recalls in his diaries that the Soviet ambassador to Washington, Anatolii Dobrynin, hinted at Soviet willingness to compromise on a full Israeli withdrawal.[35] In June 1970, the Soviet Union informed the US administration that the state of war would end with the signing of a peace agreement, and that this could take place before an Israeli withdrawal.[36] Later in the month, the Soviet Union called for an 'indefinite extension of the cease-fire into a "formalized state of peace", similar to the arrangement that existed between the Soviet Union and Japan'.[37]

However, Soviet pragmatism and flexibility had its limits with two factors in particular acting as constraints on Soviet policy-making. First, the Soviet Union had to take into account the interests of its Arab allies who ultimately had to be persuaded to accept any proposed concessions. For the militant Arab states, such as Syria, Iraq and the Palestinian guerrilla organizations, their exclusive commitment to the military option precluded any hope for a favourable reception of Soviet diplomatic initiatives. The Soviet Union, therefore, had to rely almost exclusively on Nasir, his willingness to consider peaceful avenues for a settlement, and his power to forge an Arab consensus around his policies. Yet, Nasir was himself only partially in favour of a peaceful settlement, judging that a mixture of military pressure and diplomatic manoeuvring would be the most profitable route. Thus, Nasir demanded Soviet support for his military campaigns, in particular for the War of Attrition, in exchange for Egyptian support of Soviet diplomatic moves.

The Soviet leadership had little option but to support Nasir's military as well as his peace strategies. The strength of Nasir's bargaining position was revealed most pointedly in late January 1970, when Nasir threatened to resign in favour of a pro-American administration unless he received Soviet arms and support against Israeli deep penetration raids, which were directly undermining the stability of his regime.[38] Given Soviet dependence on Egypt for its position in the Middle East, the Soviet Union, albeit reluctantly, acceded to these demands.

This underlying dependence of the Soviet Union on Egypt provides the background to the second major constraint against Soviet diplomatic flexibility and moderation. In contrast to the Soviet Union, the United States did not suffer from such a structural weakness in its relationship with Israel, since Israel had no one but the United States to turn to. In addition, given lack of Soviet influence in Israel, the Soviet Union was critically dependent on US willingness to exert pressure on Israel to make territorial concessions, in exchange for Soviet pressure on the Arab states to recognize Israel in the form of a peace agreement. But the Soviet leadership knew that US reciprocity was by no means guaranteed. Indeed, given the United States' exclusive relations with a confident and militarily victorious Israel, Soviet diplomats were highly sensitive to the United States being tempted to gain unilateral advantage by encouraging Israeli intransigence and forcing the Arabs to capitulate, either by impelling them to further military defeats or by inducing them to accept a unilateral US peace plan which would be to Israel's advantage. Soviet willingness to collaborate with the United States was, therefore, determined by Moscow's perceptions of the degree of US reciprocity and its self-imposed restraint from pursuing unilateral advantage.

In combination, these two constraints defined the limits to which the Soviet Union was willing to pursue pragmatic and flexible policies towards a settlement of the Arab–Israeli conflict. When it perceived that the US was genuinely engaging in reciprocal collaboration, the Soviet Union was willing to place pressure on its Arab allies and substantially distance itself from Arab maximalist demands. However, when the Soviet Union judged that the US was failing to apply pressure on Israel and when it seemed to be seeking unilateral advantage and to diminish Soviet influence, the Soviet Union sought to consolidate its position in the Arab world and indicate its powers of obstructionism through support of Arab militancy.

It is these wider regional and international considerations which provide the key to understanding the shifts which occurred in Soviet policymaking towards the PLO from 1968 to the Jordanian crisis in 1970. The first of these shifts occurred in 1968 when, in contrast to the earlier Soviet disregard and at times explicit criticisms of Palestinian guerrilla actions, there emerged a far more positive portrayal of these activities. The guerrillas were favourably depicted as 'partisans', resisting Israeli occupation and exploding the myth of the 'willingness of the enslaved Arab population to co-operate with the occupiers'.[39] Fatah was also directly praised as an 'organization waging a dedicated struggle against the invaders', and whose ranks were naturally being swelled by the people in the occupied territories exercising their lawful right to wage a liberation war.[40] Israeli retaliatory attacks into Jordan were condemned as unjustified and only served to 'arouse new groups of Arab patriots to join the fighters for the liberation of the territories occupied by Israel.'[41]

It was, though, the wider international and regional political developments during 1968, rather than any change in the underlying Soviet attitude towards the Palestinian guerrilla organizations, which promoted this first shift in Soviet policy. On the international level, negotiations were stalled as the Johnson administration, in its last year of office, was unwilling to put political capital into the peace process and the UN negotiations, headed by Gunnar Jarring, lacked the authority to make any significant breakthrough in the diplomatic deadlock. The lack of diplomatic progress increased Arab frustration, and enthusiasm for a peaceful settlement accordingly declined. In this political vacuum, the Palestinian guerrilla activities found an enormous popular resonance, particularly after their much publicized involvement in the battle of Karameh in March 1968. The Arab public embraced the Palestinian revolutionaries as the symbols of Arab hope and pride, and the source of the resurrection of the Arab spirit after the June 1967 disaster.

With this newly found Arab enthusiasm, the Soviet Union had little option but to provide reasonably positive reporting of these guerrilla activities. In this, Moscow was only following the lead given by the Arab states. Nasir had been converted to the Fatah cause at his meeting with Arafat in April 1968 and sanctioned the takeover of the PLO by the guerrilla factions. Even King Husayn was forced to accede to the guerrilla demands and provide greater freedom of action for their activities from Jordanian territory. In addition, the Soviet Union could be reassured that there was not much to be lost through such support in a period when negotiations were stalled and there appeared to be no immediate threat of an upsurge in hostilities.

But the Soviet Union could not completely conceal its scepticism of the Palestinian armed struggle. The Soviet commentator, Georgii Mirskii, ended an otherwise favourable report with the qualification that 'needless to say, guerrilla warfare cannot redeem the Occupied Territories. For this, political factors must be brought into play.'[42] The Soviet Union also reaffirmed its rejection of a narrowly Palestinian nationalist struggle and the goal of the liquidation of Israel.[43] But, in the less official but nevertheless Soviet-sponsored journal *World Marxist Review*, a far more biting and critical assessment was permitted. In a hard-hitting article, Fahmi Salfiti, Politburo member of the Jordanian Communist Party, argued that the conditions in the Occupied Territories were not ripe for guerrilla activity and that, since the organizations operate from outside the territories, their activity was strictly redundant and should be subsumed into the 'regular Arab commandos'. Pessimistically Salfiti concluded that 'when the premises for armed action appear, the character of the fedayeen organization and the lack of realism in their programmes limit their possibilities for effective participation in the resistance.'[44]

The fact that the Soviet Union fundamentally concurred with Salfiti's analysis became clear in the early part of 1969, when the Soviet attitude towards the Palestine Resistance reverted to its earlier more negative stance. As the new US administration under President Nixon started actively to collaborate with the Soviet Union over a peace settlement in the two-power and four-power talks, the Soviet Union distanced itself from Arab militancy. The PLO's rejection of the December 1968 Soviet Peace Plan, and its adamant opposition to the two- and four-power talks, exasperated the Soviet leadership. Criticism was made of the PLO's methods of struggle and their aim to create a democratic secular state, which was described as 'failing to take into consideration the present situation in the Arab East and the correlation of forces in the world arena'.[45] The Palestinians' refusal to contemplate a realistic compromise was likened to the attitude of Leon Trotsky at Brest-Litovsk. They were accused of acting as typical Maoists, attempting to 'put the cart before the horse'.[46]

The Soviet Union also expressed its displeasure by refusing a Fatah request for arms and reportedly threatening to stop arms supplies to the Arab states if they did not halt their provision of Soviet arms to the guerrillas.[47] The Palestinian response was fierce. In a Fatah broadcast it was stressed that 'there was no room for forgiveness or understanding towards the Soviet Union' and its own advice to the four-power talks was that they should concentrate on the 'uprooting of the Zionist entity and not the withdrawal of Zionist forces'.[48]

Despite this serious deterioration of Soviet relations with the Palestine Resistance, in late 1969 there was to be a further shift in the Soviet attitude back to a far more favourable position. In a new departure, Politburo member Aleksandr Shelepin stated that the Soviet Union regarded the 'Palestinian patriots' struggle . . . as a just, national-liberation, anti-imperialist struggle, and we will render support to it.'[49] The elevation of the Palestine Resistance to the status of a national liberation movement was paralleled by a more enthusiastic reporting of its guerrilla activity, which was heralded as the 'fifth front of the Arab struggle against Israeli aggression'.[50] The culmination of this new warmth in relations was the first invitation for a PLO delegation to visit Moscow, which then took place on 9–20 February 1970.

However, the reasons for this further shift in relations were again driven by wider global and regional factors. While in the first half of 1969 the Soviet Union were confident of progress towards a peace settlement, these hopes were to recede in the latter part of the year. By September and October 1969, Nasir was suffering considerable losses in his War of Attrition, as Israel destroyed the Egyptian anti-aircraft systems on the Suez Canal and, having uncontested dominance of the airspace, began pounding Egyptian positions at will. In early September, the first US supplies of F-4 Phantom jets started arriving in Israel, which Israel then used in January 1970 to project the war into the heart of the Egyptian interior.

From the Soviet perspective, this campaign suggested US–Israeli collusion to force Nasir's capitulation, to damage Soviet prestige in the Arab world and to extend US hegemony at the expense of the Soviet Union. The Soviet Union also could not afford to alienate Nasir at his most critical hour and was unwilling to contemplate his military defeat. Thus, the Soviet Union made the decision to protect

its client at all costs, including the unprecedented Soviet troop intervention to oversee and man the re-establishment of the Egyptian air
defence system.

It was this wider context of a Soviet Union desperate to protect its
prestige and influence in the region which primarily explains Moscow's willingness in late 1969 and early 1970 to elevate its relations
with the PLO to a new diplomatic level. By promoting the Palestinian
struggle to the ranks of the legitimate national liberation movements,
the Soviet Union was making a symbolic gesture that it was the true
protector of Arab interests and that it was not going to submit to US
pressure. It was also a signal to the United States that the Soviet Union
also had the option of radicalizing the region, of unilaterally promoting its influence, if its interest were too openly flouted. What, however, this elevation of the Palestine Resistance did not represent was
any genuine Soviet conversion to the ideology, political programme or
methods of the PLO and its various factions.

THE JORDANIAN CRISIS

The reception given to the first official visit by the PLO in February
1970 also indicated the continuing Soviet scepticism towards the aims
and objectives of the organization. The low-key nature of the visit
reportedly upset Arafat, who had become accustomed to the full red
carpet treatment in the Arab world. In the summer of 1970, a further
shift in Soviet attitudes highlighted the qualified nature of Moscow's
elevation of the PLO as a progressive force. Again, direct criticisms
of the Palestine Resistance were publicly expressed. These were mainly
provoked by PLO denunciations of US–Soviet collaboration to seek a
cease-fire between Israel and Egypt for the War of Attrition.[51] When
the PLO publicly rejected the Rogers Plan for a cease-fire, which Nasir
accepted in July 1970, Soviet dissatisfaction grew in strength. The Soviet
commentator, Igor Belaev, noted in some exasperation:

> Such an appraisal is puzzling to say the least.... Does this not
> accord with the interest of the Arab population of Palestine? And
> does the prospect of liberating the Arab territories which were seized
> by the Israelis in June 1967 militate against their interest?.... And
> there can be no solution of the Middle East crisis other than the
> political. Those who cherish the interest of the Arabs, including the
> Arab population of Palestine, should not forget that.[52]

The PLO's rejection of the Rogers Plan also had wider regional implications which were to cause considerable political and diplomatic problems for the Soviet Union. It was this PLO rejection which ignited the Palestinian confrontation with the Jordanian authorities, leading to a major inter-Arab conflict involving some of the Soviet Union's closest allies. After King Husayn decided to follow Nasir in accepting the Rogers Plan, the Popular Front for the Liberation of Palestine (PFLP) hijacked three international planes, two of which were flown to a desert airstrip in Jordan and over 500 hostages were taken. In the ensuing crisis, the Palestinian guerrillas were given the open support of Syria and Iraq, who amassed troops on the Jordanian borders. In response, the United States made a series of escalating military moves and expressed its determination to support the Jordanian monarch.

Emboldened by this external support, King Husayn decided to confront the Palestinian guerrilla challenge directly and, on 16–17 September, the Jordanian army initiated a concerted attack on the armed Palestinian positions. On the next day, a Syrian tank division came to the help of the Palestinians but the Jordanian airforce successfully attacked the Syrian force and enforced its withdrawal from Jordan. Freed from the threat of external intervention, King Husayn now had the decisive advantage against the Palestinian forces and he was able to sign, from a position of strength, an Egyptian-sponsored cease-fire agreement with the PLO on 27 September. This cease-fire only provided a short breathing space before the Jordanian army inflicted further decisive blows on the Palestinian factions, leading to their full expulsion from Jordanian territory in February 1971.

The Jordanian crisis presented a series of difficult challenges for the Soviet Union. Despite the pro-Western orientation of the Jordanian government, the Soviet Union had little interest in seeing the overthrow of the Hashemite monarchy. Ever since the June 1967 war, Jordanian–Soviet relations had been improving as King Husayn aligned his policies with Nasir, supporting the Egyptian approach to the peace process, and accepting UN resolution 242 and the Rogers cease-fire plan of July 1970.[53] In fact, the Soviet media made a favourable comparison between the Jordanian acceptance, and the PLO's rejection, of that plan. At the same time, the failure of the PLO to normalize its relations with Jordan was blamed exclusively on 'the extremist wing of the Palestinian movement which persisted in its irresponsible course. . . . Objectively this could only play into the hands of Tel Aviv, which is out to undermine the Arab efforts to fight the occupation by inciting internecine strife among them.'[54]

From the Soviet perspective, the Palestinian challenge to King Husayn's authority threatened not only to derail the peace process but also to lead to an escalation of the conflict, including possibly a superpower confrontation. The Soviet Union in no way wanted the Jordanian monarch to be replaced by a radical Palestinian leadership, including the pro-Chinese George Habash of the PFLP, which would destabilize the region and focus Arab energies on military confrontation with Israel. Such a scenario would be a decisive victory for the militant Arab approach and would considerably limit Nasir's ability to collaborate with the Soviet Union towards a peace settlement.

The overriding Soviet objective was, therefore, to contain the crisis as quickly as possible and to ensure that the Nasir–Husayn partnership was preserved in the interests of a peace settlement. But the Soviet Union had to overcome the problem that those forces agitating for the overthrow of King Husayn – Syria, Iraq and the PLO – were objectively Soviet allies and could not be completely alienated. The Soviet Union could not afford a rift with them and thus needed to exert pressure privately, while publicly not directly criticizing their actions.

The diplomatic approach the Soviet Union adopted reflected this need to preserve its influence among the radical Arab states and yet also ensure that they did nothing to escalate the crisis. Publicly, the blame for the crisis was placed on Israel and Western imperialists who were attempting to 'divide and rule' by 'provoking civil war'.[55] The PLO was not blamed directly for the crisis, and 'moderate' elements in the organization were praised for trying to defuse it. But the Soviet Union exercised no such restraint in condemning the 'extremists', who were blamed for the escalation of the conflict, particularly by their acts of terrorism such as the hijacking of civilian airliners. George Habash and the PFLP were singled out as the principal culprits.[56] However, the Popular Democratic Front for the Liberation of Palestine (PDFLP) was also condemned alongside the PFLP as an extremist Maoist organization, suffering from Lenin's diagnosis of 'the childish disease of leftism'.[57]

There was no such direct criticism of the Syrian and Iraqi military manoeuvres during the crisis. However, the *Tass* statement of 19 September indirectly warned Syria and Iraq, as well as the US and Israel, against 'foreign military intervention' into Jordan being planned by 'certain circles in some countries' which 'would not only endanger the independence of Jordan and other Arab countries, but would essentially complicate the international situation'.[58] Behind the scenes, the Soviet Union advocated restraint to its allies and opposed the Syrian intervention, which at least partly accounted for the eventual failure of the incursion.[59] At regular intervals during the crisis, the Soviet Union informed the US administration that it was doing all in its power to contain the crisis.[60]

As the crisis was subsiding, the Soviet Union looked back with evident satisfaction at its contribution to the control and resolution of the conflict. On 23 September, the Soviet Foreign Ministry summed up its diplomatic activity in Amman, Damascus and Baghdad by stating that it had been 'in contact' with the governments concerned and had expressed to them 'the USSR's firm conviction' that 'everything has to be done to stop the civil war in Jordan' as soon as possible and that the war would only 'play into the hands of forces not interested in establishing peace in the Middle East'.[61] The PLO was implicitly included in the category of those 'not interested' in establishing peace, and the Soviet Union could feel reassured that it had circumscribed the potentially destabilizing consequences of the Palestinian challenge without unduly alienating the PLO or its radical Arab sponsors.

However, the Soviet strategy towards the Jordanian crisis failed in one crucial aspect. It failed to persuade the US administration that the Soviet Union had not been involved in the escalation of the conflict and in supporting the Syrian intervention. As William B. Quandt has convincingly shown, the Syrian crisis was a decisive turning point in the evolution of the US approach to the Arab–Israeli conflict and the US administration's perception of the role of the Soviet Union in the Middle East.[62]

Nixon and his National Security adviser, Henry Kissinger, had taken direct control of the US response to the crisis and had concluded that they were confronted with a Soviet-sponsored attempt to overthrow King Husayn and to implant a radical Palestinian leadership in collusion with the PLO, Syria and Iraq. Furthermore, Nixon and Kissinger saw the eventual outcome of the crisis as confirmation of the strategic value of a strong US–Israeli alliance, which would obstruct Soviet attempts to destabilize the region and weaken Soviet influence amongst its radical Arab allies.

Thus, the United States came to see the role of the Soviet Union in the crisis in a very negative light. While the USSR had hoped the crisis would convince the US of the value of joint collaboration for the resolution of similar disputes, the United States saw the crisis as confirming the need for US unilateral action, in alliance with Israel, to weaken Soviet influence and the power of radical Arab militancy. As a consequence, the US effectively lost interest in co-operation with the

Soviet Union and this undermined any chance that the Soviet strategy of a collaborative superpower settlement of the Arab–Israeli conflict could be realized.

The Jordanian crisis revealed the indirect and unintended costs of the official Soviet support for the PLO. The Soviet Union had developed these relations for tactical reasons, to emphasize its revolutionary credentials and to protect its influence in the Arab world. It was determined, though, that these relations would not harm its strategic interest in forging an Arab–Israeli peace settlement. It had thus distanced itself from the militancy of the PLO's political programme and the organization's methods of struggle. It had also sought to differentiate between the more acceptable 'moderate' elements within the PLO, such as Fatah, as against the more 'extremist' factions such and the PFLP and PDFLP, of whom the Soviet Union indicated its extreme distaste.

The trouble was that this delicate balancing act was too subtle to allay the suspicions of the US administration. Instead, American officials were tempted to see Soviet support for the PLO as direct encouragement of Arab militancy. The PLO also did not help since it refused to submit to Soviet advice and actively sought to destabilize the existing political order in the Arab world. The end result was that the PLO's actions in Jordan tarnished the credentials of the Soviet Union and encouraged the United States to engage in a policy deliberately aimed at diminishing Soviet influence in the region. For the next three years (1970–3), the Soviet Union was effectively excluded by the United States from the peace process. The subsequent October 1973 war brought the Soviet Union frighteningly close to the one eventuality it feared most – a military escalation to superpower confrontation. To a certain degree, these developments can be traced back to the Soviet Union's tactical decision to support the PLO and the wider ramifications of that support in the specific context of the September 1970 Jordanian crisis.

3 The Relationship Blossoms: 1971–6

In the period from 1971 to 1976, the October 1973 war was the central determining event in the Middle East which had a profound impact on the Soviet position in the region and necessitated significant shifts in the Soviet strategic approach to the Arab–Israeli conflict. This chapter analyses the evolution of one of the most important of these shifts – the fundamental reorientation of Soviet thinking towards the Palestine question. While prior to the war the Soviet Union focused its diplomatic energies on securing an Israeli withdrawal from the territories occupied in 1967 and had considered the Palestinian question as a secondary and predominantly refugee issue, in the aftermath of the war the Soviet Union became committed to the creation of an independent Palestinian state and argued that, without such a state, there could be no effective resolution of the Arab–Israeli conflict. The status of the PLO in Soviet strategic thinking was to enjoy a similar transformation. In contrast to the highly qualified and lukewarm support it had received before the war, the PLO was elevated in Moscow to the ranks of a strategic ally and was accorded a central role in the Arab national liberation movement.

At least initially, however, the Soviet Union showed some reluctance either to change its policies towards the Palestine question or to elevate its relations with the PLO. The first section of the chapter recounts how the Soviet Union, in the immediate aftermath of the 1973 war, sought to resolve the issue of whether to demand the PLO's participation in the superpower-sponsored international peace conference scheduled to take place in Geneva. The Soviet leadership made clear to the PLO that it would only sponsor its participation at the conference if it agreed to change its political programme to the demand for a Palestinian mini-state, living alongside rather than instead of Israel. When the PLO refused to give this commitment, the Soviet Union dropped any demand for Palestinian representation at the conference and reverted to its traditional position which asserted that the Palestine question was principally a refugee issue.

It was only a year later in 1974 that the Soviet Union eventually crossed the political Rubicon and fully committed itself to a Palestinian state and the right of the PLO to be the legitimate representative of the Palestinian people. The second section of the chapter argues that there were a number of factors behind this shift. These included Soviet dissatisfaction over the increasingly close ties between Egypt and the United States and the growing evidence of Kissinger's drive for US-sponsored bilateral agreements. The Soviet Union also responded positively to the more moderate policies adopted by the PLO in 1974. However, these factors were not in themselves sufficient to engender a fundamental change in the Soviet position. It was only in the period immediately before the Rabat Summit in October 1974, when it became clear that an Arab consensus had been forged to recognize the PLO as the sole legitimate representative of the Palestinian people, that the Soviet Union finally took the plunge and elevated its relations with the PLO and unambiguously demanded the creation of a Palestinian state.

The final section describes the evolution of Soviet–PLO relations in the aftermath of the Rabat Summit up to the beginning of the Lebanese civil war in late 1975. Generally in this period, the Soviet Union looked with growing favour at the benefits of its new strategic relationship with the PLO, despite continuing frustrations over the PLO's refusal to recognize Israel. In particular, the Soviet Union was satisfied at how the Palestine question, and the increased authority of the PLO, had become major constraints obstructing the US unilateralist drive for a comprehensive peace settlement. Some Soviet officials even adopted an optimistic expectation that the PLO might become the principal catalyst for the radicalization of the region and that, like Nasir's Egypt in the past, the PLO might be an independent force ensuring that the region remained committed to an anti-imperialist and progressive path.

THE OCTOBER 1973 WAR AND THE GENEVA CONFERENCE

The outcome of the Jordanian crisis in 1970–1 was to place the peace process on the diplomatic back burner. Perceiving Soviet machinations behind the crisis, the US administration lost interest in diplomatic collaboration with the Soviet Union. In addition, with Israel having seemingly demonstrated its strategic value in resolving the crisis, there was little US resolve to enforce Israeli concessions for a settlement with the Arab states. In this period of diplomatic stagnation, Soviet frustration was more than matched by Arab disenchantment and a growing conviction that a further war was unavoidable.

The Soviet leadership was acutely aware of the belligerent mood in the Arab world and made considerable diplomatic efforts to avoid the outbreak of a further war. In a dramatic display of brinkmanship at the San Clemente US–Soviet Summit in June 1972, Brezhnev woke up Nixon late in the evening and demanded an immediate settlement of the Arab–Israeli conflict, warning darkly of the global consequences of another Middle East war. Nixon fended off this extraordinary diplomatic challenge and Kissinger subsequently reflected that 'we were not willing to pay for *détente* in the coin of our geopolitical position.'[1] After the failure of this *démarche*, the Soviet leadership appears to have concluded that it could no longer oppose the Arab determination to wage another war against Israel. In a sombre mood, the Soviet leadership steeled itself for a further Arab defeat.[2]

The actual outcome of the October 1973 war exceeded Soviet expectations. Although the Arab armies had not won a military victory, they had surprised Israel and had been on the offensive for the earlier part of the war. These early successes had, as Soviet commentators were quick to point out, destroyed the myth that Israel was militarily invincible.[3] The Arabs consequently had a stronger bargaining position in the negotiations for a political settlement. Although Israel had eventually regained the initiative, this only compelled the United States to collaborate with the Soviet Union over the implementation of a cease-fire so as to prevent the escalation of the conflict to superpower level. On 21 October Kissinger flew to Moscow and secured a joint US–Soviet agreement on a cease-fire-in-place, together with a call for negotiations based on UN Resolution 242, which was a few hours later adopted by the Security Council in UN Resolution 338.

A crucial concession that the Soviet Union obtained from Kissinger's visit was that both sides would serve as co-chairmen of an eventual peace conference. For the Soviet leadership, this concession was viewed as a formal US recognition of the legitimate interests of the Soviet Union in the Middle East and most especially its right to be included, on an equal and reciprocal basis with the United States, in any peace negotiations between Israel and the Arab states. It was hoped that this development had concluded the years of exclusion from the peace process and that the US would genuinely accept the Soviet Union as a legitimate partner and co-equal in the diplomatic search for peace.

One key question which confronted Soviet policy-makers was the role that the PLO might play in the proposed international conference. The problem was that by 1973 the Soviet relationship with the PLO had developed to such a degree that this issue could not be simply avoided. In spite of the débâcle in Jordan, Arafat returned to Moscow as the head of a PLO delegation in October 1971 and then in August 1972. After the second of these visits, the Palestinian press noted that 'there was a completely new atmosphere to the talks', which had been symbolized by the greeting of the head of the Soviet delegation that 'we recognize your movement with the highest level of recognition.'[4] Although Palestinian enthusiasm tended to exceed the actual political realities, the Soviet Union did noticeably upgrade its relations with the PLO.[5] During 1972, there were reports that the first arms supplies to the PLO had been received.[6] Soviet diplomacy also expended considerable political capital to ensure that the final communiqué of the Nixon–Brezhnev Summit in June 1973 included joint support for the 'legitimate interests of the Palestinian people'.[7]

However, the Soviet Union had not made any binding or substantively new commitment to the PLO in the period prior to the 1973 war. Like the period from 1968–71, the reasons for these moves have to be seen as primarily tactical in nature. At a time when the Soviet Union was excluded from any role in the peace process, support for the PLO confirmed Moscow's radical credentials. In addition, the PLO visits to Moscow in 1971 and 1972 closely followed developments in the Arab world which appeared to threaten Soviet interests. In 1971, the PLO delegation arrived after the wide-scale purge of Sudanese communists, and the 1972 visit took place in the aftermath of Anwar Sadat's decision to expel all Soviet units from Egypt. Public demonstration of Soviet support for the Palestinian struggle was an effective way of bolstering Soviet prestige after these potentially damaging developments.

The Soviet Union was not, therefore, unconditionally committed to support PLO participation in the proposed international conference, which eventually took place in Geneva in December 1973. If the Soviet Union were to contemplate promoting the inclusion of the PLO, it would only be on the basis of the PLO adopting a realistic and moderate political programme. This was made clear in a memorandum sent to the PLO in October 1973 demanding that the PLO must adopt a unified stance around a commitment to a Palestinian mini-state as a precondition for Soviet support for PLO participation in the conference.[8] Such a Palestinian mini-state, existing alongside rather than instead of Israel, implicitly required recognition of Israel, which the PLO's political programme explicitly ruled out.

Although the formal demand that the PLO should move towards a mini-state was new, Soviet officials had been exploring with the PLO the possibilities of a Palestinian state even prior to the 1973 war. In early 1971, there were reports of a series of meetings between Arafat and the Soviet ambassador to Jordan on this issue.[9] In the August 1972 PLO visit to Moscow, Soviet officials stressed that the PLO leadership must offer a definite plan to counter King Husayn's suggestion for a United Arab Kingdom (UAK), which envisaged a federation between the West and East Banks of Jordan. The King's plan was thought in Moscow to have 'some realism' and that the Palestinians must submit 'a plan consistent with international conditions'.[10] In early 1973, the Lebanese President, Raymond Eddé, informed the press that an important Soviet leader had suggested that a solution to the Palestine question could be based on the implementation of the scheme for a Palestinian state.[11] The Soviet media guardedly promoted this idea during 1973, as in the *Radio Moscow in Arabic* broadcast of 5 March 1973 which suggested that the Palestinians themselves 'can deal with the question of the forms of exercising their right to determine their own destiny' and then discussed the 1947 partition plan as concerned about 'the creation of an Arab state on the basis of this right . . . to determine their own future'.

However, the Soviet Union continued to keep its options open and was only willing to commit itself to a Palestinian state if the PLO, with the support of the rest of the Arab world, were to make this objective, with its implied recognition of Israel's right to exist, its central political demand.[12] It was to pursue this avenue that the Soviet Union invited all the principal Palestinian factions to Moscow in November 1973. The Soviet leadership was also determined that any PLO decision must gain the support of all the factions, since it had regularly argued that 'the unification of the ranks of the Palestinian Resistance within the framework of a national front' was the pre-condition for the creation of a 'mass base without which the movement cannot develop'.[13] The Soviet Union had been encouraged by the PLO's more positive attitude to the participation of the Jordanian Communist Party, whose members dominated the Palestine National Front (PNF) which had been established in August 1973 to co-ordinate activities on the West Bank.[14] It was hoped that the PNF had established a precedent for PLO unified action in the post-1973 war period.

Thus, the Soviet Union made sure that its invitation to talks in Moscow included all the major PLO factions. The delegation which arrived in Moscow on 19 November 1973 included representatives from Fatah, the PFLP, the Popular Democratic Front for the Liberation of Palestine (PDFLP), the Syrian-sponsored al-Sa'iqa, and the Iraqi-sponsored Arab Liberation Front (ALF). One of these participants has given a first-hand account of the advice which the Soviet delegation, under the leadership of CPSU Secretary Boris Ponomarev, gave to the PLO leadership.[15] The fundamental premise of the Soviet position was that a final settlement was inevitable, that this would take place at the Geneva Peace Conference and that the Palestine Resistance must attend the Conference if its interests were to be safeguarded. To ensure its participation, the onus was on the PLO to adopt a flexible and realistic set of political objectives. In particular, the PLO must make provision for the creation of a Palestinian mini-state, which 'would not necessarily be the one envisaged by the 1947 partition plan.' Ponomarev suggested that it was premature to proclaim a provisional government, since that would alienate Jordan and make the task of convening the Conference more difficult. The Soviet Union did not want to be in the position of having to recognize such a government since it 'would run the risk of provoking a crisis at the conference.'

The Soviet delegation did reassure its guests that, whatever decisions were made by the Palestine Resistance, it would continue to support the Palestinians' national rights at the political and material level and to recognize the PLO as the legitimate representative of the Palestinian people. However, it did not minimize the real dangers if the PLO failed to participate at Geneva. Ponomarev argued that the other parties to the dispute might reach a settlement without resolving the Palestine question. In such an event:

> There is a danger of seeing several Arab governments bringing pressure to bear on you and hounding you, exiling and perhaps liquidating you. Would it not be wiser and more realistic for you to play an integral part in these talks and in a final settlement in order to stop a solution liable to be detrimental to your interests?[16]

Despite the forcefulness of the Soviet presentation, it failed to elicit the desired response from the Palestinian side. For the PFLP and the ALF such political moderation was completely unacceptable. Holding firm to the ideal of the liberation of all Palestine, George Habash, the leader of the PFLP, directly criticized the Soviet stance since it meant that 'Israel would survive even if the maximum achieved at the Geneva Conference was the acceptance of the Soviet point of view, since that it is the Soviet understanding of a just settlement.'[17] After this outburst, the PFLP's relations with the Soviet Union rapidly deteriorated and were only restored in the late 1970s. Habash refused to participate in subsequent PLO visits to Moscow, and the PFLP and the Soviet Union exchanged propaganda attacks on each other.[18]

While the Soviet Union failed to make any progress with the adamantly rejectionist PFLP and ALF, it might have hoped for a more
positive response from the PDFLP, which had before the October war
recommended that the PLO adopt an interim goal of a mini-state. Yet,
even the PDFLP questioned the premises of the Soviet position. Naif
Hawatmah, the leader of the PDFLP, disagreed that a settlement would
be likely to be attained at the Geneva Conference and rather saw greater
prospects in continued armed struggle in a long war of liberation. He
also warned that the Soviet position on a mini-state included recognition of Israel and counselled the PLO to be careful that the 'current
rights of the Palestinians should not substitute the ultimate rights of
the Palestinians' – meaning that any partial gains should not be attained at the expense of the ultimate objective of the liberation of all
of Palestine.[19]

Soviet hopes for a diplomatic breakthrough were further upset by
the failure of Fatah, the largest and most influential Palestinian organization, to adopt a clear-cut stance on the Geneva Conference and the
idea of a mini-state. Fatah's problem was that, though it was dominant
in terms of number of members, its ability to define unilaterally a new
political agenda was strictly limited. Being a politically heterogeneous
organization, with members adopting widely diverging ideological positions, its policy formulation was dependent on attaining a consensus
with the other smaller guerrilla organizations. Without such a consensus, Fatah was unable, and unwilling, to enforce a unified stance. Arafat's
response to the Soviet Union was, therefore, a request for more time
to smooth over the differences between the different factions. At a press
conference in late November, Arafat showed his evident exasperation
at Soviet pressure for political concessions: 'We must take time, hold
consultations, and discuss and deliberate. . . . We do not want to be
massacred under pressure from any quarter. We want to make our own
decision. We want to face our own fate.'[20]

By the end of the visit, the Soviet Union had failed to persuade the
PLO adopt a political stance which might permit PLO officials to participate at the Geneva Conference. Rather than reaching a unified and
clear political stance, the PLO had split into rival factions with irrec-
oncilable political and strategic programmes. The Soviet Union, however, was not willing to allow its overriding strategic interest in convening
the Geneva Conference to become a victim of the PLO's inability to
adopt realistic objectives. In the Soviet redraft of the US letter to the
UN Secretary-General on the convening of the Conference, there was
no explicit mention of the Palestinians. All that the final draft recom-

mended was that the invitations to Syria, Egypt, Jordan and Israel should be 'without prejudice to possible additional participants at a later stage'.[21] In Gromyko's speech to the Conference on 21 December, there was only a passing reference to the Palestine question and the sole concession to the issue of Palestinian representation was that 'it is not possible to consider and decide upon the Palestinian problem without the participation of the representatives of the Arab people of Palestine.'[22] There was no mention of the PLO or that the Palestinian question might be anything more than a refugee issue.

At the end of 1973, therefore, the Soviet Union was keeping its distance from the PLO and leaving its options open over the future destiny of the Israeli-occupied territories in the West Bank and Gaza Strip. Rather than adopting any new position, the Soviet Union forcefully reasserted its traditional stand towards the prerequisites for a political settlement. In a keynote speech to the World Congress of Peace-loving Forces on 26 October 1973, Brezhnev reiterated Soviet commitment to UN Resolution 242 and a 'just settlement of the 'problem of refugees', that is the ensuring of the legitimate rights of the Arab people of Palestine'.[23] At his speech at the Geneva Conference, Gromyko had underlined that Israel's international borders were those of June 1967. The Soviet attitude to the PLO was that it had to come to terms with these international realities and only then could it expect to have its interests taken into account. Until that time, the Soviet Union would give its considered advice. The PLO could only expect full Soviet support if it actually incorporated this advice into its political programme.

TO THE RABAT CONFERENCE

Despite the Soviet restraint at promoting the claims of the PLO, any optimism in Moscow that the Geneva Conference would initiate intense US–Soviet collaboration towards a peace settlement was swiftly dispelled during the course of 1974. Kissinger had, in fact, never seen the Geneva Conference as anything other than a 'useful fiction' which would satisfy the minimal Soviet demands for a formal role in negotiations and thus prevent the Soviet Union from obstructing unilateral US initiatives for bilateral interim agreements between Israel and the Arab states.[24] The first success for Kissinger's strategy came on 18 January 1974 when Israel and Egypt signed a disengagement agreement, which had been negotiated exclusively through US mediation. Kissinger then immediately turned his attention to the Syrian front, visiting President Asad on 20 January, and subsequently engaging in an intense mediation effort between the Israeli and Syrian governments, which finally resulted in a Syrian–Israeli agreement on the disengagement of forces on the Golan Heights signed on 31 May. Bolstered by these successes, President Nixon embarked on a triumphant tour of the Middle East in June 1974 and was rapturously received in the Arab capitals he visited, including Damascus.

By the middle of 1974, Soviet influence and prestige in the Middle East appeared to be in tatters. The United States had seized the diplomatic initiative and had confirmed its unique capability to mediate between Israel and the Arab states. The Soviet Union had, in contrast, been forced to watch impotently from the sidelines as Egypt started publicly to attack the Soviet Union, Syria openly flirted with the West, and Jordan and Israel remained firmly embedded in the Western alliance. Soviet diplomatic and propaganda activity in this period revealed its feeling of frustration. Kissinger's diplomatic achievements were ridiculed as 'involving monumental effort producing pitifully small results'.[25] Brezhnev condemned the resulting 'ersatz plans' as substituting partial agreements for an all-embracing comprehensive settlement and accused Kissinger of violating the agreement that negotiations would be conducted in Geneva under joint US–Soviet auspices.[26] On 26 March, Kissinger had a three and one-half hour meeting with Brezhnev and his aides over the question of whether negotiations should return to Geneva, which he described as the 'toughest and most unpleasant' he had ever had with the Soviet leader.[27]

It was this unexpected turn in events, with the United States seemingly ascendant in the region, that the Soviet Union again sought to consolidate relations with the PLO after their temporary severance during the period of the Geneva Conference. In these new circumstances, the value of Soviet patronage of the PLO became more self-evident. With all the Arab confrontation states engaging in extensive diplomatic consultations with the United States, the PLO was the sole actor totally dependent on Soviet support. More critically, the growing Arab support to promote the PLO as the sole legitimate representative of the Palestinian people threatened to undercut Jordan's claims to the West Bank and to undermine the prospects of a US-sponsored peace agreement between Israel and Jordan. If such an option could be pre-empted, this would obstruct Kissinger's attempts to reach a comprehensive settlement through the accumulation of interim agreements and, the Soviet Union hoped, would enforce a return to the Geneva Conference.

It was for this reason that the Soviet Union gradually increased its support for the Palestinian cause during 1974. In March, Brezhnev pointed to this new level of Soviet support by changing the traditional slogan of support for the Palestinians' 'legitimate rights' to support of their 'national legitimate rights'.[28] During the same month, the Soviet media noted favourably the Arab claim that 103 countries had granted the PLO full recognition as the sole legitimate representative of the Palestinian people.[29] The sympathetic Soviet coverage of the terrorist actions in Kiryat Shemona and Maalot in May 1974 also reflected a new-found resolve not to antagonize the PLO, with the accounts primarily blaming Israeli provocations and complicity.[30] This was in stark contrast to the uninhibited condemnations of the Palestinian terrorist attacks at the Rome and Athens airports just prior to the Geneva Conference.[31]

However, the Soviet Union was not willing to be rushed into any unqalified recognition of the PLO or the need to establish a Palestinian state. While the rest of the Arab world was still to make up its mind on the status of the PLO and the sovereign destiny of the West Bank and Gaza Strip, the Soviet Union was not going to anticipate any final Arab decision on these matters. In addition, Soviet diplomats did not want the PLO to be granted a role in the peace process if its political programme, due to its extremist demands, would necessarily exclude the organization from serious negotiations. Thus, during this period, the Soviet Union was determined to keep its options open. A delegation from the Jordanian Communist Party (JCP) on a visit to Moscow in May 1974 was to have a direct experience of this Soviet ambivalence. The JCP delegation had arrived in Moscow to receive what it thought would be a formal confirmation of the unanimous decision of its Central Committee to establish a separate Palestinian Communist Party. Much to the delegation's surprise, Ponomarev stated that, while respecting the decisions made by the JCP Central Committee, the CPSU believed that such a move would be premature given the existing international conditions. Fearing that a Palestinian party would not receive Soviet recognition, the JCP did not implement its decision.[32]

The Soviet Union also hoped that its studied ambiguity on the Palestine question would encourage the PLO to make substantive reforms in its political programme. On the day of the opening of the 12th Palestine National Council (PNC) in June, when the Soviet Union hoped the PLO would initiate such policy reforms, the first semi-official support for a Palestinian state was given by the commentator Igor Belaiev but with the pointed qualification that Palestinian interests could be accommodated by 'some other variant'.[33] Gromyko, in his talks with Arafat in Egypt and Syria on a number of occasions during 1974, repeatedly asserted that the Soviet Union expected a decision to be taken on the borders of a Palestinian state on the West Bank and Gaza Strip and that full Soviet support was dependent on reaching such a decision.[34]

The 12th PNC did introduce some changes to the PLO's political programme. The establishment of 'the people's independent national authority over any part of the Palestinian territory which was liberated', which was a significant move towards the mini-state idea, was defined as an interim objective. There was also an indirect commitment to attend the Geneva Conference, so long as it was not based on UN Resolution 242 and included explicit recognition of the national rights of the Palestinians.[35] However, these tentative moves in the direction of moderation fell short of Soviet expectations. There was no recognition of Israel; Resolution 242, the legal basis of the Geneva Conference, was unambiguously rejected; and the conception of a 'national authority' only partially obscured the PLO's ultimate objective of the liberation of all of Palestine. Soviet reporting of the PNC only gave lukewarm approval of the new political programme and attention was focused on the differences between the Rejection Front (the PFLP, PFLP-GC and ALF) and the other more moderate factions. Overall, the PNC was summed up by one Soviet commentator as 'an important but cautious step forward, and now history will tell how correct it was'.[36]

Given the ambiguous and limited nature of the PLO reforms to its political programme, the Soviet Union continued its propaganda campaign to secure greater PLO moderation. Just prior to a PLO visit to Moscow in August 1974, Lev Tolkunov, editor of *Izvestiia*, wrote a long article on the Palestine Resistance, highlighting the class differentiation among the Palestinians and the attendant dangers of reactionary capitulation and extremist petty-bourgeois terrorist activity. Tolkunov stressed that this disunity must be overcome and that the Palestinians 'need to have of necessity well-defined tactical goals – in other words, must formulate a programme which would keep faith with the international efforts towards the just settlement of the Near Eastern dispute.'[37]

However, such admonitions failed again to induce the desired Palestinian response. The final statement on the visit showed that the Soviet Union had made no progress on securing PLO agreement to attend the Geneva Conference on the basis of UN Resolution 242 or to accept a Palestinian state with defined borders.[38] As a consequence, the Soviet Union downplayed the significance of the visit and the Soviet media did not give the publicity to the visit which Gromyko had earlier promised. Nevertheless, in the final communiqué the Soviet Union expressed its 'approval' of the decisions of the Algiers and Lahore Conferences to recognize the PLO as the sole legitimate representative of the Palestinian people.[39] The Soviet Union also must have tacitly approved the East German government's decision, a week after Arafat left Moscow, to offer full and unambiguous recognition of the PLO.[40]

However, Soviet attempts to keep its options open in the hope of securing further concessions from the PLO were to be finally concluded in September 1974. In this month, the Soviet Union officially announced its commitment to the creation of a Palestinian state and to recognition of the PLO as the legitimate representative of the Palestinian people. The principal catalyst for this Soviet shift was Sadat's decision to end the search for a compromise with King Husayn over Palestinian representation and to give full support to the PLO at the forthcoming Arab Summit in Rabat in October. With Sadat's change of direction, an Arab consensus in favour of the PLO had been forged which King Husayn could not oppose. With this new strategic reality, the Soviet Union was determined to be at the forefront, and the main external sponsor, of this unified Arab consensus born around the elevation of the PLO as the sole legitimate representative of the Palestinian people. From the Soviet perspective, such support not only emphasized Soviet support for the Arab cause. It also highlighted the failure of the United States to forge a settlement of the West Bank through an Israeli–Jordanian deal and confirmed the need to return to the Geneva forum to attain a truly comprehensive settlement.

The first official indication of the new unambiguous and clearly defined Soviet position on the Palestine question came on 8 September, when President Podgornii, in a speech in Bulgaria, made the first official statement in favour of the Palestinian right 'to set up their own state in whatever form'.[41] In a keynote speech on 11 October in Kishinev, Moldavia, Brezhnev confirmed that the Soviet Union was pursuing 'friendly solidarity . . . with the leadership of the PLO' and that there was the need to satisfy 'the legitimate rights of the Arab people of Palestine, the right to their national hearth'.[42]

The stage was now set for full Soviet support for the decisions of the Rabat Summit of 28 October to elevate the PLO as the sole legitimate representative of the Palestinian people.[43] In the aftermath of the Summit, Soviet diplomatic resources were fully exploited to support the invitation by the Arab states for a PLO delegation, headed by Arafat, to participate at the 29th session of the United Nations General Assembly in November. The Soviet representative to the UN, Iakob Malik, praised the decision to permit the PLO to participate in the discussions, since it confirmed 'the growing international recognition of the justice of the goals that the Arab people of Palestine are struggling for'. Malik also stressed the growing authority of the 'leading force of the Palestinian struggle – the PLO' and that 'the Palestine Resistance Movement is becoming ever more mature and has now turned into a weighty and realistic factor of the political situation in the Near East.' As a consequence, 'no settlement on the backs of or bypassing the interests of the Palestinian people can be either just or long-lasting.'[44]

The Soviet Union also took an active role in securing the successful passage of General Assembly Resolution 3236, which affirmed the rights of the Palestinians to self-determination and to national independence and sovereignty. Soviet reporting of this resolution emphasized that it reaffirmed the original UN resolution in 1947 to give the Arab people of Palestine the right to set up their own independent state. In the Soviet reporting, therefore, the Palestine question was presented as reassuming its rightful position as the central element in the Arab–Israeli conflict, from which, for one reason or another, it had been dislodged in the intervening 27 years.[45]

THE PALESTINE QUESTION AND SOVIET DIPLOMACY AFTER RABAT

Although the Soviet Union presented its decision to support the creation of an independent Palestinian state, under the authority of the PLO, as a natural evolution in its policy-making, in reality the 1974 decision represented a major change in its overall strategic approach to the Arab–Israeli conflict. As such, there was a fundamental 'paradigm shift' in the Soviet approach to the Palestine question.[46] The period from September to November 1974 marked the transition from the traditional Soviet stance that the Palestine question represented a refugee issue to the commitment to create an independent Palestinian state. It also brought to an end Soviet reserve over the status and legitimacy of the PLO. From now on, Soviet officials and commentators continually stressed that no solution of the Palestine question was possible without the participation of the PLO.

The extent of this 'paradigm shift' can be seen by comparing the Soviet position in late 1974 with an earlier articulation of the Soviet stance in 1971, which was set out clearly in a document providing the minutes of a meeting in Moscow in May 1971 between the Syrian Communist Party (SCP) and Soviet Politburo members, Mikhail Suslov and Boris Ponomarev.[47] The catalyst for this meeting was the Soviet leadership's unease over the SCP's draft political programme which was considered to pay too much attention to the Palestine issue. As a result, Suslov and Ponomarev repeatedly stressed that the Palestine question was not the central issue facing the Arab world. Instead of focusing on Palestine, the Syrian communists were told to engage in the more important aspects of the struggle, such as 'supporting the progressive regimes, increasing fighting capacity, intensifying the revolutionary process, etc.' In relation to Israel, the Arab struggle was 'to change the colonialist character of the state of Israel, not the elimination of Israel as a state'. This objective was a long-term problem requiring profound changes both within Israel as well as the Arab states.

As regards the specifics of the Palestine question, Ponomarev stated that UN Resolution 242 'provides a solution to the Palestine problem' through its provisions for the return, or compensation, of the Palestinian refugees. If in a more ambiguous manner, it can be inferred that the Soviet Union continued to favour the return of the West Bank to Jordan as it was stressed that 'the right to self-determination does not necessarily imply a separate state.' More directly, there emerges throughout the discussions a highly negative Soviet appraisal of the Palestinian guerrilla factions. There was explicit condemnation of George Habash and other 'extremists'. But, more damagingly, the Soviet leaders dismissed the Palestinian guerrilla activity as a military failure and that 'Israel could even have ignored it.' It was further argued that the failure to forge a mass base had been brutally exposed by the 1970 Jordanian crisis, when the Jordanian authorities were able to wipe out the movement, despite the fact that '60 per cent of the population are Palestinians'.

In 1971, therefore, the leading authorities of the Soviet communist party were encouraging their Syrian comrades to treat the PLO and its activities with scepticism and to cease viewing the 'Palestine problem as the pivot of the Arab liberation movement'. However, three years later in 1974, the Soviet Union was ignoring its earlier advice and had placed the Palestine question as a central, if not the defining, feature of the Arab struggle. This was to receive its most authoritative confirmation in the Soviet peace proposals, unveiled by the Soviet leader, Leonid Brezhnev, in November 1974, which established three pillars for a peace settlement which were to remain the essential foundations of all later Soviet peace proposals right up to the disintegration of the Soviet Union in 1991. The second, and the distinctively new, of the three pillars of this plan was the 'legitimate right of the Palestinian

people to create their own state, to self-determination'. The Palestine
question was thus elevated alongside the two other more constant features of Soviet objectives – the withdrawal of Israeli forces from territory occupied in 1967 and the provision of external 'guarantees of the
security and independence of all states involved within the sphere of
the conflict'.[48]

However, with this new definitive articulation of the Soviet approach
to a peace settlement, the challenge facing the Soviet Union was how
to translate its greater commitment to the Palestinian cause towards
promoting its broader policy objectives, the most important of which
was the reconvening of the Geneva Conference. In an indirect manner,
through undermining Kissinger's diplomatic momentum, the Soviet
manipulation of the Palestinian card brought immediate and gratifying
dividends. To Kissinger's considerable disquiet, the elevation of the
PLO as the sole legitimate representative of the Palestinian people struck
a fatal blow to the possibility of a US-sponsored Jordanian agreement
with Israel. A few months later in March 1975, Kissinger aborted his
four-month attempt to forge a second Egyptian–Israeli disengagement
agreement and angrily asserted that there would be a 'reassessment' of
the US strategic position in the Middle East. Although a number of factors have to be taken into account for this failure, including most notably
the weakness and divisions of the new Israeli government under Premier
Yitzhak Rabin, one important element was Soviet support for the formation of a Syrian–Jordanian–PLO axis in opposition to Sadat. The PLO
played a significant role in cementing this axis by accepting the Syrian
invitation of 7 March to unify its political leadership and military command with Syria. The Soviet-sponsored Syrian–Jordanian–PLO front highlighted Sadat's isolation in the Arab world, limiting his room for
manoeuvre and preventing him from displaying flexibility towards Israel.

Although this caused a major setback to US diplomacy, it only
temporarily delayed Kissinger from reaching a second Egyptian–Israeli
disengagement agreement which was formally signed in Geneva on 4
September. Further wounds to Soviet prestige were then inflicted in
March 1976 by Sadat's decision unilaterally to abrogate Egypt's Treaty
of Friendship and Co-operation with the Soviet Union. Soviet displeasure
over these developments were forcefully expressed by Brezhnev to
President Ford at the Helsinki Summit in July 1975 when he stated:
'we understood that you were going to include us in the peace process
and that our two countries would work together. Here you are, going
off at a tangent. That is contrary to the spirit of *détente*, and it's up-
setting us.'[49]

However, the Sinai II agreement was the last major diplomatic success brokered by Kissinger in the Middle East. Furthermore, the ensuing Soviet counter-strategy of forcibly promoting the Palestine question in collaboration with its Arab allies was again to demonstrate the potential of Soviet obstructionism. Deeply wounded by the new US diplomatic success, the Soviet Union felt no inhibitions in promoting an aggressive propaganda campaign against the United States and Israel. In this campaign, the Soviet Union co-ordinated its policies fully with the PLO and Syria. In November 1975, the Soviet Union supported the Syrian initiative to obtain a Security Council discussion on the Middle East, with the participation of the PLO, in exchange for agreeing to a six-month extension of the UN forces mandate on the Golan Heights. In a note to the US government on 9 November, the Soviet Union buttressed the Syrian offensive by demanding that an invitation should be sent to the PLO to attend the Geneva Conference. Indicating its more hardline stance, the Soviet Union also demanded that the basis of the Conference should include UN General Assembly Resolution 3236, involving recognition of the Palestinian right to self-determination, as well as Resolution 242.[50]

The Soviet Union then increased the heat by providing full support for the notorious UN General Assembly Resolution of 10 November that recognized Zionism as a form of racism. In justification of this resolution, the Soviet Union argued that Israeli refusal to recognize the PLO or to attend the Geneva Conference showed that 'the ruling circles of Israel are ruling as Zionists, that is with a racist approach to the Arab people.'[51] Gromyko also threateningly commented that Israeli intransigence over these issues meant that 'the very existence of Israel cannot be guaranteed.'[52] At the Security Council debate on the Middle East in January 1976, the Soviet Union further identified itself with the Palestinian cause by forwarding a resolution which affirmed the Palestinian people's right to self-determination and 'to establish an independent state in Palestine in accordance with the Charter of the United Nations'.[53] The subsequent US veto of the resolution was vigorously denounced in the Soviet press.[54]

Although the extreme and belligerent nature of these Soviet diplomatic tactics was condemned in Washington, the underlying message that Moscow sought to convey was ultimately taken on board. The new US administration under President Jimmy Carter, which was inaugurated in early 1977, instituted a fundamental change in US strategic objectives towards the Arab–Israeli conflict. The intellectual underpinnings for this strategy came from a Brookings Report, published in December 1975.[55] Although not fully corresponding to the Soviet peace proposals, the report was considerably closer to the Soviet position than Kissinger's approach. In particular, the report offered a more sympathetic account of the plight of the Palestinians, confirming their right to self-determination which 'might take the form of a Palestinian state . . . or a Palestinian entity voluntarily federated with Jordan but exercising extensive political autonomy'. More critically from the Soviet perspective, the report recommended a shift from Kissinger's strategy of deliberately seeking to exclude the participation of the Soviet Union to a, if only limited, degree of US collaboration with Moscow so as to pre-empt Soviet obstruction of the peace process. Finally, the report advocated moving away from partial, interim agreements to the search for a comprehensive settlement which would be ratified at a reconvened Geneva Conference.

At the beginning of 1977, therefore, the Soviet Union could feel reasonably satisfied that its strategy of promoting a Palestinian state had brought dividends. In an indirect manner, it had contributed to the shift in US strategy towards a collaborative approach for a comprehensive settlement of the Arab–Israeli conflict. But, this had been primarily a demonstration of Soviet negative powers – the powers of obstruction and blocking US unilateral diplomacy. What, however, remained substantially untested was the extent to which Soviet sponsorship of the PLO could be directed in a positive and constructive manner to contribute towards a comprehensive peace settlement. Despite all Soviet efforts, the PLO's political programme remained essentially unreconstructed and rejectionist in essence. If the Soviet–PLO relationship were ultimately to bear fruit, it would require PLO acceptance of a number of significant political compromises and concessions. Without such changes in PLO strategy, even the most stalwart Soviet support could not induce the United States, let alone Israel, to contemplate direct negotiations with the PLO leadership.

The US–Soviet collaborative drive towards the Geneva Conference during 1977 was to test most vigorously the constructive potential of the Soviet–PLO relationship. The complex negotiations of this period is the subject of Chapter 5. However, two years earlier during the course of 1975, when the peace process had lost much of its momentum, the Soviet Union was to have a foretaste of some of the inherent difficulties of promoting the inclusion of the PLO in any peace negotiations. The context of this was the Soviet attempt to promote the Brezhnev Plan of November 1974 after the Ford administration's decision in early 1975 to engage in a strategic reassessment of US policies in the Middle

East. With this US disengagement, the Soviet Union had a clear opportunity to promote its distinctive conception of a comprehensive peace settlement and to demonstrate, both to the Arab world and to Israel, that its preferred diplomatic strategy was more productive than Kissinger's incremental advances through interim agreements.

Overall, the Soviet diplomatic initiative to promote its peace proposals during 1975 was a failure. Even before the PLO delegation arrived in Moscow to present their response to the Brezhnev Plan, Soviet diplomacy had suffered a number of severe blows. Informal Soviet approaches to attempt to convince the Israeli government that the 'guarantees' provided by the Brezhnev plan would satisfy Israeli security concerns failed to elicit a favourable response.[56] Moreover, the emphasis on the Soviet commitment to Israeli security only served to alienate Moscow's Arab allies. Gromyko distinctly displeased the Syrian Foreign Minister, Abd al-Halim Khaddam, when at the welcoming dinner speech in Moscow he confirmed that 'Israel can receive, if it so desires, the strictest possible guarantees, with the participation – in an appropriate agreement – of the Soviet Union.'[57] Such explicit recognition of Israel's borders was anathema to Syria's pan-Arabist ideological commitment and Syria refused to condone the Soviet position. Although Egypt was less distressed by Soviet commitment to Israel's security, a visit by Foreign Minister Ismail Fahmi ended in an acrimonious argument over Soviet arms supplies and Egypt's debt to the Soviet Union. Fahmi made clear that Egyptian commitment to the Geneva Conference was dependent on Moscow dealing with these issues first.[58]

The atmosphere was not, therefore, auspicious for the visit to Moscow of a PLO delegation almost immediately after the unsuccessful and difficult Egyptian and Syrian visits. Indeed, a serious blow had been struck before the arrival of delegation, when Zuhayr Muhsin from the Sa'iqa organization and the PNC chairman, Khalid al-Fahum, refused to go to Moscow, presumably under Syrian pressure. Muhsin explained his position by stating that 'the Soviets committed a new blunder by offering strict guarantees for Israel's independent existence. They have fallen into the trap which portrays the Middle East problems as one of a lack of security and protection for Israel's existence.'[59] The only factions, then, which actually arrived in Moscow were from Fatah and the PDFLP, since, apart from Sa'iqa, the Rejection Front of the PFLP, ALF and PFLP-GC had refused to continue official contacts with the Soviet Union since mid-1974. Being thus isolated, Fatah and the PDFLP delegates had little room for manoeuvre or for granting political concessions.

Nevertheless, the Soviet Union clearly hoped that it might be able to salvage some diplomatic momentum from the PLO visit. To secure PLO recognition of Israel and a commitment to participation at the Geneva Conference would have been significant diplomatic coups. However, in the main, little progress was made during the PLO visit. Gromyko and Ponomarev reportedly spent over seven hours trying to persuade the PLO delegation to recognize Israel and to agree to attend the Geneva Conference.[60] They made no progress on obtaining a PLO commitment to recognize Israel but the final statement did include a PLO agreement to participate at the Geneva Conference. However, PLO officials were quick to point out that they still refused to accept Resolution 242 as the basis for the Conference and that they would only consider attending if the right of the Palestinians to self-determination was recognized.[61] This concession to the Soviet Union was, therefore, only a minimal advance on the PLO's earlier position towards the question of the Geneva Conference.

The Soviet Union was undoubtedly frustrated by the continued PLO intransigence. But, this frustration was only part of a Soviet disenchantment with the Arab world as a whole and its refusal ever to conform to the Soviet political programme. Many articles in this period indirectly reflected this Soviet exasperation by reiterating the need for Arab unity.[62] Direct criticism was also made in an Arabic language broadcast, which advised Arab politicians 'to show more flexibility, to see more readily the realities of the situation and the means available for settling existing differences and disputes. They must also be able to put aside narrow nationalist considerations in order to protect the vital interest of the entire Arab nation.'[63]

Indeed, from the Soviet perspective, relations with the PLO appeared in a relatively positive light compared to the other strategic Arab allies. Unlike Egypt and Syria, the PLO was not in a position to flirt with the United States and was far more dependent on Soviet patronage. The Soviet Union enjoyed exclusive relations with the PLO which mirrored, if in a far less significant manner, the US relationship with Israel. Thus, so long as Moscow could play its Palestinian card effectively, this guaranteed Soviet diplomatic involvement in the peace process. Given that the United States was constrained by its commitment to Israel not to negotiate with the PLO before the PLO recognized UN Resolution 242, the Soviet Union had a valuable diplomatic opening for securing its inclusion as a mediator in the conflict.

Although the PLO's political programme remained adamantly rejectionist, it had also shown a greater flexibility and potential moderation than Syria. Since the start of the decade, the PLO had made a number of significant concessions, which suggested at least a predisposition towards moderation. It had concluded its international terrorist campaigns; it had mended fences with a number of Arab regimes, most notably at the Rabat Summit; and it had moved towards recognition of Israel through the interim programme adopted at the 12th PNC in 1974. The Soviet Union had also managed in 1975 to obtain a PLO commitment to attend the Geneva Conference, if on a highly qualified basis. Although none of these moves involved a radical shift in the PLO's position, the Soviet Union could reasonably expect that, in more auspicious international and regional circumstances, the PLO might be more amenable to making the necessary compromises required to obtain peace. At the very least, the PLO showed a less extreme rejectionism than that offered by Syria.

For a Soviet leadership suffering the loss of Egypt due to its increasingly close relations with the United States, the elevation of relations with the PLO offered some sort of compensation. Egypt had been central to Soviet strategy ever since Khrushchev's first entry into the region in 1955. Soviet leaders had depended on Egypt, and Nasir's authority and charisma in the wider Arab world, to forge a pan-Arab consensus in favour of Soviet policies. Thus, Egypt's defection under Sadat had been a major blow to Soviet prestige and influence. For some Soviet policy-makers, working to an ideological framework which held that the 'correlation of forces' was ultimately heading in a progressive direction, there emerged an optimistic expectation that the PLO might even displace Egypt's earlier role, under Nasir, as the principal force reuniting the Arab world on a radical and progressive basis. The success of the Soviet–PLO relationship in undermining US diplomacy also encouraged this belief that the PLO could become a major radicalizing power in the region. An example of such an expectation can be seen in the work of Evgenii Pyrlin, a Deputy Head of the Middle East section of the Ministry of Foreign Affairs and a specialist on the Palestine question, who argued that:

> In relation to the overall Arab liberation movement the Palestinian movement is an undoubted factor in its radicalization, since it is precisely the Palestinian Arabs who are directly confronting the most odious manifestations of anti-Arab Zionist chauvinism. . . . The attitude to the Palestine Resistance Movement has for a long time been the distinctive watershed in the Arab world, which leaves on "different sides of the barricades" the advocates of the former colonialists and

the genuine patriots of the Arab nation. . . . From the attitude of the separate Arab governments to the Palestine problem it is possible to judge the extent of their anti-imperialist foreign policy orientation.[64]

However, Soviet expectations that the PLO might be an effective substitute for the loss of Egypt were destined to be disappointed. Nasir had the influence to forge a pan-Arab policy because he was the highly respected leader of the largest and most important independent Arab state. The PLO, in contrast, was a weak non-state actor, whose independence was strictly limited by its relations with its sponsors from the Arab states. The PLO was not only incapable of forging an Arab consensus, but its progress was dependent on, and was not a catalyst for, a pre-existing Arab consensus. The PLO's victories at the Rabat Summit and at the United Nations were the result of a prior pan-Arab agreement that this was advantageous to their interests. When such an Arab consensus was lacking, such as in 1975 when Syria and Egypt drifted apart, the PLO became effectively impotent. In Lebanon in 1976, the fracturing of the Lebanese nation reflected Arab divisions and the PLO was sucked into a wider inter-Arab conflict. By mid-1976, when the PLO was in direct conflict with Syria, the Soviet Union was faced with its greatest test of balancing its new-found enthusiasm for the PLO against the demands of its older and more powerful ally, Syria.

4 The Lebanese Civil War

In April 1975, a small incident in the Beirut suburb of Ain al-Rummanah sparked off a civil war which was to destroy the fragile unity of Lebanon. It also set a pattern for over fifteen years whereby the Lebanon became the proxy battlefield for the Arab–Israeli conflict and, just as importantly, for a number of destructive inter-Arab conflicts and disputes. As such, the Lebanese civil war, which lasted until autumn 1976, can be considered as the antithesis of the Rabat Summit. While Rabat had been a visible demonstration of Arab unity and collective Arab purpose, the Lebanese civil war highlighted the continuing salience of Arab disunity and the political and ideological tensions in inter-Arab relations. Both at Rabat and in Lebanon, the PLO played a central and formative role. However, while at Rabat the PLO had been the catalyst for forging an Arab unity around the Palestine question, in Lebanon it was a principal cause of a violent intra-Arab conflict which was to destroy much of Lebanon's social fabric.

On one level, the Soviet Union was clearly displeased by the developments in Lebanon, since the civil war provided another distressing display of the fragility of any Arab consensus and the apparent endless ability of the Arabs to fight between themselves rather than join together in a common anti-imperialist struggle. The coincidence of the fighting in Lebanon with the signing of the second US-sponsored Egyptian–Israeli disengagement agreement in late 1975 only served to accentuate the negative repercussions of these deep divisions in Arab society. However, on another level, the Lebanese civil war offered a number of potential benefits to the Soviet Union. In terms of Soviet ideology, the Palestinian and Muslim Lebanese alliance was clearly viewed as the progressive party in contrast to the Maronite Christian opposition. The Lebanese conflict also potentially offered the first testcase of the PLO's power to act as a radicalizing and progressive force in the region. Although Soviet policy-makers urged caution on their progressive allies, they still welcomed the prospects of a Lebanese leftist ascendance, so long as it was attained without provoking external intervention.

This chapter analyses the evolution of Soviet strategy during the period of the Lebanese civil war from April 1975 to late 1976. In the first section, there is an assessment of the early period of the conflict when the Soviet Union was able to present the conflict as a simple struggle between the forces of reaction and the forces of progress, which set the Christian Maronite forces against the Soviet Union's allies of Syria, the PLO and the Lebanese leftist coalition. The second section examines the period from spring to summer 1976 when the Soviet Union faced increasing difficulties in presenting such a simple bifurcated struggle as Syrian relations with the PLO and the Lebanese Left deteriorated into open conflict. Despite these developments, however, the Soviet Union continued to remain neutral between its warring allies. But, this policy of neutrality and even-handedness finally broke down in July 1976 when the Soviet Union shifted towards support for the PLO and expressed open and direct criticisms of Syria's involvement in the conflict. In the final two sections of the chapter, there is an analysis of the reasons for, and the implications of, this Soviet decision. In contrast to most other accounts of this shift in Soviet policy, it is argued that the support provided by Moscow to the PLO had a significant ideological dimension and was as much support *for* the PLO as a reaction *against* Syria.

EARLY STAGES OF THE CIVIL WAR

The large influx of PLO military factions into Lebanon after the PLO's expulsion from Jordan in 1970–1 has to be considered as one of the most significant causes for the Lebanese civil war. This Palestinian dimension was reflected in Soviet reporting of the early stages of the war which presented the conflict almost exclusively in terms of an attempt to curtail the freedom of action, or even to liquidate completely, the PLO and the Palestinian presence in Lebanon.[1] The Christian-rightist military offensive was portrayed as seeking to destroy the Palestinian military presence, building upon the earlier unsuccessful attempts by the Lebanese authorities in 1969 and 1973. The clear analogy was with the events in Jordan in 1970–1, when King Husayn had decisively confronted the Palestine Resistance and forced all the Palestinian fighting units to leave Jordanian soil.[2]

However, the root causes of the conflict had deeper and specifically Lebanese characteristics. The various communities cohabiting in the Lebanon had long-standing grievances independent of, and preceding, the mass immigration of Palestinians into the country. At the heart of these grievances was a dispute over the internal distribution of power. Ever since the formation of the independent Lebanese state in 1943, the Muslim communities had felt that the political system discriminated against their interests both politically and economically. The major institutions of state had been established with an in-built Christian dominance, with the Presidency reserved for a member of the Maronite community, and with all places in the government, civil service and army being filled on a quota system based on a 6–5 ratio of Christians to Muslims. This Christian political power had also been paralleled by its predominance in the economic field, especially in the powerful financial sector.[3]

Muslim dissatisfaction with the political system became more acute as demographic changes in favour of the Muslims led to the formation of a sizeable Muslim majority in the country. By the early 1970s Muslim demands for a more equitable political system had become more assertive. The charismatic Druze leader, Kamal Junblatt, had set up a powerful campaign for a radical reform of the political system, which sought to end the confessionalist structure of the state and establish a modern government which would not be subservient to the old oligarchic political structures. Junblatt also forged a number of independent Muslim parties into a powerful coalition alliance called the Lebanese National Movement (LNM).

Junblatt's political endeavours had been the principal force behind forging a more united and effective Muslim challenge to the Christian-dominated political status quo. However, the Palestinian guerrilla organizations also played a significant contributory role in this process. Most of the guerrillas felt a clear ideological affinity with the political programme of the LNM. By agreeing to add their support, they considerably boosted the political and, more importantly, the military power of the Muslim-leftist coalition. The assertive Palestinian presence in the Lebanon also gave the Muslims in Lebanon a considerable boost of self-confidence and contributed to the radicalization of the emerging Muslim proletariat, located in the so-called misery belt around Beirut, which provided the mainstay of support for Junblatt's programme of radical reforms.

Moving from its earlier exclusive concern for the Palestine Resistance, in the autumn of 1975 the Soviet Union began to address the specifically internal dimensions of the Lebanese crisis.[4] Not unsurprisingly, Moscow gave support to the LNM's political programme which was presented as a reasonable and legitimate critique of the colonial legacy of the 1943 constitution.[5] Soviet support was also predictable since its principal Lebanese allies were constituent members of the Muslim-leftist alliance. The Lebanese Communist Party (LCP) actively participated in the LNM and provided stalwart support for the idea of a deconfessionalized state and the removal of Christian Maronite hegemony. Kamal Junblatt was also a popular figure in Moscow and had been awarded the Lenin Peace prize and his party, the Progressive Socialist Party (PSP), was viewed as an anti-imperialist and progressive force. The close links between the LNM and the Palestine Resistance only confirmed Soviet support for the radical Muslim bloc.

In contrast to the LNM, the Christian Maronite opposition had little to commend itself to Soviet policy-makers. In the Soviet media, the Christian right was depicted as reactionary beneficiaries of an unjust and imposed colonial legacy. Their pro-Western orientation and links with Israel were treated with considerable distrust. It was unquestioningly assumed that the Christian militias, such as the Phalangists, were acting in collusion with Israel and the United States. In co-ordination with their allies, they were seen as engaged in a long-term campaign to preserve their oligarchic hold on power, to resist the pressures for Muslim political participation and to eradicate the Palestinian presence within Lebanon.

The Soviet predisposition to view the escalating Lebanese civil war in terms of a simple ideological struggle between progress and reaction was strengthened by global and regional developments beyond Lebanon's borders. In late 1975, *détente* was under increasing strain as the Jackson–Vanik amendment and the war in Angola led to a deterioration in US–Soviet relations. In the Middle East, Kissinger's success in enforcing a second Egyptian–Israeli agreement on 4 September 1975 was perceived as following a general pattern of a more determined and aggressive anti-Soviet American foreign policy. In this context, the Soviet Union were more openly disposed to viewing the Christian-rightist offensive as a co-ordinated US–Israeli conspiracy to create a reactionary pro-Western Lebanon, which would undermine the power of the Palestine Resistance and clear the path for Kissinger to implement a partial Lebanese-Israeli agreement.[6] Given that the Muslim-leftist forces were strongly placed both to resist and even to counteract the Christian-rightist campaign, there was a strong temptation for the Soviet Union to seek opportunistic advantage. The prospect of even a limited Muslim-leftist victory would be a significant anti-imperialist gain and would demonstrate that the Soviet-supported progressive forces in the Middle East were still capable of rebuffing and even reversing the 'Zionist-Imperialist' advance and its attempts to crush the Palestine Resistance and the Lebanese Left.

However, Soviet opportunistic exploitation of the crisis was tempered by a strong dose of caution. While the Soviet Union hoped the

crisis would provide a salutary lesson of the need for a overall settlement of the Arab–Israeli conflict, it was also concerned that the localized crisis in Lebanon should not escalate into a further confrontation
between Israel and the Arab states. There was no desire for a repeat of
the crisis in 1958 when US troops had intervened to prevent radical
left-wing gains in Lebanon. To forestall such an eventuality, the Soviet Union continually pressed for an early resolution of the crisis and
depicted the leftist forces, most especially the Palestine Resistance, as
demonstrating restraint before the Christian-rightist onslaught and constantly seeking a just settlement of the dispute.[7]

Soviet caution also reflected a sensitivity to Syria's perceived strategic interests over the situation in Lebanon. To a large part, the Soviet Union accepted the Syrian contention that 'the security of Lebanon
is inseparable from the security of Syria'.[8] Also, Moscow was sensitive to Asad's rejection of any potential partition of Lebanon. As Syria
was itself a multi-ethnic society with Asad and his closest colleagues
coming from a small minority group – the Alawites – the Syrian leadership feared that the disintegration of Lebanon would set a precedent
for the undermining of Syria's own fragile sectarian edifice. In more
immediate strategic terms, Syria feared that the partition of Lebanon
would prompt Israel to occupy South Lebanon up to the Litani river,
which Damascus believed was a long-term Zionist ambition. Such an
occupation would significantly increase Syrian strategic vulnerability
by widening the boundaries of direct confrontation with Israel. It would
also rule out the military option of Syrian forces outflanking the Israeli army by an advance through the Biqa' valley.[9]

Soviet strategic interests broadly converged with these Syrian objectives. The Soviet Union had no fundamental opposition to direct
Syrian intervention in the Lebanese crisis, so long as Syria tried to
mediate in the dispute to reach an early settlement and thereby prevent Israel or the West from becoming directly involved. Syrian diplomacy was also accepted as having an important role in ensuring that
the internal Lebanese crisis did not escalate out of control and spark a
new Arab–Israeli war. However, the Soviet Union's interests were not
completely subordinated to those of Syria – it had its own independent
relations with the PLO and LNM and it wanted to ensure that their
specific interests were also safeguarded. In particular, the Soviet Union
wanted any final settlement of the Lebanese crisis to preserve the PLO's
independence and also satisfy, at least partially, the reformist expectations of the Muslim community.

Until the spring of 1976, the Soviet Union had no especial difficulty in balancing the interests of its three allies. Moscow could be satisfied that Syria, the PLO and the LNM were acting in close co-ordination to repel the Christian-rightist offensive and to achieve their separate, if complementary, political objectives. In the Soviet media, the position of the LNM was presented as a just struggle for the reform of a political system which blatantly discriminated against their legitimate rights. Independently of this internal struggle, the Palestine Resistance, under the leadership of the PLO, was depicted as the innocent victim of an aggressive reactionary onslaught. In the face of these open provocations, the Palestinians were praised for their 'refusal to interfere in Lebanon's internal affairs and . . . their efforts to reconcile the two groups with a view to bringing peace in Lebanon'.[10] Syria's involvement was likewise depicted as an altruistic diplomatic attempt at mediation and that it had no wider ambition than 'to do everything possible to restore calm in Lebanon'.[11]

The ideal Soviet scenario was for the Syrian–LNM–PLO axis to achieve fairly swiftly some limited political gains, which could then be heralded as a decisive victory for the Soviet-supported anti-imperialist alliance of progressive forces. Developments during January and February 1976 seemed to offer such an outcome. In January, there was a limited escalation of the war as Fatah and the Syrian-controlled Yarmuq brigade of the Palestine Liberation Army (PLA) entered the war on the side of the Muslim-leftist alliance. After considerable Syrian diplomatic and military pressure, this led to a cease-fire coming into effect and, on 14 February, the Lebanese President, Sulayman Franjiyya, unveiled a Syrian-sponsored 'Constitutional Document' which stipulated a limited reform of the Lebanese political system to permit a more egalitarian sharing of power between the Christian and Muslim communities. The Soviet Union followed these developments with satisfaction and supported the constitutional reforms as a just resolution of the Lebanese crisis.[12] The Soviet Union clearly hoped that the crisis had now been diffused with the progressive Syrian–LNM–PLO camp both having consolidated their relations and made some minor but still significant political gains.

DETERIORATION OF SYRIAN RELATIONS WITH LNM AND PLO

These hopes were destined not to be realized. The start of the Soviet Union's difficulties came with the LNM and the PLO rejecting Franjiyya's

recommendations for constitutional reform. Kamal Junblatt felt that
these recommendations did not sufficiently address the Left's programme
of political reforms, and the Palestinian leadership was concerned that
they might reduce the PLO's freedom of action and licensed Syrian
control of the organization's activities. There was also a mutual perception that Syria's enforcement of the cease-fire had come at the very
point when the balance of forces had shifted from the militarily ex-
hausted Christians to the Muslim-leftists. It was this frustration which
led the leftist bloc to break the cease-fire in early March and, as expected, it made significant advances against the Christian forces. On
15 March, a leftist drive on the presidential palace at Baabda aimed
explicitly at forcing the overthrow of Franjiyya. Muslim successes on
the battlefield were such that, by the end of the month, the Maronites
retained control of only 18 per cent of the territory of Lebanon and
their plight was close to disaster.

Syria responded to these developments with increasing alarm. From
the Syrian perspective, an unacceptable prospect was emerging, involving a partition of Lebanon with a weak Christian enclave surrounded
by a radical leftist Muslim state, which would be an open invitation
for Israeli and Western intervention. Syria also directly blamed the
Muslim–Palestinian–leftist coalition for this negative turn of events.
On 15 March Asad ordered the Sa'iqa and PLA units in Beirut to defend the palace at Baabda and thus demonstrated that Syria had switched
its allegiance to defence of the beleaguered Christian camp. Syria's
complete break with its former leftist allies was now only a question
of time. After an explosive meeting with Junblatt on 27 March, Asad
severed ties with the LNM and terminated all military supplies. Asad
had been convinced in his meeting with Junblatt that the Lebanese
leader wanted a military victory at whatever cost and that it was a
'question of a heritage of feelings of vengeance going back a hundred
and fifty years'.[13]

Asad's relations with the PLO leadership were not to sink so low so
rapidly. Arafat tried to remain neutral in the Asad–Junblatt dispute
and to come to some accommodation with the Syrian leader. At first,
Arafat offered his services as a mediator between Asad and Junblatt
but, when this was rejected, he continued seeking a *rapprochement*
with Asad which finally resulted in a PLO–Syrian agreement on 19
April. Arafat also played a significant role in persuading Asad to obtain Franjiyya's resignation. In the subsequent election on 8 May, Ilyas
Sarkis was elected as the new President of Lebanon. Although Sarkis
was not the PLO's ideal candidate, the PLO leadership deferred to

Syrian wishes by publicly welcoming the election. However, a renewed
Christian offensive on Mount Lebanon a few days later, with the support of the Syrian-controlled PLA troops in contravention of the 19
April Accord, finally pushed the PLO into the anti-Syrian camp. On
12 May and almost two months after the original Syrian–LNM split,
Arafat established a joint command with Junblatt to oppose the Syrian-
supported Christian offensive.

The deepening rift between Syria and the leftist camp of the PLO
and the LNM placed the Soviet Union in a difficult position. As with
earlier inter-Arab disputes between objective Soviet allies such as the
Iraqi–Egyptian conflict in the early 1960s, open support for one side
in the conflict would only alienate the other. Faced with such a di-
lemma, the Soviet Union tried to sustain its commitment to all three
of its allies and to minimize the significance of the differences in their
political objectives. Soviet reporting of this period focused almost exclusively on Zionist and imperialist exploitation of the crisis. Responsibility for any disunity in the anti-imperialist ranks in Lebanon was
placed at the door of 'imperialist and reactionary elements' who were
trying to 'take advantage of the situation to provoke quarrels among
the various national patriotic contingents, the Palestine Resistance
Movement and neighbouring Syria, which is mediating in an effort to
put an end to the fratricidal bloodshed and find a mutually acceptable
settlement'.[14]

Soviet resolve to maintain a neutral stance was also driven by the
hope that these internal conflicts might only be temporary and short-
lived. Although Syrian–LNM relations had been irretrievably broken
by the beginning of April, Syria and the PLO continued trying to patch
up their differences until the middle of May. In these circumstances,
the Soviet Union wanted to make no precipitate statement of support
for one side or the other, which might damage the chances for a PLO–
Syrian *rapprochement*. In addition, the Soviet Union still maintained a
generally positive evaluation of Syria's involvement in the Lebanese
conflict, despite the growing Syrian tensions with the PLO and LNM.
Syria was complimented for persuading Franjiyya to step down from
the presidency and the election of Sarkis was described as contributing to a final resolution of the crisis in the country.[15] In general, Syria
was presented as a disinterested mediator between the opposing forces
and that 'the attempt to besmirch the Syrian mediation mission in Lebanon
has been another aspect of imperialist and reactionary pressures on
Damascus.'[16]

Yet, as early as May 1976 the Soviet Union was indicating that its support for Syria's involvement in Lebanon was not unconditional. In an Arabic language broadcast of 15 May, the PSP, LCP and other leftist groups in Lebanon were commended for their anti-imperialist progressiveness. It was also noted that the rightist forces hoped to 'promote hostility not only between the Palestine Resistance and Lebanon but also between the Palestine Resistance and Syria'.[17] The Soviet Union also made clear its opposition to the US mission of Dean Brown to Lebanon and Syria, which took place in April and May, with George Habash being especially praised for refusing to meet the emissary.[18] The favourable reception of Brown in Damascus must have worried the Soviet Union that Syria was co-ordinating its policies too closely with the United States. Diverging perceptions over Lebanon can also be seen in the respective Syrian and Soviet speeches given at a dinner in honour of Kosygin's visit to Damascus on 1–4 June 1976. The Syrian Prime Minister, Muhammad al-Ayyubi, asserted Syria's freedom 'to act against any clashes, whoever starts them and wherever they come. We will not be distracted by false slogans.' Kosygin, in his response, refused to give Syria such an open licence and limited Soviet support to 'maintenance of national unity and the upholding of the integrity of the Lebanese state'.[19]

However, despite these hints of disapproval, during May the Soviet Union gave Syria the green light for a much more extensive military intervention into Lebanon which commenced on 1 June, coinciding with Kosygin's arrival in Damascus. In response to the Syrian move, the Soviet media stated that the Syrian intervention had taken place at the request of the 'official authorities' in Lebanon and that it was aimed at 'restoring order and facilitating the achievement of a cease-fire' and that it had 'helped to ease the situation in a number of areas in the country'.[20] At the same time, the Soviet Union doubled the number of its surface vessels in the Mediterranean and established a naval presence on the Lebanese coast, which indicated that Moscow anticipated the Syrian intervention.[21]

But such visible, if unofficial, support for the Syrian military engagement provoked a crisis in Soviet relations with the PLO and LNM. From their perspective, the coincidence of Kosygin's visit to Damascus with the Syrian intervention could only suggest collusion with Syria's strategic ambitions. The PLO leadership immediately indicated that the Soviet position towards this development would be an acid test of the strength of the Soviet–PLO alliance. It condemned the Syrian intervention as aimed 'not at contributing to solving the crisis but rather at controlling this country so as to strike at the Palestine Resistance and

the National Movement'. It also argued that, since the central element
in Soviet policy was support of the Palestinians' legitimate rights, Syria
was not 'showing loyalty to the Arab–Soviet friendship'. Consequently,
it announced that the PLO would write to the Soviet leadership, demanding an explanation of their position and 'seeking the support of
the Soviet Union and its intervention with the Syrian regime to get it
to withdraw from Lebanon'.[22]

The Soviet Union became more vulnerable to charges of complicity
with Syria, when the Syrian advance failed to break through the Palestinian and leftist defences and Syrian troops became embroiled in a
bloody war of attrition. In retrospect, it appears likely that the Soviet
Union only backed the Syrian initiative on the understanding that it
would quickly stabilize the situation and lead to an early settlement of
the crisis. When this failed to be the case, the Soviet Union quickly
distanced itself from the Syrian move. In a *Tass* report of 9 June,
there was the first explicit criticism of Syria's actions in Lebanon:

> The Syrian Arab Republic has time and again issued statements saying
> that the mission of the troops it introduced into Lebanon is to help
> stop the bloodshed. Nevertheless, notice should be called to the fact
> that bloodshed continues in Lebanon today and that blood is flow-
> ing in ever greater streams.

A few days after this statement, the Soviet Union also sent its reply
to the PLO letter which had demanded a clarification of the Soviet
position.[23] Reportedly, the letter stated that the Soviet leadership had
been misled by the Syrian government and that it had not realized that
Syria would use this opportunity to attack the positions of the PLO.
The letter also affirmed the Soviet commitment to the Palestinian cause
and that it would do everything in its power to stem the Syrian and
Christian-rightist onslaught. However, the Soviet leadership also urged
the PLO to show flexibility and to use all its efforts to mend fences
with Damascus.[24] By insisting on this last demand, the Soviet Union
revealed that it still hoped that the PLO leadership might reach a satisfactory agreement with Syria. While there remained even the smallest
chance that this might be the case, the Soviet Union was not yet willing
to make a decisive stand between its warring allies. Indeed, in the
latter part of June, the Soviet Union ceased its overt criticisms of Syria,
noting with approval that Asad had agreed to withdraw from Beirut
and a number of other towns.[25]

THE CRISIS IN SOVIET–SYRIAN RELATIONS

However, Soviet tolerance of Syrian actions in Lebanon was not to last indefinitely. Indeed, Soviet hopes for a Syrian change of heart and a Syrian–PLO *rapprochement* were finally extinguished after the visit of the Syrian foreign minister to Moscow on 5–8 July. The minimal coverage of Khaddam's visit in the Soviet media and the absence, quite exceptional in Soviet–Syrian relations, of a joint communiqué, were evidence of an irreconcilable clash over the Lebanese crisis. Khaddam refused to agree to Soviet demands for a cease-fire and an end to the direct attacks on the Palestine Resistance and the Lebanese left. In a clear expression of Soviet frustration with Syrian intransigence, a statement issued a day after Khaddam's departure by the Soviet Afro-Asian Solidarity Committee urged 'all peace-loving forces to come out in support of the Palestine Resistance Movement and the progressive patriotic forces in Lebanon and declare their solidarity with the forces of freedom, peace and progress in the Middle East.' It also made the first direct criticism of the Syria, stating that 'the involvement of Syrian military units has further aggravated the situation.' Furthermore, it insisted that there must be an immediate cease-fire and the withdrawal of all forces from intervening countries.[26]

The Khaddam visit in early July marked a decisive turn in the Soviet position over the Lebanese crisis. While before it had tried to balance its support between its three allies, after the visit the Soviet Union increasingly sided with the Palestinian–leftist bloc against the Syrian military intervention into Lebanon. Reflecting the new mood, the Soviet media was far less restrained in criticizing the Syrian involvement and in explicitly demanding the complete withdrawal of Syrian troops.[27] Great public support was given to the PLO leadership's contention that Syria was directly attacking the Palestine Resistance Movement, with the added editorial comment that the PLO was now under attack from the 'back as well as the front'.[28] Soviet actions were not just limited to words. From mid-July onwards, deliveries of arms and spare parts to Syria were held up as well as the postponement of a number of programmes of technical assistance.[29]

The depth of Soviet disenchantment with Syrian policies in Lebanon can be most visibly seen in a letter Brezhnev sent to Asad on 11 July, which was also sent to the PLO leadership and subsequently published in *Le Monde*.[30] The principal theme of the letter was that Syria was directly, and inexplicably, violating the joint Soviet–Syrian agreement that 'the Palestine Resistance constitutes one of the principal

pillars of the struggle against Israeli aggression and imperialism.' The
Soviet leader expressed his disbelief that Syria had joined the Christian-rightist forces in attacking the Palestinian and Lebanese forces
and in imposing a blockade on Lebanese ports. The Syrian position
had also been embarrassing for the Soviet leadership since it meant
that the Soviet promise to send medicines and food supplies to the
Palestinians and Lebanese had been blocked by the Syrian-imposed
embargo. In the face of such actions, the Soviet leader concluded that
'we understand neither your line of conduct nor the objectives you are
pursuing in Lebanon.'

The letter starkly warned that 'if Syria persists in the course which
it has taken, it will give the imperialists and their collaborators the
chance to gain control over the Arab nations and the progressive forces.'
Brezhnev recommended that 'the Syrian leaders take all possible measures
to end the military operations conducted against the resistance. . . . You
can contribute by withdrawing your forces from Lebanon.' He concluded the letter by stating that 'we are still prepared to consolidate
the links of friendship between our two countries. . . . unless Syria acts
in such a way as to cause rifts in relations between our two countries.'

The severity of Brezhnev's letter clearly demonstrates the Soviet
Union's dissatisfaction with Syrian policies in Lebanon and its strong
commitment to protect the independent power of the PLO. However,
the Soviet media was careful not to depict the Syrian–PLO rift as ir-
reparable. And, when the PLO Foreign Minister, Faruq Qaddumi, reached
an agreement with Asad on 29 July, the Soviet Union hailed this accord as 'countering the US, Israeli and international Zionist attempt to
separate Syria and the Palestine Resistance Movement. . . . and cut the
ties of blood between Syria, the USSR and the Palestine Resistance
Movement.'[31] After this agreement, the Soviet Union adopted a more
balanced position between Syria and the Palestinian–leftist bloc. While
it continued to demand Syrian withdrawal, there was barely veiled criticism of those leftist elements within the PLO which rejected the 29
July agreement.[32] In an article by 'Observer' in *Pravda* on 9 September there was also the first direct criticism of 'some leftist elements in
the Palestinian movement and in the front of patriotic forces' who are
offering 'outright rejection of any and every peace proposal'.[33]

However, this greater balance in the Soviet position did not curtail
the constant reiteration of the demand that Syrian forces must withdraw from Lebanon. It also did not affect the public support that the
Soviet Union gave to the Palestine Resistance and the Lebanese leftists in their struggle against the Syrian–Christian coalition. In a further

statement by the Soviet Afro-Asian Solidarity Committee at the end of August it was stated that:

> The Soviet people actively support the position of the PLO and the Lebanese national patriotic forces which are seeking a settlement of the crisis without outside interference, and share the world-wide opinion that the withdrawal of the Syrian troops would be of major import-ance for the solution of the crisis. It goes without saying that nor-malization of the situation would to a great extent be facilitated by co-operation by Syria and her natural allies in the anti-imperialist struggle – the Palestine Resistance Movement and the national patriotic forces of Lebanon.[34]

By the beginning of September, however, the Soviet Union had to face the reality that the Palestinian–leftist coalition had suffered con-siderable losses and had been progressively weakened by the effects of a comprehensive sea and land blockade. Whether the Soviet Union liked it or not, a *Pax Syriana* was becoming a more probable outcome. Also, the Soviet Union had a more urgent need to see an end to the fighting, since Moscow hoped to present a new peace plan at the be-ginning of October, which would act as a marker to the new US admin-istration of the Soviet interest to resume negotiations in the Geneva forum.[35] In these circumstances, the Soviet Union decided to become more directly involved in attempting to reach a settlement of the Lebanese conflict. Given the PLO's weak bargaining position, the Soviet Union placed most of its pressure on the PLO to reach an agreement with Asad. On 17 September, Gromyko met with Qaddumi in Moscow and report-edly urged the PLO to moderate its position on a settlement with Syria. The Soviet statement on the meeting was also notable for not men-tioning the Syrian intervention or for demanding a Syrian withdrawal.[36]

The Soviet pressure on the PLO, which also included a number of meetings between Arafat and Vladimir Silkin, the Soviet chargé d'affaires in Beirut, seemed to bear fruit later in the month.[37] On 24 September, Arafat announced the PLO's decision to adopt a unilateral cease-fire, which was warmly praised by the Soviet Union.[38] With this clear PLO concession, the Soviet leadership expected that Syria would respond in kind. When Syria defiantly ignored the PLO move and initiated a massive offensive on Mount Lebanon on 28 September, the Soviet Union did not hide its disapproval and disappointment. From the Soviet per-spective, the Syrian move appeared calculated to inflict the maximum damage to the Soviet diplomatic position. It undermined the Soviet initiative at reaching a settlement and, as with the 1 June Syrian

intervention, suggested a degree of Soviet complicity. The Soviet Union
again had to face a barrage of criticism from its Palestinian and Lebanese allies.[39] The Syrian onslaught also overshadowed the 1 October
Soviet peace plan for the Arab–Israeli conflict and embarrassingly
demonstrated the disunity of the Soviet Union's supposedly anti-imperialist allies.

The Soviet Union expressed its disapproval of the Syrian response
to the PLO's unilateral cease-fire by issuing another statement from
the Soviet Afro-Asian Solidarity Committee on 30 September, which
announced that the Syrian participation in the military operations was
'harming not only the Lebanese people, but the entire struggle of the
Arab peoples and states against Israeli aggression and for a just settlement in the Middle East'.[40] When Syria disrupted another series of
Syrian–PLO contacts by a further offensive on 11 October, Soviet criticism of Syrian actions reached its height. An 'Observer' article in *Pravda*,
which is normally taken to reflect the authoritative view of the Politburo, stated that the new onslaught had snuffed out 'the glimmer of
hope of an improvement in the Lebanese situation. . . . What it amounts
to is that, on the one hand, Syrian representatives have agreed to hold
talks on a cease-fire, while on the other, Syrian troops are torpedoing
efforts to achieve a peaceful settlement and the bloodshed is intensifying.'[41] Soviet criticism had never been as direct and as official as this
and it vividly expressed Soviet anger at perceived Syrian deception
and double-crossing.

In the end, the Soviet Union's greatest fear was not to be realized.
A few days after the 11 October offensive, Syrian forces ceased military operations and did not press their attack to a complete annihila-
tion of the PLO and Lebanese leftist military units. However, the main
factor in forcing Syrian restraint was not Soviet pressure but rather the
Saudi threat to cut off its economic aid. Saudi Arabia successfully obtained
Asad's consent to attend a mini-summit in Riyadh on 16–18 October,
with the leaders of Egypt, Kuwait, Lebanon and the PLO. At that summit,
a settlement was reached on the Lebanese crisis, but at the price of
legitimizing the Syrian military presence in the country. The Syrian
presence was given the fig-leaf of belonging to an 'Arab Deterrent
Force' and Asad was able to leave Riyadh with.an Arab acquiescence
to an effective *Pax Syriana* in Lebanon.

The Soviet Union was initially sceptical of this Saudi-sponsored deal,
quoting an Iraqi press warning that it might compromise the Palestine
Resistance Movement.[42] However, once the agreement was confirmed
by the Cairo Summit conference a week later, Moscow grudgingly

accepted the new political reality. While still smarting from Syrian resistance to Soviet demands, Moscow gradually recognized the legitimacy of the Syrian troop presence, using the euphemism that it was acting as a 'peacekeeping force'.[43] The ending of the Lebanese crisis also led to a number of favourable developments from the Soviet perspective. Syrian and PLO relations were patched up and, at the Cairo Summit, there was a display of Arab unity not seen since the October 1973 war. Furthermore, the PLO had emerged from the Lebanese cauldron with its independence and prestige essentially intact, if a little battered. The Soviet Union greeted these developments with considerable satisfaction. Soviet reporting in late 1976 includes a noticeable sense of relief that the terrible events in Lebanon had at last been concluded and that the Arab world could finally focus its attention on the more important task of confronting Israel.

ASSESSING SOVIET–PLO RELATIONS DURING THE LEBANESE CIVIL WAR

Most analysts have expressed some bewilderment at the Soviet decision to support the PLO and to oppose Syria at the height of the Lebanese civil war. Galia Golan and Itamar Rabinovich express a common assumption when they suggest that: 'As to the PLO itself, here too Moscow's moves are almost inexplicable, for there was nothing in the Soviet–PLO relationship to suggest that Moscow saw this group as a more important, effective or dependable ally than Syria.'[44] Efraim Karsh suggests in a similar vein that the importance of Syria to the Soviet Union 'exceeded by far that of the PLO and the Lebanese Left put together.'[45]

The conventional wisdom is, therefore, that the Soviet support for the PLO was more tactical than anything truly substantive. At its most extreme, this approach even suggests that Soviet expressions of displeasure with Syria were simple exercises in dissimulation. On this analysis, the criticisms of Syria and the moral support given to the PLO and the LNM did not signal any real change in the value the Soviet Union accorded to its three allies. Criticism of Syria was purely for display, acting as a substitute for 'placing real pressure on Syria'.[46] Advocates of this viewpoint also focus attention on the Pravda statement of 8 September 1976, which blamed leftist elements for failing to accept a political settlement. This, they suggest, reveals that Moscow still gave priority to its relations with Syria over its less important allies inside Lebanon.[47]

This line of argument has a number of problems. For a start, the same *Pravda* article which attacked the leftist rejectionists also explicitly demanded a Syrian withdrawal and stated bluntly that the Syrian decision to intervene had 'turned against the Palestinian movement and allowed the right-wingers to deal telling blows against the detachments of the Palestinians and the national patriotic forces of Lebanon'. The argument also fails to explain why the Soviet Union disrupted arms supplies to Syria, which is clearly something more than mere propaganda, and why Soviet–Syrian relations remained cool well into 1977.

A more plausible explanation is offered by Galia Golan, who presents a less extreme and more plausible interpretation of these events. She suggests that the Soviet decision was not so much one in favour of the PLO but rather 'one to oppose the Syrians'.[48] Rather than deliberately siding with the PLO for reasons of altruistic solidarity, the principal Soviet objective was to signal its disapproval of Syria's jealously guarded independence and its rejection of Soviet advice on how it should act in Lebanon. Golan's argument has many valid points. As Karsh correctly points out, the Soviet Union was disappointed with the indecisive nature of the Syrian intervention and were convinced that the Syrian failure would only worsen the situation and embarrass the Soviet Union among its radical Arab allies.[49] The Soviet Union must also have been concerned that Syria had been seemingly co-ordinating its actions with the United States and with Saudi Arabia and Egypt. Asad's public visit to France in June 1976, and his support for French mediation efforts, must also have been an annoying demonstration of Asad's willingness to distance himself from the Soviet Union.

These considerations must have contributed to the Soviet decision to make public its criticisms of the Syrian move. However, they still fail to provide a complete explanation of why the Soviet Union was willing to damage its relations with Syria to the extent that it did or why, if its relations with the PLO were so much less important, it defended the Palestinian cause even when the PLO appeared to be on the point of suffering a major strategic defeat. One striking assumption of the advocates of this argument is the underlying premise that Soviet decision-making was driven purely by strategic factors. On this basis, since Syria was clearly of greater strategic importance than the PLO, Soviet decision-makers could not rationally follow a policy which elevated its relations with lesser entities like the PLO above those with Syria. Thus, any outward evidence of greater support for the PLO cannot be correctly assessed as a policy *for* the PLO but rather one *against* the particular policies adopted by Syria at that time.

The danger of giving such unwavering priority to strategic calculations is that it can blind the analyst to the ideological and often seemingly irrational factors in an actor's decision-making process. In the context of the Lebanese civil war, there are clear signs that Soviet policy-makers assumed that the crisis had, at least partly, been provoked and fomented by a US–Zionist conspiracy in league with reactionary elements inside Lebanon. Particularly after the second Egyptian–Israeli agreement in September 1975, Soviet reporting continually emphasized that there was a Zionist-imperialist plot to liquidate the Palestine Resistance and to force a partial peace settlement between a Christian-dominated Lebanon and Israel. Seen in this framework, the Lebanese conflict offered a clear example of a struggle between the forces of 'progress' and the forces of 'reaction' and the Soviet Union did not stint from showing where its ideological loyalty lay. There is also evidence that the Soviet Union expected the Muslim-leftist forces to attain a limited victory, which could be presented as a decisive turn in the correlation of forces in favour of the Soviet-supported Arab progressive and anti-imperialist alliance.

Adeed Dawisha has shown, after extensive interviews with key Syrian officials, that conspiracy thinking – the belief that the Palestinian–leftist challenge was a US–Zionist plot to undermine Syria's integrity and geopolitical position – dominated the Syrian decision-making process.[50] Although Soviet policy-makers might be expected to be less prone to such extreme conspiratorial thinking, they were not immune to the distorting prism of their particular ideological preconceptions. When the Christian-rightist camp was so clearly defined as reactionary and as acting in collusion with a Zionist-imperialist plot, Syrian support for the Christians inevitably suggested that Syria had entered into the global conspiracy against the Palestine Resistance and the Lebanese leftists. In the letter Brezhnev sent to the Syrian leadership on 11 July, there is evidence of a genuine Soviet bewilderment that Syria had agreed, however unwittingly, to play this reactionary role. The Soviet leader's assertion that 'we understand neither your line of conduct nor the objectives you are pursuing' should be taken as a genuine statement of the Soviet incomprehension at Syrian policy towards Lebanon.

This perspective on the Soviet attitude to the Syrian intervention presents a more complicated picture of the relative value the Soviet Union accorded its relations with Syria and with the PLO–leftist coalition. On strategic criteria, Syria was undoubtedly the most important ally for the Soviet Union, since it was a powerful independent state and was essential for preserving Soviet influence in the region to compensate for the loss of Egypt. In comparison, the PLO, and even more the LNM, were relatively insignificant non-state actors with only a limited degree of independent power.

However, as was argued in the previous chapter, there had emerged in Soviet thinking a strong current of opinion which viewed the Palestinian cause, and by extension the PLO, as a critical catalyst for the anti-imperialist struggle in the Arab world. Ignoring the internal weaknesses of the organization, these supporters of the PLO argued that it had a 'radicalizing' role in the Middle East, which the Lebanese events had only further confirmed. In the heat of the Syrian–PLO crisis, senior Middle Eastern commentators like Vladimir Kudriavtsev argued that the Palestine Resistance is 'objectively a link between the progressive sections of the population in different Arab countries because circumstances here have made it the most consistent fighter for the elimination of the consequences of aggression.'[51] Following this line of thinking, Soviet reports suggested that 'the Lebanese events are like a mirror in reflecting a temporary process which is taking place in many liberated countries, the process of crystallization and polarization of class forces.'[52] It therefore logically followed that the 'real yardstick of the readiness of countries of this region to work for the success of the national liberation struggle is the support of the Palestine Resistance and the coordination of action with it.'[53]

At the centre of Soviet dismay at Syrian actions in Lebanon was the fact that Syria was directly and unambiguously attacking the Palestine Resistance. The fate of the Lebanese leftists was a lesser concern and their case was much less forcibly presented. But the depth of Soviet commitment to the Palestinian cause was made clear in a number of statements in the middle of October. In an article in *Pravda*, which was signed by 'Observer' and thus could be taken as having the imprimatur of the Politburo, it was stated that

> ... Syrian troops are torpedoing efforts to achieve a peaceful settlement and the bloodshed is intensifying. Who stands to gain from this? It is no secret to anyone that the blows are now being struck against those whom international imperialism and local reaction have long been trying to rout – the Palestine Resistance, which is in the forefront of the anti-imperialist struggle in the Middle East.[54]

A couple of days later, a similar statement was issued by the Soviet Afro-Asian Solidarity Committee. Although this was a less authoritative source, the prominence given to the statement in the leading Soviet newspapers – in bold print and on the front pages – confirmed its support from the Soviet policy-making establishment. The statement included the remarks that:

> It is well known that in recent years the Palestine Resistance Movement has grown stronger, gathered strength and has become an active and stalwart fighter against Israeli aggression and imperialist intrigues in the Near East. Now in Lebanon blows are yet again falling on this movement, which is one of the vanguard detachments of the national liberation struggle, whose anti-imperialist position has for a long time drawn fire from imperialism and Zionism. And this is taking place with the direct participation of Syrian forces.[55]

The sympathy and support that the Soviet Union was willing to extend to the Palestine Resistance, driven by an ideological commitment to a movement which was deemed to be progressive and anti-imperialist, must provide some of the explanation of why the Soviet Union was willing to criticize Syria to the extent it did. Certainly it had no intention of breaking relations with Syria completely. The most acerbic criticisms were published as statements from the Soviet Afro-Asian Solidarity Committee and thus did not having the stamp of the full authority of the Soviet state. But this does not detract from the Soviet Union's resolve to make crystal-clear its disapproval of Syrian attempts to liquidate the Palestine Resistance. Moreover, it was not just a critical evaluation of Syria's actions but an open assertion of its support for the Palestine Resistance and the PLO in the overall struggle against imperialism in the Middle East.

Although ideological considerations were critical components in the Soviet decision-making process, there were also more pragmatic factors, which strengthened the Soviet resolve to preserve the independent power of the Palestinian organizations. Another important dimension to the Soviet–Syrian dispute was a straight battle for control of the PLO. Asad had for a long time indicated his resolve to subordinate the PLO into an Eastern axis with Syria and Jordan, which would be under the firm control of Damascus. Ideally, Asad wanted an enlarged Sa'iqa organization which would be indistinguishable, except in name, from the Syrian army. The Soviet Union had always, from the Syrian–Egyptian union in 1958 onwards, disliked such concentration of power. It diminished Soviet influence and gave too much independent power to individual Arab leaders. Soviet policy-makers preferred a more flexible anti-imperialist alliance with the Soviet Union as the primary sponsor and link between the different actors.

The Soviet Union realized that a Syrian-dominated PLO would lessen

Soviet influence both on the PLO and on Syria. With Syria dominating and controlling a Syrian–PLO–Jordanian axis, the need for Soviet mediation would be considerably reduced. As with the Syrian–Israeli disengagement agreement in 1974, Syria would probably deal directly with the United States who alone had influence over Israel. To prevent such an eventuality, the Soviet Union needed to preserve an independent PLO, which would be faithfully tied to Soviet diplomacy. Soviet sponsorship of the PLO provided a crucial justification for Soviet involvement in the Middle East peace process since, in contrast to the Arab confrontation states, the PLO was excluded from making direct deals with Washington. An independent PLO also made Syria more susceptible to Soviet influence, since the Soviet Union would be in a position to mediate between Syria and the PLO and Syrian diplomacy would, even if to a limited extent, have to take into account the position of the PLO.

In conclusion, it can be seen that Soviet actions against Syria during the latter part of the Lebanese conflict were not solely directed to express opposition to Syria. There was also a degree of positive support in favour of the PLO, and to the extent that it was supporting the Palestinian cause, the Lebanese leftist coalition. Yet the change in the Soviet position should not be exaggerated. The overriding Soviet interest was to preserve its good relations with all its clients – Syria, the PLO and the Lebanese left – and it was heartily relieved when the crisis was over and it could restore its battered alliance with Syria.

In retrospect, the Soviet Union must also have wondered if its decision to adopt a less neutral stance had been worth the effort. Not only had Soviet–Syrian relations suffered but the PLO did not show any particular gratitude to the Soviet position. The Fatah leader, Salah Khalaf, continually assailed the Soviet Union for its relative inaction and blamed it for failing 'to bring enough pressure on Syria and the warring parties, as well as on the international level, to bring the crisis to an end'.[56] He also criticized the Soviet Union for failing to intervene directly to break the sea blockade around the PLO and Muslim-leftist forces.[57] At the end of the day, therefore, the Soviet Union had lost out with both its allies and alienated them both to differing degrees. Yet, by the middle of 1977, there was also the reassurance that the damage had been limited and that the Soviet–Syrian–PLO axis had been restored to its earlier strength. From late 1976 to 1977, Arab attention had also turned decisively from the Lebanese cauldron to the quest for the reconvening of the Geneva Conference.

5 An Opportunity Missed: 1977-80

Although the Lebanese civil war had greatly tested the Soviet Union's new alliance with the PLO, and had threatened to undermine Soviet relations with Syria, the onset of 1977 appeared to promise a restoration of Soviet fortunes. In the latter part of 1976, the major Arab states made a number of diplomatic moves to resolve their differences and to resurrect a pan-Arab strategy towards the reconvening of the Geneva Conference. This was officially confirmed at the quadripartite Riyadh Summit on 9-10 January 1977, when Egypt, Syria, Jordan and Saudi Arabia agreed to co-ordinate a common political programme. This Arab resolve towards a more unified stance also coincided with, and was a direct response to, the inauguration of a new United States administration under President Jimmy Carter. Like the Arab states, the Soviet Union was at least cautiously optimistic that the new administration would seek to reinvigorate the peace process. In particular, Moscow hoped that the change of administration would seek to transcend Kissinger's legacy and promote a more all-embracing and comprehensive peace, which would potentially include, rather than deliberately exclude, the participation of the Soviet Union.

Developments in the peace process during 1977 were partially to realize Soviet hopes and expectations. The Carter administration did make strenuous efforts to reconvene the Geneva Conference and to promote a comprehensive resolution of the Arab–Israeli conflict. Unlike its predecessor, the administration also proved to be more sympathetic to the Palestinian cause and actively sought the inclusion of the PLO in negotiations. In late August 1977, the US Secretary of State, Cyrus Vance, also invited the Soviet Union to co-operate with the United States in drafting a joint statement as the basis for the reconvening of the Geneva Conference. The publication of the joint statement in October 1977 represented the high point of US–Soviet collaboration towards the settlement of the Arab–Israeli conflict. Although the historic significance of this moment was not apparent at the time, the Soviet Union was never again to be invited by the United States to play such a close collaborative role.

This chapter first analyses Soviet policy-making in this period up to

October 1977 when Moscow came closest to being accepted by the United States as an active and responsible participant in the peace process. It is argued that during this period the Soviet Union sought to act in a broadly constructive manner. This is particularly demonstrated in the evolution of Soviet policy towards the PLO, which was central to Soviet pretensions to be treated as an equal to the United States in the peace process. Although the Soviet leadership did fail to achieve its principal objective, which was PLO recognition of Israel, it did succeed in gaining PLO support for the joint US–Soviet declaration and a commitment to participate at the Geneva Conference. More importantly, the Soviet Union persuaded the PLO to agree that, once it had sat down with Israel at the reconvened Geneva Conference, this would amount to a *de facto* mutual recognition between Israel and the PLO. From the Soviet perspective, these achievements were not inconsiderable. At the very least, Moscow hoped that they demonstrated concrete evidence of the Soviet Union's positive and constructive position towards collaboration with the United States.

The final section of the chapter charts the developments in Soviet–PLO relations from Sadat's journey to Jerusalem in November 1977 until the end of the decade, when the Soviet Union and the PLO found themselves completely excluded from the US-dominated diplomatic drive for an Israeli–Egyptian peace. During this period, Soviet–PLO relations appeared to grow increasingly close and to blossom into a full-blown strategic alliance. However, the underlying reality was rather different. Although Moscow did elevate its relations with the PLO, it was the Soviet relationship with Syria, with whom the PLO continued to have difficult and strained relations, which was increasingly accorded strategic primacy as the centrepiece of Soviet policy in the Middle East. In addition, in the late 1980s, the Soviet Union began to foster clear reservations concerning the loyalty and ideological reliability of the political leadership of the PLO, particularly as regards to Yasir Arafat and his close Fatah colleagues. This was, at least in part, fuelled by Syrian and leftist Palestinian criticisms of Arafat's policies which increasingly confirmed Soviet suspicions of Fatah's ideological heterogeneity. Thus, even at the end of the 1970s, the seeds of Soviet distrust of the PLO, which was to become such a major feature of Soviet–PLO relations in the 1980s, had already been sown.

THE NEW US ADMINISTRATION AND SOVIET DIPLOMACY

Despite the extreme Soviet displeasure over the second Egyptian–Israeli agreement in September 1975, throughout the following year the Soviet Union continued to send out subtle signals that it remained interested in superpower collaboration in the Middle East. In March and October 1976, modifications and revisions to Brezhnev's 1974 three-pronged peace plan were set out to indicate a degree of moderation and willingness to negotiate.[1] However, the new set of proposals given in a speech by Brezhnev on 21 March 1977, a few months after the inauguration of the new US administration, broke distinctive new ground. While the proposals still demanded a full Israeli withdrawal from the occupied territories, Brezhnev agreed that the withdrawal could be gradually phased over a number of months. He also made clear that the borders between Israel and its Arab neighbours should be 'finally established and inviolable', and that the final settlement should include not only an end to the state of war but also the 'establishment of relations of peace'. In addition, the Soviet leader accepted the principle of demilitarized zones on both sides of the borders, overseen by UN forces or observers. However, the part of the Soviet initiative which generated the most favourable response in the West and in Israel was the absence of any mention of the PLO and Brezhnev's insistence that the Soviet Union did not intend to impose its ideas.[2] Shimon Peres, the Israeli defence minister, responded to the Soviet initiative by saying that he was taking it 'very seriously', especially Brezhnev's comment that it was not an 'imposed peace plan'.[3]

Although the favourable Israeli response was a bonus, the Soviet peace initiative was primarily directed towards the United States. It was a clear response to the signs that the Carter administration was adopting a less hostile attitude to the Soviet Union and Soviet involvement in the Middle East. Even before his election, Carter had committed himself to refocusing American foreign policy away from the limiting prism of East–West confrontation and towards direct involvement with the economically under-developed Third World. This was based on a strongly held conviction that earlier US administrations had failed to respond to 'the manifold sources of conflict [in the Third World] which arise out of tribal, religious, and ethnic border disputes . . . in their local terms, i.e., with an awareness of their local significance . . . and not purely in the game theory projection of the East–West encounter'.[4]

The Middle East was viewed as a prime example of the failure of earlier US foreign policy to address itself to the real underlying sources of conflict in the region. This, it was argued, was the ultimate cause of Kissinger's failure to reach an all-encompassing settlement of the Arab–Israeli conflict. For the new Democrat team determining Middle East policy, Kissinger's mistake had been to focus his energies primarily on containing Soviet expansion and not on grappling with the fundamental roots of the conflict. Carter and his entourage were determined not to make the same mistake and to initiate a more ambitious and radical approach, which would tackle the very heart of the conflict and reach a comprehensive settlement which would satisfy the interests of all sides in the dispute. This would mean the end to the search for partial, limited agreements and the return to the Geneva Conference forum, which would necessarily include the participation of the Soviet Union as co-chairman with the United States. At that reconvened Geneva Conference, an all-embracing peace agreement would be ratified.

The new comprehensive approach to a settlement found its intellectual underpinnings in the Brookings Report, published in December 1975. Some of the principal members of the Carter administration had participated in the formulation of the report – most notably Zbigniew Brzezinski, the National Security Adviser, and his assistant on the Middle East, William Quandt. In terms of policy prescriptions, the report advocated a comprehensive settlement through an American-dominated diplomatic drive to gain substantive agreements between the various parties which would be ratified at a reconvened Geneva Conference. Israel would have to withdraw from the territories occupied in the 1967 war with only minor modifications, in return for which she would obtain a full peace with her neighbours, including diplomatic recognition and open borders. The Palestinian problem would be resolved through the satisfaction of the Palestinian right to self-determination, subject to Palestinian recognition of Israel, which might 'take the form of a Palestinian state . . . or a Palestinian entity voluntarily federated with Jordan but exercising extensive political autonomy'. Finally, the report recommended that the Soviet Union must be involved, at least to a limited degree, in the negotiations, since otherwise it would obstruct the peace process.[5]

The Soviet Union reacted positively both to the Brookings Report and the evidence in early 1977 that the new administration was taking a more balanced approach towards a resolution of the Arab–Israeli conflict.[6] In particular, Moscow was impressed by the administration's more sympathetic attitude to the Palestinian problem. In his memoirs, Cyrus Vance reflected the administration's view that 'rejected from their homes, embittered, radicalized, living in squalor and desperation, the Palestinians remained the central, unresolved, human rights issue in the Middle East.'[7] Directly flowing from such beliefs, Carter broke new ground with a controversial speech on 16 March 1977 that stated that a 'homeland' had to be set up for the suffering Palestinian refugees.[8] Carter also had a less hostile attitude to the PLO than had been the case with his predecessors. As Quandt has suggested, at least in the first half of 1977, Carter used the terms 'PLO' and 'Palestinians' almost interchangeably.[9] His position on the PLO was that, so long as it recognized Israel, there was no reason why it could not be a legitimate participant in the peace negotiations.

Both the PLO and the Soviet Union could, therefore, be reasonably satisfied that the new Carter administration was more favourable to their participation in the peace process than the previous administrations. However, both parties also had their reservations. First, neither the PLO nor the Soviet Union were willing to place their unconditional trust in US good intentions. For the PLO, Carter's promotion of a Palestinian homeland was a definite advance but was still far from representing the commitment to a Palestinian state which was the minimal Palestinian demand. The Soviet Union had a similarly wary attitude. Moscow had reacted negatively to Carter's arms reduction proposals of March 1977 and to the administration's human rights campaign and its public defence of Soviet dissidents. As Garthoff points out, throughout 1977 the Soviet Union remained uncertain of Carter, evolving from an 'an uncertainty based on unfamiliarity to uncertainty based on inconstancy'.[10] In the Middle East, the Soviet leadership remained acutely concerned that US public advocacy for a reconvening of the Geneva Conference was merely an elaborate feint for the subsequent pursuit of Kissinger-style unilateral diplomacy.

The Soviet Union and the PLO also had fears relating to the relative weakness of their bargaining positions in the diplomatic process towards a reconvening of the Geneva Conference. Among those with claims to seats at the conference, the PLO and the Soviet Union had the least secure guarantees of their participation. The PLO, as a non-state actor which had not originally been a participant at the earlier session of the Geneva Conference in November 1973, was in a particularly vulnerable position. Israel refused to have any dealings with the organization and the Arab states, though formally committed to PLO participation, were in practice far more ambivalent.[11] The Soviet Union was in a stronger position, since it was recognized as a great power which had been co-sponsor of the 1973 convening of the conference. However, in comparison with its rival superpower, the Soviet

Union had embarrassingly poor relations with the major regional actors in the Arab–Israeli conflict. Israel, Jordan and now Egypt were firmly in the US camp and, after the deterioration in Soviet–Syrian relations during the Lebanese civil war, even Syria's willingness to acquiesce to an American-inspired settlement could not be discounted.

It was primarily to overcome this mutual sense of vulnerability that led to a joint Soviet and PLO desire to enhance bilateral relations. For the PLO, the benefit of Soviet sponsorship of its interests was that such sponsorship offered protection from Arab and American pressures and from the Israeli resolve to deny its legitimacy. For the Soviet Union, promotion of the PLO opened up the one potential weak link in the US armoury. The PLO was the one party in the Middle East conflict with which the United States could not deal directly, given its promise to Israel in 1975 to refrain from all official contacts until the PLO recognized Israel. In contrast, the Soviet Union had close bilateral relations with the PLO and a measure of influence on the organization. If, as expected, the question of Palestinian representation were to be a central obstacle to the reconvening of the Geneva Conference, the Soviet relationship with the PLO would be something the US could not ignore indefinitely. So long as the Soviet Union could convince the US administration that it had the key to securing PLO moderation, this would be a strong incentive for US assent to the principle of collaborative diplomacy.

However, the Soviet Union knew that it had a number of obstacles to overcome if it was to play its PLO card effectively. First, the Soviet Union had already experienced difficulties in trying to promote PLO moderation and to gain its recognition of Israel. It remained to be seen whether the Soviet Union could find some new creative way to break the strong PLO resistance to accepting the legitimacy of the state of Israel. A further potential problem was that the United States, Israel and the Arab states might somehow be able to circumvent the problem of PLO participation at the Geneva Conference. Israel was adamant that it would not negotiate with the PLO and that it preferred to deal directly with a Jordanian delegation, which would have non-PLO Palestinian delegates. The Arab states also hinted from time to time that direct PLO participation was not essential and that Palestinian interests could be represented by some pan-Arab body, like the Arab league. The Soviet Union, by contrast, needed to ensure that the PLO was directly represented in the conference and that it had the power to make its own independent decisions.

There was, however, one more potential obstacle. The Soviet Union

was aware that, since the PLO had no overriding ideological commitment to the Soviet Union, its loyalty to Soviet patronage could not be
guaranteed. The possibility could not be ruled out that the PLO would
be sufficiently reassured of US intentions that it would accept US conditions for a dialogue in exchange for American protection of its interests. The Americans would thereby be able to snatch the one card
unambiguously held by the Soviet Union and thus potentially have a
full deck. It would confirm Sadat's oft-repeated claim that the United
States held 99 per cent of the cards in the Middle East. The Soviet
Union, therefore, had to convince the PLO that it was only under exclusive Soviet sponsorship that its rights could be adequately safeguarded and that to consider accepting the American embrace was
tantamount to political suicide.

All these various obstacles meant that the Soviet Union had a careful balancing act to perform to secure its objectives. First, it had to be
able to induce the PLO's moderation of its political programme so
that, in some form or other, the PLO would be committed to recognition of Israel. Second, it had to ensure that the PLO was represented
at the Conference and that Palestinian interests were not delegated to
Jordan or some other non-PLO body. Third, it had to secure the PLO's
loyalty to the Soviet Union and that the leadership was not seduced by
US promises to protect its interests. All these factors meant that the
Soviet Union had a complex diplomatic task to make sure that it used
its PLO card most effectively and in a manner which would most ad-
vantageously promote the central Soviet interest of being granted a
substantive role in the diplomatic peace process. For the Soviet Union,
the stakes were high and this gave an urgency and seriousness to Soviet–
PLO bilateral relations which had not been present in earlier times.

SETTING THE SCENE FOR THE JOINT US–SOVIET STATEMENT

The most immediate task facing the Soviet Union was, therefore, to
secure the PLO's agreement to participate at the Geneva Conference
on a more moderate and acceptable political programme. In the early
part of 1977, the Soviet media presented this as an almost foregone
conclusion, suggesting that the Palestinians had already broadly accepted the need to recognize Israel and to limit their political ambitions to the creation of a state on the West Bank and the Gaza Strip
alongside, and not instead of, Israel.[12] The favourable response of the

Palestinian leadership to the Brezhnev peace proposals of 21 March was also taken as a sign of the PLO's growing maturity.[13] It was readily assumed that the forthcoming 13th PNC in Cairo would make some far-reaching but 'responsible' decisions.[14]

However, Soviet expectations for a radical change in the PLO's position were not to be fulfilled at the PNC session. There were some advances but they did not go much beyond the concessions the PLO leadership had already made to the Soviet leadership during the two PLO visits to Moscow in 1975. The political programme of the PNC stated that the PLO would attend any international conference so long as it was invited on the basis of UN Resolution 3236, which unlike 242 explicitly included recognition of the right of Palestinian self-determination. This indirect agreement to participate at the Geneva Conference had, however, already been included in the joint PLO–Soviet statement after the March 1975 visit. Similarly, the PNC confirmed the November 1975 joint Soviet–PLO statement, which promoted the Palestinian right to establish an independent state rather than the more ambiguous 'national authority' conception which had been adopted at the previous PNC in April 1974.

From the Soviet perspective, these advances were certainly valuable but did not represent any substantive breakthrough. On the critical question of recognition of Israel and acceptance of UN Resolutions 242 and 338, the PNC endorsed the rejectionist position. There was to be no acceptance of 242 and 'no recognition, no peace [*sulh*]' with Israel.[15] The Soviet Union expressed its displeasure with this political radicalism by devoting minimal media attention to the PNC. The reports which were given almost exclusively dwelt on the positive aspects of the political decisions, particularly the agreement to attend international conferences on the Palestinian question. The rejectionist elements were generally ignored.[16] Soviet commentators also tried to put a brave face on the proceedings by suggesting that, despite the lack of any major breakthrough, 'on the whole, the Palestinian position is now more flexible.'[17]

This optimistic gloss on the PNC decisions indicated that the Soviet Union had not given up hopes of inducing PLO moderation. A few weeks after the PNC, from 5 to 8 April, Arafat headed a PLO delegation to Moscow which was received with greater official enthusiasm and support than any earlier visits. Arafat was granted his first official meeting with Brezhnev, which was accorded a front-page photograph in *Pravda*. Brezhnev also praised the PLO by describing it as 'having become one of the vanguard detachments of the Arab National Liberation movement', and he expressed the Soviet Union's commitment that representatives of the PLO should participate at the Geneva Conference.[18] Non-Soviet sources also suggested that the Soviet leadership had promised not to attend the Conference if the PLO was not invited.[19] Faruq Qaddumi, the head of the PLO's political department, summarized the achievements of the visit by stating that 'the Soviet Union will not be satisfied with anything that does not satisfy the Palestinians.'[20]

However, on the core substantive issue of the PLO's willingness to recognize Resolution 242, the Soviet Union yet again was confronted by the Palestinian leadership's refusal to countenance such a concession. Faruq Qaddumi, Zuhayr Muhsin from Sa'iqa and Naif Hawatmah from the DFLP noted that during the visit the USSR continued to disagree with PLO policy on 242 and tried to induce a change in the PLO's position. Muhsin even claimed that the Soviet Union had threatened to resume relations with Israel over this issue.[21] In any case, the Soviet Union had little success with its threat or its diplomatic pressures. In an interview given shortly after the visit, Qaddumi reaffirmed the PLO's rejectionist stance, stating that Palestinian demands would not be satisfied by a mini-state on the West Bank and Gaza Strip and that even 'Tel Aviv is in dispute, Jaffa is in dispute.'[22]

However, although the PLO leadership adopted a rigid stance towards Resolution 242, it did show some flexibility over a number of secondary issues concerning the Geneva Conference. The PLO reportedly agreed that it would not insist on participating in the first session of the conference, so long as it was involved in later sessions when the substantive negotiations would take place.[23] This brought the PLO into line with Gromyko's suggestion to Vance in late March, when he reportedly asked, 'Why can't we decide on [PLO] representation at the Conference itself.'[24] This was widely interpreted to suggest that the Soviet Union would not object to the first session being limited to the original participants invited to the 1973 session. The PLO also agreed to be flexible over the nature of its representation at the Conference and would not necessarily object to being included in a unified Arab delegation, though its preference was for an independent delegation.[25] The Soviet Union had also been agreeably surprised by Arafat's willingness to accept a confederation between a Palestinian state and Jordan.[26]

However, the most significant outcome of the Soviet–PLO discussions in April became known in early May. The news was leaked to the Western press that the Soviet ambassador in Washington, Anatolii Dobrynin, had informed the State Department that the PLO would accept

242 if Israel simultaneously recognized the right of the Palestinian people
to a national homeland.[27] This suggestion gained a positive response
from Carter, who hinted that, if the PLO recognized Israel, Israel might
respond by recognising the PLO.[28] Further confirmation of the PLO's
willingness to contemplate the idea of mutual Israeli–PLO recognition
came after a PLO–Rakah meeting in Prague in early May, when the
Rakah delegation stated that the PLO was willing to recognize Israel
in return for Israeli recognition of the Palestinians' right to self-determination.[29]

The PLO leadership vigorously denied that it had made this commitment to mutual recognition during its April visit to the Soviet Union.[30]
It is difficult to determine whether the Soviet Union had misinterpreted
the PLO's position, or, as is probably more likely, the PLO had been
embarrassed by the public revelation of a private agreement. However,
whatever the exact position held by the PLO, the issue of mutual recognition again came to the fore when a PLO delegation revisited Moscow from 29–31 August. As with earlier visits, the Soviet leadership
attempted to secure the greater prize of PLO recognition of Israel.
And, as before, these efforts failed to make the decisive breakthrough,
despite Gromyko engaging in a marathon session of over five hours.[31]
Palestinian participants in the talks were to confirm that they had been
placed under intense pressure to moderate their stance on 242.[32] Soviet displeasure with PLO intransigence was reflected in the sparse
coverage of the visit in the Soviet media and the lack of any meeting
with Brezhnev. The final statement on the visit revealed the divergence in the Soviet and PLO positions by failing to produce any joint
position on the prerequisites for a just settlement.[33]

However, the Soviet Union did not come out empty-handed from
the discussions with the PLO. The PLO committed itself to remaining
loyal to Soviet diplomatic moves in forwarding the prospects for a
reconvening of the Geneva Conference. The final statement on the visit
gave a frank admission that the Soviet and PLO positions were mutually vulnerable and that there was a need to cement their relations to
oppose all attempts to 'deflect attention from the [Geneva Conference]
by all sorts of ideas for considering the Near East questions without
the participation of representatives of the PLO and the Soviet Union'.[34]
Perhaps more importantly, the PLO leadership, in compensation for its
refusal to recognize 242, fully committed itself to the idea of mutual
Israeli–PLO recognition and that this would be the basis for its acceptance to participate at the Geneva Conference.[35]

Although the Soviet Union would have much preferred the PLO to agree explicitly to recognize Israel before the opening of the Geneva Conference, Moscow was forced to concede that the idea of informal mutual recognition between Israel and the Palestinians was the most substantial concession that the PLO was willing to make. Although far from ideal, this at least partially satisfied broader Soviet ambitions. In particular, the Soviet Union felt that it had some diplomatic leverage to pursue its objective of securing US acceptance of the need for superpower collaboration, on the basis that Washington would ultimately have to concede that it was only the Soviet Union which could deliver the Palestinians to the negotiating table.

However, to the considerable surprise of the Soviet Union, the US administration did not need much convincing on the strength of this argument. Indeed, it was Cyrus Vance who first suggested to the Soviet ambassador in Washington, Anatolii Dobrynin, that the Soviet Union and the United States should start work drafting a joint statement for the reconvening of the Geneva Conference. The principal reason for this US *démarche* was the realization that its earlier attempts unilaterally to convene the conference had failed to make much headway. In particular, the US had failed to overcome the problematic question of Palestinian representation at the conference. In May, Vance had attempted to resolve this obstacle by suggesting that a working party group should be convened prior to the Geneva Conference, which would have excluded the PLO and the Soviet Union. This idea had been effectively torpedoed by a Syrian rejection.

With the working group idea having failed, Vance then tried unilaterally to resolve the Palestinian conundrum by offering US recognition of the Palestinian right to a homeland in exchange for PLO recognition of 242.[36] These negotiations were carried out through the offices of Saudi Arabia and their eventual failure was due to a number of factors, including misunderstandings between the US and the PLO and pressures from Syria and Israel. However, the direct and indirect pressure exerted on the PLO from the Soviet Union was also a critical factor. In a series of letters from the Soviet leadership to Arafat, there was strong Soviet advice to delay making a final decision on recognition of 242.[37]

The general thrust of the Soviet advice was that it was foolhardy for the PLO leadership to trust the United States over such a crucial issue. To place its faith in US promises would leave it vulnerable to American and right-wing Arab pressures to make unacceptable political compromises. As such, Moscow argued that it would be far wiser to coordinate any policy concessions with the Soviet Union who was genuinely committed to protecting Palestinian interests in the event of the reconvening of the Geneva Conference. When the PLO Executive Committee met on 17–18 August to discuss the American initiative, its acceptance of the Soviet advice can be seen in the final statement which urged 'greater vigilance against imperialist conspiracies ... and an ability to differentiate between the enemy and friends, headed by the Soviet Union.'[38] At least in part, it was the Soviet Union's success in ensuring the loyalty of the PLO which acted as a catalyst for the United States to consider engaging the Soviet Union more substantively in the negotiating process towards the reconvening of the Geneva Conference.

However, the exact nature of the intentions of the US administration in making the offer to work with the Soviet Union remain a subject of controversy. On the face of it, the resulting joint statement issued on 1 October was a relatively anodyne political document. There was no mention of a Palestinian state, or even of a Palestinian homeland, and there was no reference to the PLO. The only concession made by the United States was an agreement to secure the 'legitimate rights of the Palestinian people', while previously there had been only a US willingness to take into account Palestinian 'interests'.[39] US officials replied to the subsequent vehement Israeli rejection of the joint statement by maintaining that it was an exaggerated response to a nonexistent threat. The joint statement was, in their view, merely a procedural matter without any substance.[40]

In fact, there is substantial evidence that justifies the Israeli conviction that the US–Soviet joint statement was not as innocent a document as US officials professed. As early as May 1975, Bzrezinski had contributed to an article in *Foreign Policy* which had argued that the publication of a joint US–Soviet statement at a time when negotiations were at an impasse would 'put great pressure on the Arabs and Israelis, especially if it was then endorsed by Western Europe and Japan. This might not have an immediate effect on Israeli policy ... but a public US posture in favour of such a settlement would exert powerful influence and would probably gain both domestic and international support'.[41] Carter made a similar point in a *Time* interview in early August 1977 when he said:

> I think that if a particular leader of one of these countries should find his position is in direct contravention to the position of all the parties concerned, *including ourselves and the Soviet Union*, and was a narrowly defined question in his own country, there would be a great impetus on the leader to conform with the overwhelming opinion. ... [emphasis added][42]

There is little doubt that the leader he had in mind was the Likud leader of the new Israeli administration, Menachem Begin. It also became clear in later statements that the issue which Carter believed the Israeli leadership was not addressing adequately was the question of Palestinian representation and the role of the PLO. In a press conference given a few days before the publication of the joint statement, Carter stated that 'it's obvious to me that there can be no Middle East peace settlement without adequate Palestinian representation. The Arab countries maintain that the PLO is the only legitimate representative of the Palestinians' interests.' He then added that, though the PLO was not the sole legitimate representative of the Palestinian people, it was nonetheless 'a group that represents, certainly, a substantial part of the Palestinians.'[43]

Whatever the real motives of the Carter administration, the Soviet Union had a clear understanding of the function of the US–Soviet joint statement. For the Soviet leadership, the function of the statement was to break the impasse over Israel's refusal to recognize the PLO and the PLO's refusal to recognize Israel, which the Soviet Union believed, along with its superpower partner, was the most serious obstacle to the reconvening of the Geneva Conference. From the Soviet perspective, this impasse was also built into the very framework of the Geneva Conference since all parties to the dispute were obliged to accept UN Resolutions 242 and 338 to be permitted to participate in negotiations. But with 242 and 338 as the bases for the conference, there was no prospect for engaging the PLO or for guaranteeing that the Palestinian question would be adequately addressed. The only satisfactory solution, therefore, was to modify or adopt a new set of bases for the resumption of the Geneva Conference, which would include a reference to the need to satisfy Palestinian rights. In Soviet eyes, the joint US–Soviet statement had precisely this function.

This assessment of the function of the joint statement was founded on the earlier Soviet idea of a mutual and simultaneous recognition between Israel and the PLO. It had become clear in the subsequent months that neither party was willing voluntarily to take such steps. The Soviet Union had thus concluded that it would only be under joint US–Soviet pressure that the two sides could be forced to make the necessary gestures. For the Soviet Union, the joint statement was a US and Soviet agreement to force Israel and the PLO to negotiate with one another and to recognize each others' legitimate interests. On the basis of the joint statement, the United States would pressurize Israel to attend the Geneva Conference and the Soviet Union would enforce

PLO participation. Neither Israel nor the PLO would be forced to recognize each other before sitting down at the same table in Geneva. But, once they started negotiating between themselves, this would be judged as amounting to an implicit mutual recognition.[44]

The Soviet Union, therefore, believed the joint statement was the key to unlocking the problem of Palestinian representation and for leading to the swift convening of the Geneva Conference. From the Soviet perspective, the critical factor was the extent to which the United States was willing to exert pressure on Israel and to be committed to respecting Palestinian rights. In a meeting with Senator George McGovern in late August, Gromyko stressed that the United States must stop being too lenient on Israel and must be less ambiguous on the Palestinian issue.[45] The American willingness to enforce Israeli acquiescence to the joint statement was seen in Moscow as a test-case of the US commitment to collaborative diplomacy.

For its part, the Soviet Union wanted to convince the United States of its essential moderation towards Israel and the reasonableness of its commitment to the Palestinian right to self-determination. In the formulation of the joint statement, the Soviet Union showed considerable flexibility to the extent that, as Carter himself noted, they conceded on every substantive issue which differentiated the Soviet from the US positions.[46] In the joint statement, there was no mention of the PLO or of a Palestinian state and the Soviet Union agreed to accept the US formulation of a full peace between Israel and its Arab neighbours. Even though the Soviet Union officially continued to promote a Palestinian state, Gromyko reassured Carter that 'if we can just establish a miniature state for the Palestinians as big as a pencil eraser, this will lead to a resolution of the PLO problem for the Geneva Conference.'[47] As a whole, the Soviet Union went to considerable lengths to align its position with that of the United States and to come to a mutually acceptable compromise over the basic outlines for a just settlement.

The Soviet Union was also determined to ensure that the PLO should unreservedly accept the joint statement. As Fahmi noted in his memoirs, immediately after the publication of the joint statement, the Soviet Union enforced PLO acceptance of the statement and urged the PLO leadership to persuade the other Arab parties to give a similarly positive response.[48] The favourable PLO reception of the statement was to surprise many Arab and Western officials and commentators. Vance found the PLO's position most unexpected, since the statement had included no reference to the PLO or to a Palestinian state.[49] The Soviet success in gaining PLO support was a significant achievement and the PLO was to continue expressing its loyalty to the statement in the following months.[50] The PLO leadership later made clear that it was willing to participate at the Geneva Conference on the basis of the joint statement.[51]

The Soviet Union, therefore, felt that it had essentially honoured its side of the bargain in the collaborative diplomatic effort to formulate and implement the joint US–Soviet statement. It had shown diplomatic moderation and gained PLO acquiescence to the joint statement's outlines for a settlement. It was naturally a great disappointment when, a few days after the joint statement was issued, the United States appeared to retract from its agreed position with the Soviet Union in the face of strong Israeli pressure. On 5 October, the United States and Israel issued a joint statement which stated that UN Resolutions 242 and 338 remained the agreed basis for the resumption of the Geneva Conference and that acceptance of the joint US–Soviet statement was 'not a prerequisite for the reconvening and conduct of the Geneva Conference'.[52] A US–Israeli working paper adopted at that time also excluded any mention of the PLO. For the Soviet Union, the US–Israeli agreement undermined the fundamental basis of the joint US–Soviet statement and was a testament to the American failure to gain Israeli acceptance of PLO representation at the Geneva Conference. Soviet dismay at the US reversal was intense. In subsequent Soviet literature on the Middle East, the US failure to stand by the joint statement was depicted as a major turning point in US–Soviet relations, representing a US failure to honour an agreed commitment to engage in genuine collaborative diplomacy. As such, it was viewed as having harmed the spirit of *détente* and increased the distrust between the two powers and being directly linked in a causal chain which was to lead eventually to a renewed Cold War.[53]

At the time, however, the Soviet Union showed, at least initially, that it was not unsympathetic to the American predicament. The Soviet media focused most of its criticism on Israel and the Zionist lobby. With the United States remaining committed to the resumption of the Geneva Conference, the Soviet Union still contributed its diplomatic efforts to that end. It gave repeated assurances to Israel that its intentions were honourable and that the Soviet Union was committed to guaranteeing Israeli security and the attainment of full peace in the region.[54] The Soviet Union also supported the PLO's continuing interest in gaining admittance to the Geneva forum, which led to significant concessions such as the selection of Edward Said, an American Palestinian academic, to represent the Palestinian side in negotiations.[55]

But the Soviet Union was aware that its diplomatic position had been weakened by the US retraction. Syria became adamantly opposed to the resumption of the Geneva Conference and there was little the Soviet Union could do to change Syria's stance. Syrian pressure on the rejectionist elements in the PLO also circumscribed Arafat's more moderate tendencies. When Sadat finally broke away from the Arab ranks and made his controversial decision to fly to Jerusalem on 19 November, the Soviet Union traced back Sadat's treachery to the US failure to confront Israel and honour its commitment to the principles of substantive superpower collaboration.

TO THE CAMP DAVID TREATY

Sadat's journey to Jerusalem represented a watershed in the Arab–Israeli peace process which left the Soviet Union and the PLO impotently on the sidelines as the United States engaged in a sustained unilateral diplomatic offensive to reach a bilateral agreement between Egypt and Israel. The PLO's response was swift and unreservedly hostile. At a conference in Tripoli on 4 December 1977, the six principal Palestinian guerrilla factions issued a joint statement which unambiguously rejected 242 and 338 and any conferences based upon these resolutions.[56] The Carter administration reacted to this development by confirming that the PLO had thus excluded itself from any role in the peace process. Brzezinski provided the final farewell by concluding an interview in *Paris Match* with the words 'Bye Bye PLO'.[57]

The Soviet Union initially took a more cautious attitude to Sadat's move and refused explicitly to condemn Egypt or the United States. However, in response to the Begin–Sadat meeting in Ismailiyya on 25–26 December, the Soviet Union escalated its anti-Egyptian campaign, condemning Sadat's journey to Jerusalem as a 'trip to Canossa' and unambiguously siding with Syria, Iraq and the PLO in their complete rejection of the Egyptian diplomatic initiative.[58] In an interview in *Pravda*, Brezhnev defined the Soviet position by explicitly criticizing the 'notorious' Israeli–Egyptian talks, defining them as a 'negative' factor impeding a genuine comprehensive settlement.[59] The Soviet media made clear that in no way would the Soviet Union be a participant in these 'illegitimate' meetings which were nothing but a 'cover-up for separatist deals' under the aegis of the United States.[60]

With the Soviet Union and the PLO converging in their opposition to the US-directed Israeli–Egyptian contacts, there was a clear mutual interest in enhancing bilateral relations. For its part, the Soviet Union judged that the weakest link in any US-brokered Egyptian–Israeli agreement would be the Palestinian question. The Soviet commentator, Georgii Mirskii, argued as early as December 1977 that even if, as was likely, Sadat were 'to submit – that is to concede a separate settlement on terms advantageous to Israel. . . . it implies that the Palestine Question – the main, key and decisive issue of the entire Middle East settlement – will remain unsolved, and that consequently, the Arab–Israeli conflict will remain unsolved.'[61] This meant that the Soviet Union had a direct interest in underlining its commitment to the Palestinian cause by energetically promoting the international legitimacy of the PLO. By taking an uncompromising stance on the Palestine question and on the PLO, the Soviet Union hoped to isolate the United States and Egypt and increase Soviet influence in the rest of the Arab world.

The PLO also had its own reasons for wanting to consolidate its relations with the Soviet Union. Even for the Fatah leadership which had traditionally sought to maintain a position of non-alignment and ideological neutrality, the new adverse circumstances suggested that, in Salah Khalaf's words, the 'time has come for a turn to the Soviet Union.'[62] In August 1978 a Fatah delegation made its first visit to Moscow and among its number was the right-wing figure of Khalid al-Hasan who was later approvingly to comment that Moscow was 'more Arab than the Arabs themselves'.[63] The more leftist-inclined PLO leader, Khalaf, even argued, in an unusual display of collective Arab self-criticism, that 'we should be ashamed of ourselves for our disgraceful treatment of the Soviet Union in our political relations and general relations.'[64] The change in the PLO's stance towards the Soviet Union was clearly noticeable in the strongly worded resolution of the 14th PNC in January 1979, which affirmed 'the importance of the alliance with socialist countries, first and foremost with the Soviet Union, since this alliance is a natural necessity in the context of confronting American–Zionist conspiracies against the Palestinian cause.'[65]

Given the coincidence of Soviet and PLO interests in the aftermath of Sadat's journey to Jerusalem, it is not surprising that Soviet–PLO relations were visibly to be enhanced. The real breakthrough came after the signing of the Camp David Accords on 17 September 1978, when Arafat headed a PLO delegation to Moscow from 29 October to 1 November. At the conclusion of this visit, the final communiqué included the Soviet Union's recognition of the PLO as the '*sole* legitimate representative of the Palestinian people'.[66] This was the first time that the Soviet Union had officially accorded the PLO such exclusive representation. In previous years, the Soviet Union had refrained from granting this exclusive recognition so as to maintain a lever of influence for encouraging political compromises. On this occasion, however, the Soviet leadership gave this final recognition without any substantive political concessions in return.

The Soviet embrace of the PLO became even warmer towards the end of 1978. On the occasion of the UN-sponsored International Day of Solidarity with the Palestinian People on 29 November, Brezhnev personally signed a telegram to Arafat, stating that 'thanks to its staunchness, courage and fidelity to principle in this hard struggle the PLO has won Arab and international recognition as the only lawful representative of the Palestinian people and has become an advanced force of the Arab National Liberation movement.'[67] In response to the UN initiative, the Soviet Union also established a Soviet Committee for Friendship and Solidarity with the Palestinian people, which was a clear demonstration of the Soviet desire to give greater prominence to its support for the Palestinian cause and its relations with the PLO.[68] Arafat responded enthusiastically to these developments by confidently asserting that 'it was with Soviet arms that we triumphed and it is with Soviet arms that we shall triumph again'.[69]

However, the outward appearance of an ever-increasing solidarity and closeness of relations between the Soviet Union and the PLO belied a number of continuing tensions and sources of bilateral conflict. Although the Soviet Union fully supported the PLO's rejectionist stance towards the Egyptian–Israeli negotiations, the Soviet leadership remained greatly frustrated by the PLO's refusal to contemplate recognition of Israel. Indeed, the Soviet leadership's exasperation noticeably increased as the PLO's non-recognition of Israel effectively undermined Soviet *démarches* to the United States. The extent of Soviet frustration can be seen clearly in a document seized by the Israelis during the 1982 Lebanon war, which contains the full minutes of Gromyko's meeting in Moscow with a PLO delegation on 13 November 1979. At the conclusion of the meeting Gromyko had this to say:

> How is it possible for us to recognize the PLO and the establishment of an independent Palestinian state when the PLO does not recognize Israel and the well-known UN Resolutions? We heard the very convincing argument from your side regarding the motives for your refusal to accept these resolutions. . . . These reasons are known. But in our talks with the Americans, we always confront this obstacle and this limitation which cannot be overcome. . . . In every

statement, the Americans say: How can we recognize an organization while they are not ready to recognize anything?

Gromyko's advice to the PLO was unambiguous. It is also clear that it was advice which he had given on many earlier occasions.

Here I wish to ask you a question. Are you considering certain tactical concessions in return for getting recognition from the hostile camp? Are you considering recognizing these international resolutions? And are you also considering recognizing Israel's right to exist as an independent sovereign state?.... Is your position to reject all concessions on this problem, even those not involving principles? What matters to you is the establishment of a Palestinian state, and, notwithstanding the differences that may exist, the establishment of a Palestinian state is the foundation and contains all the other things.[70]

However, continuing Soviet frustration over the PLO's refusal to recognize Israel was not the only source of tension which threatened to undermine the outward show of Soviet–PLO solidarity in the face of the Camp David peace process. In the aftermath of the signing of the Israeli–Egyptian Peace agreement in 1978, the Soviet Union initiated a strategic reassessment of its Middle Eastern strategy, which had a direct impact on Soviet attitudes to the PLO. The principal catalyst for this reassessment was driven not only by developments in the Middle East but also by markedly more conflictual and hostile US–Soviet relations throughout the Third World. The United States adopted a more antagonistic and confrontational stance. In 1978, Brzezinski warned that the Soviet Union was engaged in a drive for geostrategic advantage through capitalizing on the 'arc of crisis' which included those countries 'along the shores of the Indian ocean, with fragile social and political structures in a region of vital importance to us threatened with fragmentation.'[71] These US fears only increased in 1979 as the Iranian revolution reached its climax with the ousting of the Shah and the inauguration of Ayatollah Khomeini's unreservedly hostile Islamic republic of Iran. In this context, the Soviet invasion of Afghanistan in December was perceived as an unashamed Soviet drive for geopolitical advantage, symbolizing the final epitaph on the period of Soviet–US *détente* and the start of a period of extreme distrust between the two superpowers.

In this new geostrategic environment, Soviet policy-makers reassessed the strategic importance of their alliance with the PLO. In a more hostile regional and global environment where the United States was determined to pursue an aggressive campaign in the Middle East to exclude the Soviet Union, Moscow had become more dependent on those allies with genuine politico-military power to oppose US attempts at hegemony. In this context, the PLO's strategic value declined. And, as the PLO's importance declined, Syria's primacy in Soviet strategic planning was consolidated. Syria was the only ally of the Soviet Union which directly confronted Israel, and Damascus was resolved to use all its available resources to oppose Israeli and American attempts to impose a settlement contrary to its interests. Also, after Sadat's journey to Jerusalem in November 1977, Asad ended his attempts to preserve a degree of independence between the two superpowers and literally begged for a close political and military alliance with the Soviet Union. To demonstrate the seriousness of his allegiance to the Soviet Union, Asad became the most stalwart defender of Soviet interests, most notably providing much appreciated Arab support for the Soviet occupation of Afghanistan.

Although the Soviet Union did not immediately elevate Soviet–Syrian relations to the level Asad was demanding, the strains and tensions which had plagued earlier bilateral relations were gradually overcome. By the time of Asad's visit to Moscow in October 1978, the Soviet Union had accepted the legitimacy of the Syrian presence in Lebanon and that Syria's involvement was directed towards 'the normalization of the situation in Lebanon on the basis of the guaranteeing of its sovereignty, independence and territorial integrity'.[72] After the Egyptian–Israeli peace treaty of March 1979, the Soviet Union also finally began to supply the sophisticated arms which Asad believed were essential to provide an effective deterrent against Israel.[73] The increased importance of Soviet–Syrian relations was given its formal confirmation in a bilateral Treaty of Friendship and Co-operation, which was signed between the two countries on 8 October 1980.[74]

The Soviet decision to accord strategic primacy to Syria had significant implications for Moscow's relations with the PLO. With Syria now recognized as the 'the leader of the Arab nation in the struggle to remove the consequences of Israeli aggression and against US expansionism', the PLO was expected to subordinate its strategy to Syrian demands.[75] As compared to the period of the Lebanese civil war, when the Soviet Union had tilted decisively towards the PLO in its conflict with Syria, the Soviet Union had now clearly indicated that its priorities lay firmly with support for Damascus. Although Soviet–Syrian relations remained relatively unproblematic up to the 1982 Lebanon war, mainly because the PLO was itself dependent on Syrian support for its Lebanese base, the Soviet Union's strengthening of its relations with Syria did involve a relative weakening of its links with the PLO.

However, the declining fortunes of the PLO were not solely due to the changing international geopolitical situation. In the context of increasing East–West confrontation, Soviet policy-makers became more concerned about the loyalty and fidelity of their chosen allies. In the late 1970s, Moscow had been persuaded through Asad's persistent advocacy that Syria had become genuinely loyal to the Soviet Union and would not follow Egypt's example and, at the first opportunity, switch allegiance to the United States. In contrast, by the start of the new decade, the Soviet Union became increasingly unsure about whether it could count on the loyalty of the PLO, particularly the loyalty of the Fatah-dominated PLO leadership.

Soviet policy-makers, reared on the Marxist-Leninist ideals of monolithic unity, had always considered the fissiparousness of the Palestine Resistance Movement as its 'Achilles' heel', which undermined its potential power as an influential anti-imperialist force in the Middle East.[76] Such concerns were similarly, if not more strongly, expressed in commentaries on Fatah, whose weaknesses as an organization were felt to correspond to the 'class heterogeneity of the organization and the lack of clarity of its ideological platform.' This was viewed as the result of Fatah's support for 'contacts with all Arab states friendly to the Palestinian cause, taking material aid both from "right and left."' As a result, Soviet ideologues divided the class structure of Fatah into its leftist, centrist and rightist elements. In this analysis, Arafat, Qaddumi and most of original members of Fatah were presented as belonging to the centrist 'petty-bourgeois' wing rather than the more progressive leftist wing, which constituted those members 'coming from the working classes, the poor peasantry and the progressive trades union officials'.[77]

Up until the late 1970s, the Soviet Union had broadly supported Fatah and the Fatah-dominated PLO leadership because it represented the most powerful faction within the PLO and its political stance was recognized to be relatively moderate, at least in contrast to the more extreme rejectionist groups. However, in the more ideologically demanding period of greater East–West confrontation, the Soviet Union progressively tilted towards the avowedly leftist factions within the PLO. Ties with Hawatmah's DFLP, with whom the Soviet Union had since the 1973 October war developed strong relations in response to the increasing Marxist orientation of the DFLP's programme, were strengthened. In 1978 there was also a reconciliation between Moscow and George Habash's PFLP, which had been condemned in the early 1970s as an extremist Maoist organization but which had in the late 1970s also adopted a more orthodox Marxist colouring. After the invasion of Afghanistan, both Habash and Hawatmah gained Soviet gratitude by providing propaganda support for the 'international assistance given by the Soviet people to the people of Afghanistan and the anti-imperialist revolution'.[78]

This stalwart support from Habash and Hawatmah contrasted unfavourably with the PLO–Fatah response to the Soviet invasion. The right-wing Fatah leader, Khalid al-Hassan, stated that the 'Soviet Union had denied its friends the ability to defend its actions'.[79] A *Time* interview in January 1980 also quoted Arafat as saying that the Soviet Union sought to 'establish control over Middle Eastern oil', to which a *Tass* commentary retorted by publicizing Arafat's claim that it was a 'gross distortion' which sought to 'drive a wedge between the Soviet Union and its friends'.[80] Yet, the Soviet Union could not ignore the fact that Arafat had failed to praise the Soviet invasion and had headed a delegation to the Islamic Conference Organization in Islamabad in January 1980, which condemned the Soviet occupation of Afghanistan.[81]

The Soviet Union's growing *rapprochement* with the PFLP and DFLP also involved a greater awareness of and sympathy for their disaffection with the Fatah leadership of the PLO. In part, this was driven by the PFLP's and DFLP's scepticism that the Fatah leadership was not taking a sufficiently stalwart position towards the Camp David process and was developing too close and intimate relations with right-wing regimes like Jordan and Saudi Arabia.[82] In part, the disaffection was due to a bitter conflict over the distribution of power within the PLO. At both the 14th and 15th PNCs in 1979 and 1981 respectively, the PFLP and the DFLP focused their energies on trying to force the Fatah leadership to accept a greater degree of collective leadership. Their argument was that Arafat and his Fatah associates dominated all the structures of the PLO and that there was a lack of real democratic diffusion of power within the organization. Hawatmah even went as far as to attack Arafat personally for his autocratic tendencies and his 'capitulationist illusions'.[83]

The PFLP and DFLP were not, however, the only allies of the Soviet Union who were presenting an increasingly negative assessment of the Fatah leadership. At the same time, the Palestinian communists, who had separated from the Jordanian Communist Party and formed their own independent party in 1982, were engaged in a similar assault on

Fatah. Their specific criticism was that Fatah had come under strong
Saudi pressure to lessen the communist party's activity in the West
Bank, 'primarily by undermining the Palestine National Front (PNF),
in which our comrades played an outstanding role. This is a rightist,
reactionary class policy.'[84] The Palestinian communists' fear of a right-
wing assault was to grow stronger in the following years and were not
entirely unjustified. At the Baghdad Summit in November 1978, the
PLO and Jordan received $150 million to be spent jointly in the Occu-
pied Territories and the Fatah leadership used this as an opportunity to
expand its influence among the inhabitants on the West Bank. As a
consequence, Fatah came into direct conflict with the communists and
a bitter dispute ensued. The Fatah leadership obstructed the communist attempt, which was supported by the PFLP and DFLP, to revive
the PNF and engaged in an offensive on the traditional communist
strongholds in the labour unions and student and youth movements.[85]
The PLO–Fatah leadership also resisted the continual demands by the
Arab communist parties that the Palestinian communists should be represented on the PLO's Executive Committee.[86]

Although the Soviet Union was careful not to alienate Fatah given
its dominance within the PLO, Moscow broadly shared the criticisms
of the Fatah leadership as expressed by its closest allies in the Palestine
Resistance – the DFLP, the PFLP and the Palestine Communist Party.
In addition, the poor relations of the Fatah leadership with Syria added
to Soviet reservations. Unlike the DFLP and the PFLP, who mended
their fences with Damascus after the Lebanese crisis, Asad retained a
strong personal animosity towards Arafat and was adamantly opposed
to practically all of the PLO–Fatah diplomatic initiatives. With Asad's
desire to subsume the Palestine Resistance within Syrian decision-making
and his growing obsession to attain strategic parity with Israel, he became
increasingly hostile to the PLO's diplomatic independence and its
flirtations with the West. In Asad's eyes, Arafat was deliberately trying to undermine Syria's strategic ambitions by seeking a dialogue
with the West and thereby advancing a political settlement of the Israeli–
Palestinian conflict. Given the military imbalance between Israel and
the Arab world, Asad believed any moves towards a diplomatic settlement
were tantamount to treachery, since they would split the Arab front of
resistance and result in effective capitulation to Israeli demands.

Given the strategic primacy Moscow increasingly conferred on Syria,
these criticisms of the Fatah leadership of the PLO had considerable
weight. When added to the highly vocal complaints of the leftist groups
within the PLO, Arafat and his Fatah loyalists appeared to Moscow at

best as ideologically suspect and, at worst, on the brink of capitulation. There is also evidence that, in the period immediately before the 1982 Lebanon war, direct Soviet suspicions of Arafat had intensified. Oleg Gordievskii, the KGB double agent who defected to Britain in 1985, noted that at some point in the early 1980s Moscow became 'increasingly disturbed by intelligence reports of secret meetings between PLO leaders and Western officials. Arafat, it was suspected, was giving way to Western efforts, greatly resented in Moscow, to exclude the Soviet Union from a Middle Eastern settlement.'[87]

It seems probable that the meetings which attracted Soviet attention were those between Arafat and the young American John Mroz, who had been authorized by Reagan and Haig in August 1981 to initiate a secret dialogue with the PLO leadership. From August 1981 to May 1982, Arafat reportedly met Mroz on 50 different occasions and their talks focused on the US terms for initiating a dialogue.[88] The fact that the Soviet Union knew about these contacts can be seen in the media reports given in July and August 1981, warning that the United States was trying to look for a 'secret and indirect contact with the PLO' and that it was attempting to draw out 'conciliatory elements in the PLO . . . to weaken and split the Palestine Resistance Movement politically'.[89] Further evidence can be found in a book written in 1986 by the foremost Soviet specialist on the Palestine question, where it was noted that 'in the second half of 1981 to the first half of 1982' the United States engaged in 'active political manoeuvres on the Palestinian question, which with hindsight can now be seen as a deception of world public opinion in as much as Washington had already knowledge of the preparations for Israeli aggression in Lebanon.'[90]

Thus, by the time of the 1982 Lebanon war, the outward strength of the Soviet–PLO strategic alliance masked an underlying substantive deterioration in relations. Not only had the PLO been relegated to a secondary and subordinate role in Soviet policy-making in the Middle East but the Soviet leadership began to have serious reservations over the loyalty and trustworthiness of Arafat and the PLO leadership. The fact that the facade of Soviet–PLO solidarity remained publicly undamaged reflected the PLO's continuing official loyalty to the Soviet Union and its stated opposition to separatist settlements in the mould of Camp David. From the Soviet side, Gordievski notes that Moscow continued to give Arafat 'unenthusiastic' public support but only because he was judged to be 'the only man capable of holding the PLO together'.[91]

However, the reality of the decline of Soviet–PLO relations was not to be hidden indefinitely. The Israeli invasion of Lebanon in 1982, with the deliberate intention of driving the PLO out of that country, could not but affect the dynamics of the Soviet–PLO relationship. Indeed, in the period after 1982, the Soviet Union and the PLO could no longer disguise their more problematic and difficult relationship.

6 The Relationship Deteriorates: 1981–5

Soviet concerns over the loyalty of the PLO and the strategic value of Soviet–PLO relations grew in intensity as the vulnerability of the PLO's principal base in the Lebanon became increasingly exposed. By the early 1980s, the PLO's position in Lebanon was under pressure from a number of directions. The right-wing Likud government in Israel, under the leadership of Menachem Begin, had made clear its determination to destroy the PLO in Lebanon. Within Lebanon itself, the quasi-independence of the territory under PLO control – the so-called 'Fatahland' – had alienated the local Muslim community, particularly the Muslim Shi'i population of the South, which had earlier been a bedrock of support for the PLO within the country. And, for its part, Syria, which had gained Arab legitimation for its presence in Lebanon, exerted considerable pressure on the PLO to reduce its independent decision-making and to subordinate its policies to Syrian strategic oversight.

The first section of this chapter analyses the Soviet response to the deteriorating strategic and political situation that the PLO found itself in Lebanon, which culminated in the Israeli invasion in 1982. It is argued that when the Israeli invasion finally took place, the PLO leadership should not have been surprised by the Soviet refusal to intervene on their behalf. The Soviet leadership had repeatedly confirmed that it could and would not contemplate such an option. However, Soviet inaction during the war did have a psychologically damaging effect, undermining Soviet prestige in the region generally and among the Palestinians in particular.

The Soviet Union did, though, seek to compensate for its relative impotence during the war with a concerted attempt to regain its position. The second section assesses this Soviet attempt to retrieve its influence in the Middle East. Under the more activist leadership of Iurii Andropov, Soviet diplomatic activity focused on ensuring that Israel's intervention in Lebanon should end in failure and that the US administration's attempts to secure advances in the peace process – through the Reagan plan – should be rebuffed. In both these endeavours, the Soviet Union co-ordinated its activities with Syria and strategic Soviet–Syrian co-operation grew in intensity. In contrast, the Soviet

114

Union became increasingly disillusioned with the PLO as the PLO leadership flirted with the Reagan plan and joined its diplomatic efforts with Jordan. Although these PLO initiatives failed, partly due to Soviet–Syrian pressures, Soviet suspicions of the PLO's loyalty and credibility were significantly increased.

The third and fourth sections of this chapter chart the further precipitous decline in Soviet–PLO relations. The third section provides an assessment of the internal dispute within Fatah in Lebanon during 1983 which escalated into an indirect Syrian–Fatah conflict, with Syria providing support to the Fatah dissidents. Although the Soviet Union attempted to remain officially neutral, it could not disguise its underlying support for the Syrian position which contrasted with the support that the Soviet Union had given to the PLO eight years earlier in 1976 when it had first directly confronted Syrian military power in Lebanon. While in 1976 the Soviet Union had judged the PLO to be the progressive party against the reactionary policies of Syria, in 1983 it was Syria which was clearly designated as the progressive anti-imperialist power with the PLO's credentials being under far greater suspicion. For the Soviet Union, the capitulationist direction of the PLO was confirmed by the signing of the Jordanian–PLO Agreement in Amman in February 1985. As the fourth section illustrates, this PLO initiative left Soviet–PLO relations at their nadir, where there was real concern expressed in Moscow that the PLO had irrevocably joined the imperialist and reactionary bloc in the Arab world.

THE 1982 LEBANON WAR

The deteriorating situation of the PLO base in Lebanon in the late 1970s was a source of considerable concern for Moscow. The rising power of the Lebanese Christian Right, under the charismatic leadership of Bashir Jumayyil, and the corresponding decline of the Muslim-leftist forces had left the PLO in a weaker strategic position. The growing tensions between the Palestinians and the indigenous Muslim population, particularly the Shi'i community, added to the PLO's vulnerability. Given that the PLO also faced a more determined and assertive enemy under Menachem Begin's government, which had made no secret that it ultimately sought the destruction of the PLO, only added to the bleakness of the PLO's political and military position in the region. Soviet analysts knew that, in the face of a determined Christian–Israeli offensive, the PLO's 15,000 poorly armed combatants could not realistically be expected to offer anything but the most minimal resistance.

For a political and military leadership habitually cautious in its assessment of the 'correlation of forces', there was no question that the Soviet Union would be prepared to defend militarily the PLO's highly vulnerable Lebanese base. The Soviet Union stated this to the PLO leadership clearly and without any ambiguity. In all their contacts with Palestinians, Soviet officials constantly emphasized that they would not intervene in Lebanon to defend the PLO.[1] More directly, the Soviet Union insisted that the PLO should do nothing to provoke Israel and that it must adopt a strictly defensive stance.[2] In line with this prescription, the Soviet Union refused to supply the PLO with the sophisticated weapons which it was constantly demanding for fear of an escalation of the conflict with Israel.

The weapons issue was to be a continual source of friction between the Soviet Union and the PLO as can be seen during Arafat's visit to Moscow on 19–21 October 1981. Arafat reportedly made a desperate plea for sophisticated surface-to-air missiles to act as a deterrent against the Israeli aerial attacks.[3] But, as the Palestinian leadership was ruefully to admit, the Soviet Union only agreed to supply 'ordinary arms'.[4] One Palestinian leader indirectly expressed his dissatisfaction with Soviet parsimony by noting that China and Saudi Arabia were the PLO's main arms suppliers.[5] The only concession Moscow made was to permit East Germany to supply 34 Second World War T-34 tanks and a number of Katusha rocket launchers of a similar vintage.[6]

Through the restrictions placed on arms supplies, the Soviet Union made clear that the primary onus was on the PLO to protect its Lebanese base. The Soviet Union also stressed that its primary commitment was to the Lebanese state and that Soviet relations with the Lebanese state authorities were formally and legally prior to any commitments to the PLO's politico-military Lebanese base. In references to Lebanon made by the Soviet government, it was always stated that the USSR was committed to Lebanon's 'sovereignty, independence and territorial integrity'.[7] The corollary of this legal position was that, for the Soviet Union, the PLO, as a national liberation movement, could expect to have no necessary legal rights to a territorial base in Lebanon or elsewhere and that such rights were only accorded by prior agreement with the host state. This meant that it was the PLO's responsibility to maintain good relations with the Lebanese state. In Arafat's meeting with Gromyko and Ponomarev in November 1979, the latter made this point clear that when he stated that the PLO must have good relations 'not only with anti-imperialist organizations in Lebanon, but also with the other forces, like Franjiyya, for instance. . . . you, with your presence in Lebanon, must take care that your relations with the Lebanese state should not worsen because then your situation would be difficult.'[8]

The Soviet Union also stressed that the PLO must resolve its security problems through reliance on its Arab allies. In the Lebanese context, this implied close co-ordination with Syria, who alone had the potential capability to protect the PLO against a Christian–Israeli assault. These recommendations for PLO reliance on Syria was also a logical extension of the Soviet Union's own strategic and military alliance with Syria, which was strictly limited to the defence of Syria against a direct attack on its sovereignty. Soviet officials emphasized that the Friendship and Co-operation Treaty did not apply to Syria's involvement in Lebanon.[9] However, the Soviet Union was providing essential guarantees of Syria's domestic security and thereby giving it the opportunity to act more forcefully within Lebanon. Just as Syria was being backed by the Soviet Union, Soviet officials recommended that the PLO seek its security through close alliance with Syria.[10] In this way, a strong Soviet–Syrian–PLO axis would be created which would considerably decrease the PLO's vulnerability in Lebanon.

The bottom line in all these various pieces of advice to the PLO was that the Soviet Union would in no circumstance directly intervene in Lebanon. It should not, then, have been a great surprise to the PLO leadership that the Soviet Union provided almost no material support to alleviate the PLO's predicament in the face of the Israeli invasion into Lebanon on 6 June 1982. In fact, as Rashid Khalidi's careful analysis of PLO decision-making during the war reveals, the PLO leadership were fully aware of the limits of Soviet support. They knew that Moscow 'could not and would not do anything on its behalf which violated Lebanese sovereignty, or had not been formally requested by the Lebanese authorities.' Given that President Sarkis supported the Christian camp, this was only a polite way of saying that the Soviet Union would do nothing. Khalidi continues by saying that the PLO was also 'made aware' that the Soviet Union was 'unwilling and unable to assist Syrian forces inside Lebanon, and that any guarantees they might extend would only apply to Syrian territory.'[11] In the rest of his account, Khalidi found that the PLO leadership never had any real expectation that the Soviet Union would change its non-intervention stance.

It would be a mistake, though, to suggest that the Soviet Union was completely inactive during the war. However, its activities were primarily devoted to ensuring that there should be no major Syrian–Israeli escalation of hostilities and that Syrian military arms losses should be compensated. To achieve these objectives, the Soviet Union acted with vigour to secure a cease-fire on 26 June between Syria and Israel and to initiate a massive arms resupply which brought Syria back to its pre-war levels by mid-September. However, no such Soviet intervention was provided to ease the desperate plight of the PLO as it lay besieged in Beirut. However, Brezhnev did send a number of messages to Reagan, attempting to shame the US administration to take more forceful action. He darkly warned that if the US failed to act 'the tragedy of Lebanon, and especially of the population of its capital, will remain an indelible stain also on the conscience of those who could stop the aggressor but do not do so.'[12] Although Reagan was reportedly angered by this suggestion of US complicity, it did not change American policy towards the need for a PLO withdrawal essentially on Israeli terms.[13] Faced with this inflexible US stance, the Soviet Union bowed to the inevitable and accepted that the PLO would have to submit to terms for withdrawal set by Philip Habib, the US mediator between Israel and the PLO. On 21 July, the PLO leadership made one last desperate plea for help from the Soviet Union, but were swiftly told that 'there was nothing that the USSR can do, since it could act only via Syria, and this was not possible.'[14]

The PLO leadership had, in fact, expected no more favourable Soviet response. They had known 'the limits to which they can go and help us' and that it could not and 'will not help militarily before the Arabs'.[15] However, even taking this known Soviet reluctance into account, the PLO leadership still felt disillusioned by the degree of Soviet inaction during the Lebanon war. PLO leaders such as Salah Khalaf, who had previously been one of the most enthusiastic in promoting close Soviet–Arab relations, could not suppress his fears that the Soviet Union had colluded in ending Syria's participation in the war. He stated: 'I do not understand the Soviet stance really. Is it due to lack of information? I wonder, doesn't Syria want to fight, or don't the Soviets want the Syrians to wage war?'[16] Na'if Hawatmah, normally the most loyal Soviet supporter, was more explicit in calling for the Soviet Union to use 'all possible means including military power', and complaining that the effect of its diplomatic and political efforts was 'limited if not zero'.[17]

The appearance of Soviet inactivity also meant that Moscow faced a major public relations problem in the wider Arab world. Moscow knew that the Soviet Union's superpower credentials had been badly tarnished by the abysmal failure of Soviet-supplied Syrian arms and its impotence at preventing a close ally being humiliatingly defeated and expelled from its major territorial base. Even respected Western analysts were suggesting that this marked a 'superpower in eclipse'.[18] To counter these critiques, the Soviet Union engaged in a propaganda offensive to defend its stance on the Lebanon crisis. In an unusual break from precedent, Primakov fielded a press conference at the Ministry of Foreign Affairs on 4 July where he stressed that the Soviet Union was giving material aid to the Arabs, which 'naturally included military aid'.[19] In a response similar to that given after the June 1967 Arab defeat, Soviet officials indicated privately to their foreign visitors that it was not Soviet weaponry which was at fault but rather the Arabs' use of it.[20]

On the fate of the Palestine Resistance, the Soviet Union tried to put a brave face on its military defeat. The PLO's brave resistance was applauded but the inevitability of its defeat was conceded, given that the PLO's military potential was limited to few poorly armed partisan groups.[21] Moreover, it was argued that this was not the important issue. Though the Palestinians had undoubtedly suffered a military defeat, they had in fact won a moral victory.[22] In an interview Brezhnev gave to *Pravda* on 21 July, he made this case when he argued that:

> However complicated the Palestinian problem may be, through whatever difficulties the Palestinian people may go, one thing is clear: the Palestinian problem is no Gordian Knot, and it cannot be cut with a sword. The staunchness displayed by the Palestinians under such tragic circumstances shows with fresh force that they are defending the living cause of a living people and they cannot be subdued. Thus, a definite conclusion can be drawn: the aggression of Israel is turning into a major political and moral defeat, a deepening isolation in the international arena.

He continued by reconfirming the Soviet commitment to create a Palestinian state to be agreed upon through 'collective efforts of all sides concerned, including the PLO, as the sole legitimate representative of the Palestinian people'.

Brezhnev's remarks, supported by many other Soviet officials, reveal that the Soviet Union was far from contemplating a withdrawal from the Middle East. It had certainly been disappointed by the lack of Arab unity during the war and frequently pointed out that this was the ultimate cause of the Arab failure to confront Israel with any real effectiveness.[23] Soviet exasperation at the demands for direct intervention was also sometimes expressed, as with the response of Vadim

Zagladin, Deputy Head of the Central Committee International Department, during an unusually critical Hungarian interview: 'There is a war between Israel and one of the Arab countries, aggression against an Arab country. Under these circumstances, what can the Soviet Union do? Should it attack Israel? This is an impossible situation.'[24]

However, for the most part, the Soviet leadership kept its cool and focused on the long-term strategic implications of the US-supported Israeli invasion of Lebanon. Schooled in the Clausewitzian-Leninist traditions, the Soviet leadership knew that military victories do not necessarily translate into political victories. Even before the war, Moscow had been predicting that the ultimate US objective was to use 'Israel's military bludgeon and come out at the same time as peacemaker, mediator, and carrier of the keys, so to speak, to the settlement of the Middle East settlement.'[25] In his *Pravda* interview, Brezhnev was stating clearly that the Soviet Union would be determined to obstruct any such attempt at enforcing American dominance in the region. For the Soviet Union, the Lebanon war might be a US military victory but the underlying reality was that it marked only the first stage in a far more bitter political struggle. The real battle was yet to come.

THE REAGAN PLAN

For the Soviet Union, President Reagan's unveiling of a new US plan for a Middle East settlement on 1 September represented the start of the predicted US–Soviet political struggle for influence in the region. Reagan's initiative coincided with the final withdrawal of PLO troops from Beirut, which Reagan characterized as a significant US diplomatic victory and a 'day that should make us all proud'. The plan he unveiled on this occasion did not significantly deviate from the diplomatic positions of earlier US administrations. There was a reaffirmation that UN Resolution 242 applied to all fronts; that there should be a freeze of Israeli settlement activity on the Occupied Territories; and that the Palestinians, in line with the Camp David agreement, should be granted a transitional period in which to exercise full autonomy over their internal affairs.

However, Reagan also made explicit that Israel would not have to withdraw fully to the pre-1967 borders, when 'Israel was barely 10 miles wide at its narrowest point'. He also made clear that the US did not support the creation of an independent Palestinian state and that Palestinians would only be permitted to exercise self-government 'in association with Jordan,' thus implying that negotiations on the fate of the West Bank and Gaza Strip would require Jordanian–Palestinian co-ordination. Finally, the Reagan plan was marked by the signal failure to make any specific mention of Syria or its territorial claims to the Golan Heights or even its right to participate in negotiations.[26]

A week later the Arab states at their summit in Fez responded with a plan which predictably demanded a full Israeli withdrawal, the creation of a Palestinian state and the recognition of the PLO as the sole legitimate representative of the Palestinian people. However, the Fez initiative went further than earlier Arab peace proposals in providing the first, if indirect, recognition of Israel's right to exist in peace with its neighbours.[27] The Soviet Union waited for the outcome of the Fez Summit before promoting its specific proposals for a settlement of the conflict. Moreover, when Brezhnev unveiled these proposals on 15 September during a visit by South Yemeni leader, Ali Nasir Muhammad, they almost completely mirrored those set out at Fez, except that recognition of Israel was directly, rather than indirectly, stated. There are also reports that Soviet officials had tried to persuade Saudi Arabia to permit the Soviet Union to be a signatory of the Fez plan.[28] Although Riyadh had rejected this suggestion, the Soviet media sought to emphasize a common Soviet–Arab stand by repeatedly stating that 'the Soviet initiative coincides with the basic principles of the plan for a Middle East settlement adopted recently by the Arab summit conference in Fez.'[29]

The Soviet Union's determination to align its proposals with the Arab consensus reflected an essentially defensive and reactive policy towards the Reagan initiative. In the aftermath of the Lebanon war, the United States was politically and diplomatically in the ascendance and Soviet diplomats were acutely aware that, despite the Fez resolutions, a number of Arab countries were attracted by Reagan's proposals and were 'even speaking of the positive features of this plan'.[30] King Husayn of Jordan, in particular, had gone on record saying that in his opinion the Reagan initiative was 'the most courageous stand taken by any American administration since 1956. I believe it to be a very constructive and a very positive move and I would certainly like to see it continue and evolve.'[31] However, the most worrying development for the Soviet Union was the evidence of the PLO's interest in exploring the Reagan initiative. PLO officials had confirmed that they had found some positive elements in the initiative, in particular its recognition of the Palestinian problem as a political rather than a humanitarian problem and its express opposition to Israeli sovereignty, and to Jewish settlements, on the West Bank and Gaza Strip.[32]

The PLO leadership also quickly showed an interest in exploring the prospects of Jordanian–PLO co-operation as recommended in the Reagan plan. Arafat, liberated from Syria's restrictions on his freedom of action, initiated in October 1982 a series of intensive, high-level discussions with King Husayn and the Jordanian government. Significant progress was made and, at the end of November, Arafat and Husayn agreed to the formation of a Higher Jordanian–Palestinian Committee to discuss their future relationship. This committee then announced on 14 December that it had agreed to' 'move politically on all levels' to regain Palestinian rights.[33] Arafat's diplomatic flexibility was not limited to Jordan. He also authorized PLO contacts with the arch-enemy of the radical Arab world – Egypt. The political objective of this diplomatic *démarche* was barely disguised. A PLO spokesman in Cairo unambiguously asserted that the PLO was willing to negotiate on the basis of the Reagan initiative since 'the PLO believed that the US was the sole power capable of putting pressure on Israel to induce it to withdraw from the occupied Arab territories.'[34] For the Soviet Union, such statements had a disturbing affinity with Sadat's oft-repeated remarks that the United States held 99 per cent of the cards in the Middle East peace process.

At the end of 1982, the Soviet Union was preparing itself for a reactive counter-attack to derail the Reagan plan and to reassert Soviet influence in the region. Soviet resolve in this respect was considerably enhanced by the succession of Iurii Andropov to the position of General Secretary after the death of Brezhnev in November 1982. Soviet foreign policy during the Lebanon war had undeniably been affected by the immobilism of the last months of Brezhnev's rule and the concurrent succession struggle. Once Andropov was securely in power, he immediately defined a more aggressive and determined Soviet stand against US encroachments into the Middle East. In contrast to earlier attempts to persuade the United States to engage in bilateral collaboration, Andropov defined an overt and deliberate policy of obstruction and the pursuit of unilateral competitive advantage.

The main arm of this Soviet strategy was a speedy and massive rearmament of Syria. In his first month in office, Andropov concluded a new large-scale arms deal with Asad and he accelerated the earlier Soviet pledge to dispatch Soviet air defence units to Syria.[35] By January 1983, two highly sophisticated SAM-5 surface-to-air missile brigades had been deployed on Syrian territory with the Soviet advisers, technicians and manpower to man them. This qualitative increase in Syria's military power was paralleled by an increased assertiveness in Soviet

pronouncements on the Middle East. On 31 March 1983 a Soviet government statement warned Israel about its 'criminal designs' and that it
should 'stop playing with fire' since 'Syria is not alone. On its side
are Arab patriots, the socialist countries and everyone who values peace,
justice and honour.'[36] Shortly after this announcement, a visiting delegation of Israeli parliamentarians to Moscow were warned that if Israel
attacked Syria, there would be 52,000 Soviet soldiers on the Israeli
border within 24 hours.[37]

The significant increase in the Soviet commitment towards the defence of Syria considerably enhanced Asad's regional standing. It
provided the essential protective backing for Syria to confront the
US attempt to forge an Israeli–Lebanese agreement and to obstruct
the implementation of the Reagan Plan for a comprehensive peace settlement. With no role specifically envisioned for Syria in the American initiative, Asad unambiguously rejected it and called for the Arabs
to bury their differences and build a 'Syrian–Soviet–Arab strategic
consensus against our Arab nation's enemies, the United States and
Israel.'[38] Asad also used all his available diplomatic and coercive resources to try to enforce Jordanian and Palestinian rejection of the
Reagan Plan.

The Soviet Union fully supported Syria in this diplomatic offensive
and complemented Asad's efforts with its own diplomatic initiatives to
obstruct the American peace plan. In early December 1982, Andropov
had a private meeting with King Husayn, who was leading a delegation from the Arab League, during which the Soviet leader dropped
the traditional diplomatic niceties to explain the Soviet opposition to
the US peace initiative. He warned that 'I shall oppose the Reagan
plan, and we will use all our resources to oppose it. With due respect,
all the weight will be on your shoulders, and they aren't broad enough
to bear it.'[39] King Husayn was also to admit that he had come under
strong Soviet pressure over the question of the Palestinian–Jordanian
relationship and the issue of an international conference. His replies,
which had failed to satisfy the Soviet side, were that the Jordanian–
Palestinian relationship was 'not subject to discussion on the international level' and that, though the idea of an international conference
was desirable, it was a 'problem in the US arena . . . and we are duty-
bound to deal with this arena.'[40]

Andropov failed to convince the Arab League delegation explicitly
to condemn the Reagan plan but this only strengthened his resolve to
increase the diplomatic pressure, especially on objective allies like the
PLO. Arafat did not help his case by stating to the press, immediately

before a scheduled PLO visit to Moscow on 11–13 January 1983, that 'it appears the Soviet Union does not comprehend the situation; it is new to the region.'[41] Andropov brushed aside such condescension by presenting the Soviet position in an uncompromising and abrasive manner during Arafat's visit. He argued that the Reagan plan was an imperialist-Zionist plot and that there could be no justification for PLO ambivalence over its anti-Arab and anti-Palestinian solution to the Middle East conflict. Andropov continued by asserting that this was not the time for unilateral concessions, such as recognition of Israel.[42] He advised that the PLO should only accept recognition of Israel if it could be assured of reciprocal Israeli recognition of the Palestinians' right to self-determination.[43] Since there was almost no chance of the Begin administration accepting such terms, the PLO was recommended to remain opposed to any pressures to accept UN Resolution 242. Andropov's hardline stance conspicuously contrasted with the Soviet position in the 1970s, as outlined in previous chapters, when the PLO had frequently been recommended to accept 242 unconditionally.

The wording of the final communiqué issued on the visit also suggests that there had been considerable Soviet scepticism over Arafat's diplomatic strategy after the Lebanon war. There was no mention of an 'identity of views' having been reached. Instead, it was merely noted that Arafat had 'informed the Soviet leaders about the main directions of the political activity of the PLO', confirming that no one except the PLO had the 'right to speak on behalf of the Palestinian people' and that the PLO favoured the establishment of a confederation with Jordan 'on the basis of voluntariness between the independent Palestinian state after its creation and Jordan'. In a clear expression of a degree of Soviet ambivalence over the PLO's strategy, there was only the weak confirmation that 'the Soviet side showed an attitude of understanding to this position'.[44]

After the departure of the PLO delegation, the Soviet media went to considerable lengths to clarify the exact Soviet understanding of the PLO's position on confederation. It was stressed that it was diametrically opposed to the American and Israeli plans to 'transform Jordan into a supposed Palestinian state by settling the greatest number of Palestinians in Jordan'.[45] Rather, any decision on confederation would only come after the establishment of an independent Palestinian state, which would be attained through a comprehensive settlement with the participation of the PLO on an equal basis and as the recognized sole legitimate representative of the Palestinian people.[46] This Soviet interpretation of the idea of a Jordanian–Palestinian confederation indicates that the Soviet Union was only giving Arafat a strictly limited licence to develop his relationship with King Husayn. Most probably, it was only because the Soviet Union had proposed such confederal arrangements in the past that it felt obliged to support Arafat's recent conversion to the idea. Faiq Warrad, the First Secretary of the Jordanian Communist Party, probably reflected Soviet reservations when he suggested that:

> In the present situation, we are opposed to such plans, holding that they are premature. The cart cannot be put before the horse. . . . A Palestinian state is as yet non-existent. The statements about its preconditional association with Jordan are used by Israel to further its expansionist designs, to return and annex the Occupied Territories, and abolish the rights of the Palestinian people.[47]

Despite all his efforts, Andropov failed to secure Arafat's outright condemnation of the Reagan plan. However, it was jointly agreed that the plan sought to prevent the creation of a Palestinian state and to remove the PLO from the peace process. Arafat did furthermore agree to oppose all 'attempts to replace an all-embracing just settlement with separate deals of the Camp David type suiting the aggressor and on its terms'.[48] At the 16th PNC session in Algiers on 14–22 April 1983, Arafat also succeeded in gaining a less than absolute rejection of the Reagan plan. The plan, as it stood, was judged to 'conflict with international legality' and thus could not be considered 'a sound basis for a just and lasting solution of the cause of Palestine and the Arab–Zionist conflict'.[49] Senior PLO officials said this still left open the chance for negotiating amendments and subsequent reconsideration.[50]

However, the combined pressure from the leftist Palestinian organizations, from Syria, and from the Soviet Union severely limited Arafat's room for manoeuvre in developing his Jordanian connection. As he was unwilling to contemplate a complete schism between Fatah and the other leftist factions, Arafat was forced to negotiate with King Husayn on a highly restrictive agenda. There was to be no derogation of the PLO's exclusive representative rights, no recognition of UN Resolution 242 and no acceptance of the Reagan plan unless it was substantially modified. This was far from acceptable to King Husayn, who in spring 1983 was impatient to secure a positive PLO commitment to recognition of 242 and a favourable response to Jordanian–PLO co-operation over the Reagan plan. Given the widely diverging positions between the King and Arafat, the talks held between them in early April were predestined to fail. On 10 April, the Jordanian

government announced that, though Arafat and King Husayn had negotiated the final text of an agreement, this had been rejected by Arafat's
colleagues from the PLO leadership. As a consequence, Jordan announced it was formally rejecting the Reagan plan and that 'we in
Jordan, having refused from the beginning to negotiate on behalf of
the Palestinians, will neither act separately nor in lieu of anybody in
Middle East peace negotiations.'[51]

The Soviet Union enthusiastically acclaimed the breakdown of the
Palestinian–Jordanian talks and the Jordanian rejection of the Reagan
initiative. This was presented as the conclusive proof that the Reagan
plan was incompatible with 'the overall Arab plan for a Middle East
settlement approved by the Arab summit in Fez'.[52] Following its earlier analyses, the principal reason offered for the failure was that it
denied the Palestinians the right to self-determination and statehood.[53]

Soviet officials could also be satisfied that its pressures on the PLO
leadership had borne fruit. Soviet media reports leading to the 16th
PNC had highlighted the explicit rejection of the Reagan plan by leftist leaders like Habash, Hawatmah and Khalid al-Fahum, while conspicuously failing to quote from Arafat.[54] The dangers of the
Palestinian–Jordanian connection falling into the US–Israeli trap were
also explicitly stated.[55] Furthermore, Soviet officials were reported to
have lobbied members of Fatah and other factions to ensure that 'Arafat
did not fall into the trap of the Reagan Plan'.[56]

Soviet pressure on the PLO was, though, only one factor, and not
the most significant, in the demise of the Jordanian–PLO dialogue. A
more important reason was the disillusionment felt by both Arafat and
King Husayn to US policy in the Middle East in the first half of 1983.
The Reagan administration had conspicuously failed to develop its peace
initiative and had instead become embroiled in the attempt to forge an
Israeli–Lebanese agreement, which was eventually signed on 17 May
1983. The sense of US collusion with Israeli strategic ambitions in
Lebanon, and its failure to secure an Israeli withdrawal from that country,
undermined Jordanian and Palestinian hopes that the US would have
the political resolve to secure Israeli withdrawal from the West Bank
and Gaza Strip.

However, the Soviet element, though a secondary factor, was certainly
felt to be a powerful constraint on the development of the Jordanian–
PLO *rapprochement*. King Husayn was convinced that 'pro-Soviet hardliners in Arafat's entourage' had been 'responsible for this inability to
reach an agreement'.[57] This display of Soviet power was also to convince him that any further Jordanian initiatives would have to take

into account Soviet interests, since 'Moscow can contribute to achieving stability in the region.'[58] By mid-1984, the King was arguing that any Middle East peace process must include an international conference which would include the Soviet Union.[59]

Similarly, Arafat was under no illusion that, if he wanted to preserve a consensus in his organization, it would be facilitated by gaining Soviet approval for his diplomatic initiatives. Developments since the Lebanon war had shown that, despite his relative freedom from Syrian control, combined Soviet–Syrian opposition to his diplomatic strategy was still a powerful obstructive force. In the latter half of 1983, Arafat was also to learn the potential costs of alienating his Soviet ally.

THE FATAH SCHISM

Arafat's diplomatic strategy had not only failed to achieve any significant breakthrough on the peace process, it had also caused severe internal problems within the PLO. At the 16th PNC in February 1983, the differences and tensions between the leftist factions and the Fatah leadership had only barely been papered over. A few months later, this uneasy alliance finally unravelled as a full-scale rebellion against Arafat's leadership emerged inside Lebanon. The initial catalyst for the revolt was Arafat's decision to appoint two Fatah officers to command Palestinian forces in Lebanon, who were widely considered to have discredited themselves by fleeing from their posts during the Israeli invasion of Lebanon. A number of senior Fatah officers, led by Sa'id Musa (Abu Musa), refused to accept these appointments and they were supported by some Fatah Central Committee members based in Damascus, most notably Nimr Salih and Samih Abu Kuwayk.

These Fatah dissidents made clear that their dissatisfaction with these military appointments was only part of a more comprehensive critique of the PLO and Fatah leadership. They argued that Arafat's decision was only one symptom of a much deeper malaise, which required a number of radical reforms to resolve. They proposed that there should be a restructuring of the Fatah organization, which would include Arafat's removal from the leadership. They also demanded Fatah to adopt a radical rejectionist political programme, which would assert the primacy of armed struggle and the complete rejection of political negotiations.

Opposition from within the Fatah ranks to Arafat's leadership was not a new phenomenon. In April 1978, there had been a revolt by the left wing of the organization against Arafat's acceptance of UN Resolution 425, which had established a United Nations peacekeeping force in South Lebanon (UNIFIL). Arafat had, at that time, been able to assert his authority relatively quickly. In the circumstances of 1983, Arafat's capability to quash the revolt was far more limited. Most of the loyalist forces had, after the evacuation from Lebanon, been relocated in a number of other Arab countries. Also, on this occasion, the Fatah revolt had taken place on Syrian-controlled territory and it rapidly became apparent that Syria was providing logistical and military support to the dissident forces. Syrian-controlled factions, such as Sa'iqa and the PFLP-GC, joined with the Fatah dissidents and supported their demands. These combined forces, with Syrian backing, were more than a match for the remaining loyalist Fatah forces and they gained a number of military successes.

The Soviet Union had been aware of the ideological heterogeneity of Fatah, and had conceptually divided the movement into its rightist, centrist and leftist elements.[60] It had also not hidden its ideological preference for the leftist faction, hoping that it would act as a catalyst for the radicalization of the rest of the organization. Nimr Salih, in particular, had been a regular and highly regarded visitor to Moscow. As a result, a number of Soviet commentators initially provided positive evaluations of the Fatah dissidents' demands. Igor Beliaev, the Middle East expert on *Literaturnaia gazeta*, hardly disguised his implicit support for the 'representatives of the Left Wing in the Fatah organization' who 'believed that the talks held by Yasir Arafat . . . with King Husayn were a departure from the policy of struggle against Israeli aggression and were a kind of compromise, so to speak, not just with King Husayn, but with Israel too.'[61] Other accounts also praised the dissidents' demands as essentially reasonable, with their emphasis on the need for collective leadership, for a review of military appointments and a re-evaluation of the tactical aims of the PLO and its military strategy.[62] Sa'id Musa, who was to become the effective leader of the dissident faction, was to maintain that relations with the Soviet Union remained close.[63]

But, in the early period of the crisis, the Soviet Union was also careful to continue in supporting the Fatah leadership and to distance itself officially from the Fatah dissident position. Salah Khalaf made two visits to Moscow in June and he was reassured that the Soviet Union continued to support Arafat's leadership of the PLO. In a press conference, Khalaf stated that Andropov had sent two personal messages to Arafat to underline the Soviet Union's steadfast commitment to the PLO leadership.[64] Also, as it became clear that the Fatah dissidents were seeking a military solution to resolve their differences with the Fatah leadership, the Soviet position hardened. It was noted that the use of force was an 'illicit form of resolving political questions' and that now there were 'fewer people who doubt that Yasir Arafat is conducting the correct political line, and is fighting to prevent a plot by those who would like to break up the Palestinian Resistance Movement from within.'[65]

Soviet support for the PLO leadership was not, though, unconditional. The Soviet position was, in fact, most closely aligned with the position taken by the DFLP and the PFLP. These two organizations had refused to join forces with the Syrian-backed rebels and had tried to adopt a mediatory position. They supported the demands for a collective leadership and for a more rejectionist political programme but had refused to sanction the use of force to depose Arafat and stated that Arafat's position as leader could only be changed through the proper legal channels. They also argued that Arafat was an important symbolic head of the Palestine revolution and that the real struggle was to ensure that he returned to the correct political path rather than on insisting on his deposition.[66] In an authoritative article in *Pravda* on 25 August 1983, Soviet support for the PFLP–DFLP position was implicitly given. It was argued that there were two contrasting tendencies in the Palestine Resistance, which were equally damaging. First, there was the right wing pushing the PLO to self-liquidation, working through intermediaries such as Jordan. Second, there was the extremist tendency which sought to resolve all issues by military means. Such divisions could only 'aid the US and Israel' and they could only be resolved by taking a realistic but anti-imperialist stance.

However, the Fatah rebellion posed additional difficulties for the Soviet Union since, as well as being an intra-Palestinian conflict, it gradually developed into a major Syrian–PLO dispute. The Soviet Union had followed with increasing dismay the breakdown in the Syrian–PLO alliance in the aftermath of the Lebanon war. Asad had been deeply offended by the PLO leadership's criticisms of Syria's early acceptance of a cease-fire during the Lebanese war.[67] Arafat's flirtation with the Reagan plan and his dialogue with King Husayn only increased Asad's suspicions of the Palestinian leader. The final breakdown in relations came with Arafat's condemnation of Syrian support for the Fatah rebellion. On 24 June, Arafat was humiliatingly expelled from Damascus and Syria unambiguously sided with the dissident cause. Asad was now determined to forge an anti-Arafat coalition which would supplant Fatah's leadership of the Palestinian movement and bring the Palestine Resistance under full Syrian control.

The estrangement of the PLO leadership and Syria over the Fatah rebellion greatly complicated Soviet policy-making. The situation had some similarity with the events in 1976 when Syria and the PLO had again been close to military confrontation and the Soviet Union had to balance the interests of its two allies. However, in contrast to the period in 1976, the Soviet Union was now far less willing to alienate the Syrian leadership. In 1976 the Soviet Union had finally judged Syria to be the 'guilty' party which had succumbed to imperialist pressures and joined the reactionary Christian offensive against the progressive leftist–Palestinian alliance. In 1983, though, Soviet strategic thinking placed Syria firmly in the forefront of the anti-imperialist struggle against the US–Israeli offensive to restructure the Lebanese state and impose hegemonic control of the Middle East. In contrast, the PLO's position was more ambivalent and ambiguous, given that the PLO leadership had openly flirted with the United States and its designs for a separatist Jordanian–Israeli settlement. In 1983, therefore, the Soviet Union was far more predisposed than in 1976 to support Syria in its regional ambitions and objectives.

The dilution of Soviet support for the PLO was reflected in the limited support that Moscow was willing to give to the PLO leadership over its difficult relations with Syria. In terms of responsibility for the deterioration in Syrian–PLO relations, the Soviet leadership placed most of the blame on the PLO. Thus, when Arafat met Andropov in Moscow in January 1983 and asked for direct arms supplies, noting Syria's refusal to pass on the Soviet supplies granted to the PLO prior to the Lebanon war, Andropov's reply had been uncompromising. Any Soviet supplies to the PLO would only come via Syria and it was the PLO's responsibility to mend its relations with Damascus.[68] Similarly, when Salah Khalaf came to Moscow in June 1983, the Soviet leadership demanded that a Syrian–LNM–PLO alliance be formed to fight for a settlement based on the Fez plan.[69]

Similar Soviet disinclination to blame or exert pressure on Syria was also evident when the PLO leadership requested Soviet support in its Lebanese proxy conflict with Syria. Andropov did send a number of messages to Asad, mirroring those sent to Arafat, stating that the two leaders should settle their differences.[70] Salah Khalaf, when he visited Moscow in June, was also promised that the Soviet Union would do all in its power to mediate between the two sides. In addition, he was recommended to travel to Havana and secure Cuban mediation.[71]

However, once Soviet and Cuban mediation were confronted with Asad's steadfast refusal to admit any complicity in the Fatah rebellion, insisting that it was a purely internal Palestinian affair, the Soviet Union refused to contemplate any more vigorous actions. At the beginning of July, the PLO leadership in Tunis received a message from Moscow stating that the Soviet Union could not pressure Syria for a settlement with Fatah. This reportedly filled the Fatah camp with gloom and despondency.[72]

The Soviet non-interventionist stance was underlined during the visit of a PLO delegation, headed by Qaddumi, to Moscow on 11–15 July 1983. In the report on Qaddumi's talks with Gromyko, Soviet neutrality was confirmed in 'its firm opinion about the impermissibility of strife and internecine dissension among the Palestinians faced with the Israeli aggressor, for they weaken the forces of the Palestinians and disunite the Arab ranks. Discord within the PLO can and must be overcome by political means, by dialogue. Attention was also drawn to the need to strengthen co-operation between the PLO and progressive Arab countries.'[73]

However, in the period from September to November, the Soviet Union's non-interventionist and officially neutral position switched towards a more critical stance with a more openly pro-Syrian tilt. This reflected, in part, the military failures of the loyalist PLO forces which had resulted in withdrawal from the Biqa' and isolation in their last base in Tripoli. But a more significant factor was that, from the Soviet perspective, the continuing PLO refusal to submit to Syrian demands in Lebanon threatened to divert Syrian energies from more urgent geostrategic challenges. During September, with the withdrawal of the Israeli forces from the Shuf region in Lebanon, the Soviet Union became increasingly concerned over the potential of a large-scale US intervention on the side of the Christian Lebanese army in its conflict with the Syrian-supported Druze forces. Such concerns were accentuated after a suicide truck-bomb on 23 October destroyed the US marines' headquarters and the US retaliated with heavy naval shelling of Syrian and Druze positions in the Shuf, as well as direct air attacks on Syrian strongholds in Biqa'. At the same time, in the waters off Lebanon the Reagan administration assembled a formidable armada of 30,000 men and 300 airplanes.

By the beginning of November, there was a real Soviet fear that the US leadership was contemplating 'a large-scale military operation in Lebanon with the objective of dealing a massive blow to the national patriotic forces of that country'.[74] In this context, the Soviet Union viewed the intra-Palestinian fighting as a senseless diversion of the

Arab struggle when the threat of US expansionism was so close. Soviet concern and its sense of frustration was unusually given prominence in the journal *Kommunist*, which normally dealt with more theoretical questions of Marxist-Leninist theory.

> One cannot but express concern over the situation within the PLO and its main organization, Fatah. We have expressed alarm concerning the events in North Lebanon, the armed clashes in the Tripoli region. All this weakens the cause of the Palestinians, as well as the national patriotic forces of Lebanon, and the cause of all Arabs. It is necessary to do everything to help stop this fratricidal clash. Both sides will lose from this conflict, and only the governments of Israel and the USA will win.[75]

For a Soviet leadership focusing its energies on the prospects of US intervention in Lebanon, there was a growing belief that the intra-Palestinian fighting was an integral part of an anti-Syrian imperialist conspiracy.[76] Soviet officials also hinted that Syria could not be held accountable because 'now it is the most important force countering the aggressive plans of the USA and Israel'.[77] Furthermore, the Soviet Union placed a large part of the blame for the upsurge in fighting after September on Arafat and the Fatah leadership. On 16 September, Arafat had returned to Tripoli in defiance of the Syrian ban and had taken direct command of the loyalist forces. Such a move was seen in Moscow, reflecting the views in Damascus, as inexcusably provocative.

The decline in the stature of the PLO leadership in Soviet eyes was to become apparent when Qaddumi revisited Moscow on 20–22 November. In contrast to the 'atmosphere of mutual understanding' which had characterized his July meeting with Gromyko, this time the atmosphere was downgraded to being 'friendly and businesslike'.[78] The statement on the Gromyko–Qaddumi talks also revealed a Soviet resistance to accept Palestinian justifications for the armed clashes, noting only that they were 'senseless and unnatural fratricidal clashes between the Palestinians. Irrespective of their causes, they undermine the positions of the PLO won in a long and difficult struggle and only play into the hands of the USA and Israel.' Even more menacingly, the statement hinted that the PLO was in mortal danger of losing its progressive status and that 'the PLO must continue to be an active anti-imperialist factor.' The pro-Syrian bias was expressed in the need for the PLO to remain united and co-operate with 'the national patriotic forces of the Arab world, above all, with Syria, which resolutely opposes the plans of the aggressors'.[79]

In the minutes of the meeting, which were subsequently published in an Arab Gulf newspaper, Gromyko supported the Syrian contention that 'the PLO and the Fatah leadership take lightly the American schemes instead of taking a firm resolution towards the Reagan plan.' He noted that 'part of the reason for the deterioration of the relations between Syria and the PLO' were the 'new thoughts among the Palestinians' which accepted a solution based on 'self-rule' and not on 'an independent Palestinian state'. Finally, he stressed Syria's absolute primacy, since 'if anything should happen to Syria, the entire structure of the struggle against the American and Israeli aggressors would totally collapse'.[80]

However, despite clearly favouring Syria in the conflict in Lebanon, Moscow still disapproved of a full-scale military assault on the loyalist Fatah forces in Tripoli and Soviet announcements emphasized that a 'peaceful' solution must be found.[81] The Soviet Union also continued to recognize that, despite all their faults, Arafat and the Fatah leadership still represented the dominant group in the Palestine Resistance and that they, rather than their Syrian-backed opponents, had the popular support of the majority of the Palestinian community. But, although the Soviet leadership felt obliged to give its formal support to Arafat's leadership, it made clear that its estimation of Arafat had been radically undermined by the developments of the year. Despite a number of rumours that Arafat would travel to Moscow in the latter part of 1983, the Soviet authorities denied him an entry visa.[82] It was, in fact, to be the start of a long five-year period before Arafat was again to be welcomed officially in the Soviet capital. There were also rumours, which have some credibility, that Asad made a secret visit to Moscow in October when he reached an agreement with the Soviet leadership that Arafat should be replaced by a more progressive and anti-imperialist Palestinian leadership.[83]

Just as Arafat's star was shining less brightly, so was the official Soviet evaluation of the position of the PLO. Gromyko's warning that the PLO must 'remain an anti-imperialist force' was frequently repeated in the Soviet media.[84] In the message sent by the Soviet Union to the PLO on the occasion of the International Day of Solidarity with the Palestinian people, there was stringent advice to secure 'the cohesion of all its detachments, as well as close co-operation between the PLO and the Arab countries, first and foremost with those who stand in the front ranks of resistance to the aggressive and expansionist designs of the USA and Israel.' It continued by saying that 'the situation now leaves something to be desired in this respect'.[85] In a similar vein,

Soviet reports at the end of 1983 stressed that the PLO would have to 'draw a lesson, a bitter lesson but a necessary one from the recent tragic events in Tripoli'.[86]

When Arafat crowned his humiliating withdrawal from Tripoli by heading straight to Egypt, marking his first visit since Sadat's journey to Jerusalem, this was precisely the lesson which the Soviet Union believed he should not have learnt. After Arafat's journey to Egypt, the former restraints on Soviet public disquiet with the Palestinian leader's policies were lifted and the putative causes for the PLO's difficulties were openly addressed. The most common interpretation given was that certain sections of the Palestinian leadership, notably the right-wing elements and 'Arafat's associates' had created a 'pessimistic mood . . . that one could hardly talk about an independent state in the foreseeable future, that this was far off, and this aim was practically impossible to achieve. Therefore, certain interim solutions were sought.'[87] This search for interim solution explained the PLO's continued interest in exploring the Reagan plan and in engaging in an intensive dialogue with Jordan.[88]

By the end of 1983, therefore, the Soviet Union was unambiguously stating that Arafat and the PLO had deviated from the anti-imperialist path. In its failure to consolidate the PLO's relations with Syria, the PLO leadership had, it was argued, alienated the most decisive factor in the struggle against imperialism and Zionism. Instead of enhancing the Syrian connection, the PLO leadership had openly flirted with the United States and with US designs for a separatist Jordanian–Israeli settlement, which Soviet analysts suggested would only provide limited self-autonomy and would not satisfy the Palestinian right to its own independent state. The clear implication was that the PLO needed to engage in a radical reorientation in its political strategy if it was to regain its position as a Soviet-approved progressive actor in the Middle East.

TO THE AMMAN AGREEMENT

However, despite the significant deterioration in bilateral Soviet–PLO relations, the Soviet Union had not written off the PLO or, more importantly, reduced its commitment to secure a central role for the PLO in any peace negotiations. This became more apparent as the international and superpower tensions in the Middle East diminished during 1984 and the Soviet–Syrian campaign to undermine US–Israeli objectives in Lebanon began to bear fruit. In February 1984, Syria and the Soviet Union could celebrate their first victory as the Reagan administration withdrew the US marines from Beirut. This was followed on 5 March when the Lebanese government submitted to the relentless Syrian campaign and abrogated the US-sponsored Lebanese–Israeli agreement of the previous year. These developments represented a considerable Soviet coup and a correspondingly humiliating retreat for the United States, greatly damaging its prestige and reputation in the region. With Reagan's energies during 1984 directed towards securing a second presidential election, the Middle East was accorded a low priority in US foreign policy.

With the United States now having effectively withdrawn from the region, the Soviet Union had one of its rare opportunities to promote its influence in the region without a strong countervailing US presence. The new Chernenko administration sought to seize this opportunity by promoting a new variant of the Soviet peace plan which was announced on 29 July 1984. In reality, the plan did not deviate significantly from previous Soviet initiatives and had a close affinity to the Brezhnev plan from 1982. It demanded a specially convened international conference under the auspices of the United Nations and with the participation of the United States and the Soviet Union. There were the traditional demands for a full Israeli withdrawal, the creation of a Palestinian state and peace and security for all states in the region, including Israel. The only significant additions were acceptance of a Jordanian–Palestinian confederation, but only after the creation of an independent Palestinian state, and the proposal for the West Bank and Gaza Strip to be handed to the United Nations for a short transitional period.[89]

However, despite its lack of any great originality, the Soviet resolve to promote its peace proposals represented a shift from the obstructionist policies of the Andropov period. In moving to a more constructive political stance, Soviet diplomats sought to expand their influence beyond the small group of faithful Soviet allies headed by Syria. In particular, attempts were made to persuade Jordan and Egypt to align themselves with the Soviet approach to a peace settlement. These moves were to have some success. Both Egypt and Jordan adopted the Soviet call for an international conference and tried to persuade the US administration to accept this proposal. The Soviet Union responded to these gestures by resuming full diplomatic relations with Egypt in July 1984 and by publicly courting Jordan, as with the visit by the Jordanian Chief of Staff's visit to Moscow in August to discuss a new Soviet–Jordanian arms deal.[90] The Soviet Union also overrode Syrian objections

to these diplomatic initiatives, resulting in a certain deterioration in Soviet–Syrian relations which was exacerbated by Soviet reservations over
Asad's implacable resolve to build a military strategic parity with Israel.[91]

Soviet diplomatic efforts to regalvanize its peace proposals also necessitated closer ties with the PLO. Paradoxically, despite the problems in bilateral relations, the Soviet plan of July 1984 had given the
organization a prominence it had not enjoyed in previous Soviet initiatives. The PLO was presented unambiguously as the 'sole legitimate
representative' of the Palestinians and that it must be an equal participant in the peace conference since 'this is a question of principled
significance, as a Middle East settlement is unattainable without the
resolution of the Palestinian problem, and it cannot be resolved without the participation of the PLO.'[92] With such a central role accorded
to the PLO, the Soviet Union was obliged to seek to regain the support of the PLO leadership and to promote the unity and integrity of
the organization which had been so split by the events since 1982.

During 1984, the Soviet Union made a number of gestures which
marked a softening of the Soviet stance towards Arafat and the PLO
leadership. At Andropov's funeral in February 1984, Arafat met un-
officially with Soviet officials and was reportedly reassured of continued Soviet support for Fatah, so long as it actively tried to restore
relations with the other factions and with Syria.[93] In May and June,
two Fatah delegations visited Moscow and the Palestinian delegates
noted the warmth of the meetings and argued that relations were improving.[94] As a signal of his personal return to favour, Soviet media
reports ended the long silence over Arafat's activities and officially
depicted him as the leader of the Palestine Resistance Movement.[95] On
7 October, Arafat also had an official meeting with Gromyko in East
Berlin, which the PLO media hailed as of great significance.[96] Soviet
reports of this period reflected the more upbeat Soviet–PLO relationship by cautiously judging that 'the split in the Palestinian movement
is beginning to be overcome' and predicting that the PLO would be
reunited on a clear anti-imperialist basis.[97]

The growing Soviet–PLO *rapprochement* was not purely driven by
Soviet needs to promote its peace plan. It also reflected, in part, the
moves made by the Fatah leadership to heal the internal divisions within
the PLO which had gained the approval of the Soviet Union. Mediated
by South Yemen and Algeria, there had been a partial reconciliation
between Fatah and those leftist groups which had remained neutral in
the fighting in North Lebanon during 1983, notably the PFLP, DFLP,
PCP and PLF which were to form a coalition named the 'Democratic

Alliance'. In June, the Aden–Algiers Accords formally marked an agreement which involved a number of political and organizational concessions from the Fatah leadership. These included more stringent conditions for developing relations with Egypt and Jordan and reforms in the organizational structure of the PLO which would provide for greater representation from non-Fatah factions. On this basis, it was agreed that a PNC would be convened where the PLO factions would be formally reunited.

The Soviet Union approved of this agreement gained under South Yemeni and Algerian mediation.[98] For its part, Moscow sought to secure the approval for this process of reunification from the Syrian-backed factions – the Fatah dissidents, al-Sai'qa, the PFLP-GC, and the PPSF – which had formed a coalition named the 'National Alliance'. However, the Soviet Union failed to make substantive progress in these endeavours, despite exerting considerable pressure on Asad. In March 1984, Politiburo member Gaidar Aliev visited Damascus and presented a Soviet memorandum for a Syrian–PLO settlement, which reportedly included Asad's ending of support for the rebel factions.[99] However, Asad unceremoniously rejected the memorandum. The joint communiqué at the end of the visit did not disguise the Soviet displeasure, noting 'a deep exchange of opinions took place concerning the situation in the Palestinian Resistance Movement'.[100] With Syria remaining intransigent, the National Alliance continued to demand the deposition of Arafat as a precondition for rejoining the mainstream, which the Fatah leadership naturally rejected. This, in turn, undermined the prospects for the convening of the PNC, since the Democratic Alliance insisted that the PNC only convene after a reconciliation with the National Alliance had been attained.

With this paralysis in the intra-PLO negotiations, Arafat broke the deadlock by unilaterally announcing that the 17th PNC would take place in Amman at the end of November. This naturally scuppered any chance of the participation of factions from either the Democratic or National Alliances. It was also a decision which greatly angered the Soviet leadership. Although Moscow might have had some residual sympathy for Arafat in the face of Syria's continuing intransigence, this did little to reduce the extent of extreme Soviet displeasure at Arafat's decision. In one stroke, Arafat had undercut the Soviet peace plan, which had been unveiled by Chernenko in July 1984 and which had been gaining in momentum during October with a succession of visits to Moscow by Arab leaders. The planned culmination of the Soviet diplomatic offensive was to have been the much awaited official visit by King Husayn. This had now to be cancelled due to Arafat's move. The PLO–Jordanian *rapprochement* had also increased Syrian hostility towards the PLO leadership and had effectively ruled out any Syrian–PLO renewal of relations, which had been the foundation stone of the Soviet peace proposals. In addition, the Soviet Union was acutely aware that Arafat's strategic intention was to construct a more flexible PLO position, in co-ordination with Jordan, for the expected new US diplomatic initiative after Reagan's expected re-election as President.

However, despite the deep sense of frustration with Arafat's decision, the official Soviet response to the convening of the Amman Summit was relatively restrained. The few media reports which were offered merely noted the views of some of the Palestinian leaders that the session was 'untimely' and that they 'have expressed their reservations about the holding of the PNC session in the present conditions.'[101] The Soviet commentary on the 20th anniversary of the Palestine Resistance on 1 January 1985 was rather harsher in tone, noting that there were sharp differences 'over methods and style and leadership and questions of tactics' and that the US and Israel were using these differences to 'impose the idea of separate deals and make the PLO abandon its clear-cut anti-imperialist and patriotic platform'. However, the article ended on a relatively optimistic note, stating that the talks earlier in the year in Aden and Algiers had resulted in 'an agreement on unity of action' and that 'these accords make it possible to avert a split in the PLO and to surmount the existing difficulties'.[102] Arafat was himself to play on this seemingly ambivalent Soviet position by arguing that it was primarily Syrian pressure which had forced the negative Soviet stance. In an Egyptian radio broadcast, he noted that 'Syria, the ally, is still more important to the Soviets than the Palestinians are. I am a politician and can understand this. There is understanding between the two sides.'[103]

However, privately and behind the scenes, the Soviet Union was far less tolerant of Arafat's manoeuvres and there was certainly no 'understanding between the two sides'. One example can be found in the Soviet obstruction of the efforts made by the Fatah leadership to try to persuade the DFLP and PCP to participate at the PNC. The Fatah leadership had been close to gaining these factions' consent but the Soviet Union exerted pressure on the two organizations to decline the invitation.[104] Soviet officials also insisted that all the leaders of the Democratic Alliance come to Moscow during the period of the Amman PNC and secured their signature to a joint statement, which stressed the continuing validity of the Aden–Algiers Accord as a 'basis for overcoming the difficulties in the PLO so that it should remain an active detachment of the Arab anti-imperialist movement'.[105] In addition, the Soviet Union refused to send a delegation to the Amman PNC and, more substantively, refused to recognize the legitimacy of the final resolutions of the PNC session or even the representative status of the newly elected PLO Executive Committee.[106] When a delegation from this new PLO Executive Committee arrived in Moscow in January 1985, it was bluntly told of this Soviet denial of its legitimacy and the Soviet media downgraded the visit to one of PLO officials 'promoting Soviet–Palestinian public ties and developing the activity of friendship societies'.[107]

The same mix of public ambivalence and private hostility was to mark the Soviet response to the Amman Agreement, which set out the basis for joint PLO–Jordanian co-operation towards the peace process and which was signed by Arafat and King Husayn on 11 February 1985.[108] Officially, the Soviet Union never directly condemned the agreement but rather noted that it had been received unfavourably by 'the Arab states that take an anti-imperialist stand and eight out of ten organizations comprising the Palestine Resistance Movement have condemned the Amman agreement. It has also been criticized by some members of the leadership of Fatah, to which Yasir Arafat belongs, notably by Faruq al-Qaddumi, the head of the PLO Political Department.'[109] Soviet analysts also issued reassuring statements that the Soviet Union was not opposed to the idea of a Jordanian–PLO *rapprochement*, as could be seen in the July 1984 Soviet plan's proposal for a Palestinian–Jordanian confederation.[110] Similarly, the Amman Agreement was not condemned for its substantive proposals, which were described as a 'masterpiece of ambiguity'.[111] Rather, it was the absence of a clearly defined position which was criticized, since it opened up the opportunity for the United States and Israel to 'continue the Camp David process . . . by organizing separate direct talks between a Jordanian–Palestinian delegation and Israel'.[112] Arafat used the indirect nature of the Soviet critique to argue that there was a *de facto* Soviet support for his agreement with King Husayn and that a critical *Pravda* article only 'spoke about the different views on the agreement, and was a review not an analysis, not an official Soviet statement'.[113]

Yet, like Arafat's optimistic gloss over the Soviet attitude to the Amman PNC, this assessment did not reflect the Soviet Union's underlying deep hostility to the Amman Agreement. Privately, the Soviet Union made clear in its communications with the PLO and with Jordan that it was utterly opposed to the agreement and that it would not contemplate any position which did not strictly adhere to the July 1984 peace plan. This unyielding stance became evident when a joint Jordanian–Palestinian delegation visited Moscow in May as part of a round of visits to China and a number of Western European capitals. Unlike the delegation's reception at their other stops, the Soviet Union refused to meet the joint delegation and insisted on separate meetings with the Palestinian and Jordanian representatives. Tahir al-Masri, the Jordanian foreign minister and head of the delegation, was bluntly told that the Soviet Union did not support the Amman Agreement. Masri also failed to impress the Soviet leadership with the Jordanian–Palestinian conception of an international conference, which had been an integral part of the Amman Agreement. The Soviet Union, as King Husayn was later to state, 'held the position that only the two superpowers should participate in the conference and not all five permanent members of the UN Security Council.' The King added that 'despite our repeated efforts', the Soviet Union refused to 'change its position'.[114]

The strength of Soviet opposition can also be seen in its response to the creation of the Palestine National Salvation Front (PNSF), which was established under Syrian sponsorship in March 1985 to act as an institutional replacement for the PLO. The PFLP, the PLF and the pro-Syrian factions were the constituent members. In the past, the Soviet Union had always resisted the Syrian attempts to create a rival Palestinian body to the PLO. This time, although it did not officially support the PNSF, the Soviet Union did reveal its implicit support by exerting considerable pressure on the remaining members of the Democratic Alliance, the DFLP and the PCP to join the Front. As Sulayman al-Najjab, a PCP Politburo member, was to recall, Soviet officials stressed that they were determined to 'give Arafat a lesson he will not forget'.[115] The DFLP and PCP refused to accept this Soviet advice, since they were resolved to preserve the institutional unity of the PLO. But the fact that the Soviet Union was taking the opposing position reveals how close it had come to adopting the Syrian stand against Arafat and the PLO leadership.

Moreover, by the summer of 1985, the official stance on the path taken by the PLO leadership came closer to the more hostile private responses. This reflected the growing concerns in Moscow that the United States might take the plunge and meet a joint Jordanian–Palestinian delegation, including members of the PLO. This concern reached its climax when Richard Murphy, US Assistant Secretary of State for Near Eastern and Southern Asian Affairs, made a trip in early August to the Middle East amid rumours of an impending US *démarche* to the

PLO. With a US–PLO dialogue seemingly close to fruition, Soviet attacks on the Amman Accord and on the PLO leadership became more acute. The Amman agreement was condemned as a 'device for impos- ing the bankrupt "Reagan Plan" on the Palestinians and other Arabs' and the PLO leadership was specifically warned not to follow the capitulationist path taken by the late President Sadat.[116] The Soviet Union also increased its diplomatic activity by inviting to Moscow a succession of Palestinian leaders from factions opposed to the Amman agreement. These included the first independent visit made by the lead- ership of the Sa'iqa organization, as well as the traditional Soviet loyalists of Na'im al-Ashhab from the PCP, Habash from the PFLP and Hawatmah from the DFLP.[117] Critics of the Amman Agreement from within the Fatah leadership, most notably Salah Khalaf, were also conspicuous in being present in Moscow at this time.[118] The convergence of all these personalities in the Soviet capital added up to a concerted Soviet cam- paign against the Amman Agreement and a US–PLO *rapprochement*.[119]

In the event, Murphy's visit to the Middle East in August failed to make the decisive breakthrough as he continued to demand, as the precondition for any talks, PLO recognition of UN Resolution 242. As the prospects for a US–PLO dialogue receded, the PLO leadership sought to reforge their relations with the Soviet Union. Palestinian hopes were raised by a more upbeat Soviet message on the International Day of Solidarity with the Palestinian People which stated that 'we are confi- dent that imperialism and Zionism will not succeed ... in diverting the Palestinian people from the road of struggle for genuine national self-determination and the establishment of an independent state of their own.'[120] On 20 November 1985, Vladimir Poliakov, the Head of the Near East Countries Department of the USSR Foreign Ministry, agreed to meet Arafat in Tunis.[121] By the end of the year, Palestinian leaders were optimistically suggesting that the crisis in Soviet–PLO relations was finally over.[122]

In reality, however, Soviet–PLO relations in the mid-1980s had suf- fered a severe deterioration and effectively remained in a state of crisis. This represented the culmination of a growing Soviet ideological sus- picion and distrust of the organization starting in the late 1970s. The progressive decline of the PLO's anti-imperialist credentials can be seen clearly in the differing accounts provided by two Soviet books on the Palestinian question written by the same person but one being published in 1978 and the other in 1986. The earlier book had been enthusiastic about the Palestinian leadership and its struggle for jus- tice on the basis of an 'anti-imperialist revolutionary nationalism' which

represented a 'revolutionary factor of the whole Arab national liberation movement'.[123] By the time of the second book in the mid-1980s,
that enthusiasm had markedly waned. Instead of a glowing account of
a powerful anti-imperialist force, the Palestine Resistance was presented
as an inherently weak entity which 'refracts not only the major contradictions ... between the Arab national liberation movement and the
policies of the imperialist powers, but also the socio-political contradictions present in the Arab world.'[124] In a similar vein, it was suggested that the contemporary weakness of the Palestine Resistance was
the result 'of the failure to overcome the isolation of the separate
Palestinian detachments and groups'.[125]

The Soviet attitude to the PLO at the end of 1985 was, therefore,
cautious, sceptical and shorn of those earlier hopes of the organization
being a powerful independent radicalizing force. Instead, the Soviet
Union saw a weak, dependent entity which was fractured by deep divisions, reflecting the ideological and political contradictions of the Arab
world generally. There was still the pragmatic conviction that the PLO,
with its mass base of support from the Palestinian people, was an unavoidable factor in any lasting settlement of the Israeli–Palestinian problem. But the Soviet Union, as it continually emphasized to the Palestinian
leadership, judged that the PLO, as presently constituted, was far from
being an acceptable participant in the peace process. There was a long
and difficult path ahead with all the factions needing to work out a
'general realistic approach to the present Middle East situation and the
mutually acceptable conditions for a settlement of the Palestinian
problem'. This would require 'serious concessions, the creation of an
atmosphere of trust between the different organizations and their leaders,
rejection of excessive ambitions and the hurling of insults, and a careful approach to the selection of allies.'[126] The clear implication was
that it was only when the PLO had reached this mature, unified and
realistic stand that it could hope to have the same warmth in its relations with the Soviet Union, which it had last enjoyed during the late
1970s.

7 The Final Rise and Fall of a Relationship: 1986–91

By 1986, the new Soviet leader, Mikhail Gorbachev, and his more established PLO counterpart, Yasir Arafat, faced the political reality that both the Soviet Union and the PLO had suffered a critical decline in their political standing in the Middle East. For the Soviet Union, the success of Andropov's campaign to undermine the Reagan plan and the US–Israeli objectives in Lebanon had turned into a pyrrhic victory. As the failure of the Chernenko July 1984 Peace plan demonstrated, the Soviet Union lacked the power and influence unilaterally to promote a substantive peace process. But, given the Soviet Union's obstructive and competitive behaviour in the aftermath of the Lebanon war, the United States was even more determined to exclude Moscow from any collaborative participation in the peace process. The end result of this was that the Soviet Union's influence was limited to a small band of 'Soviet Faithfuls' – such as Syria, South Yemen and Libya – whose radical rejectionism and predilection to terrorism had increasingly led them to be treated as international pariahs by most countries outside the Soviet bloc.[1]

In the same period, the PLO found itself faced with a similar, if not greater, degree of isolation and marginalization. A heavy blow was inflicted by King Husayn of Jordan's decision in February 1986 to break off ties with the PLO in exasperation at the PLO's failure to make the concessions necessary to permit a US–PLO dialogue. For Arafat and the PLO leadership, this represented the ultimate failure of their post-Lebanon war political strategy. In the years 1982–6, they had succeeded in not only alienating their former radical Arab allies, which had led to a major schism within the ranks of the Palestine Resistance. They had also signally failed to construct new and consolidated relations with the more moderate elements in the region, who ended up being even more distrustful of the organization than before. Thus, King Husayn, having terminated his relationship with the PLO, engaged for the next two years in an undisguised campaign to reassert Jordanian sovereignty over the West Bank. Following King Husayn's cue, the United States made clear to the PLO that it had lost faith in the organization and that there would be no more US–PLO contacts, formal or informal, until the PLO clearly and unambiguously recognized the legitimacy of Israel.

Thus, by 1986, both the Soviet Union and the PLO found themselves marginalized and relatively impotent actors in the Middle East. Over the next four years, however, there was a remarkable renaissance both in the reforging of the Soviet–PLO relationship and in the increase of the regional influence of the Soviet Union and the PLO. By 1989, the PLO and the Soviet Union had recaptured the earlier warmth of their relationship, had both implemented a number of important reforms in their political programmes, and had finally appeared to be on the brink of being accepted as legitimate participants in the peace process.

The first two sections of this chapter cover the period of the Soviet–PLO 'renaissance' from 1986 to 1989. The first section analyses the PLO's moves to heal the internal factional rifts within the organization which culminated in the 1987 PNC in Algiers when the unity of the PLO, with the exception of a few Syrian-sponsored factions, was formally confirmed. The Soviet Union played an important role in this process by insisting that a unified PLO be the principal precondition for the restoration of bilateral relations and by exerting its own pressure and influence on the various parties to this end. Although Soviet distrust remained a powerful constraint right up to the 1987 PNC, the eventual decision by Moscow to support the PLO reunification, in the face of strong Syrian opposition, represented a major turning point. For the first time since the mid-1970s, the Soviet Union demonstrated that it was willing to develop relations with the PLO independently from, and not strictly subordinate to, Soviet relations with Syria.

The second section analyses the contribution of the more intense Soviet–PLO relationship to the critical breakthrough of the PLO's decision at the 19th PNC in 1988 *de facto* to recognize Israel. It is argued that, alongside other factors, Gorbachev's enthusiasm and dynamism, allied with his promotion of 'new thinking' in Soviet foreign policy, was a significant contribution to the PLO's historic decision. However, despite the liberal internationalist rhetoric of 'new thinking', Gorbachev's Middle East policies in this period retained significant continuities with earlier Soviet diplomatic endeavours. Instead of a fundamental break from the past, Soviet–PLO relations during the period from 1987 to 1989 are better understood as a return to the period of Soviet–PLO collaboration during the first year of Carter's administration in 1977 when the Soviet Union and the PLO, sensing their mutual vulnerability and isolation, acted closely and constructively together to attempt to secure US and Israeli acquiescence to their participation in comprehensive peace negotiations. The major difference between the two periods was that in 1977 the Soviet Union failed to persuade the PLO unconditionally to recognize Israel, while in 1988 they ultimately met with success.

The final section of the chapter brings out the real significance of 'new thinking'. This was the reality, which to some extent 'new thinking' sought to masquerade, of the Soviet Union's declining Great Power status and the undermining of the ideological foundations upon which these Great Power pretensions were constructed. Without these props, Soviet interests in the Middle East, and in the PLO in particular, became subordinated to the more immediate domestic problems within the Soviet empire and the more urgent negotiations between the Soviet Union and the West. As a consequence, Soviet–PLO relations precipitously deteriorated, especially over the Soviet decision to permit the mass exodus of Soviet Jews into Israel. By the time of the eventual disintegration of the Soviet Union in 1991, the Soviet–PLO relationship was only the palest shadow of its former self.

TOWARDS THE INTERNAL REUNIFICATION OF THE PLO

In February 1986, King Husayn of Jordan and the Reagan administration made one last attempt to obtain Arafat's unambiguous recognition of Israel. As an incentive to the PLO leadership the United States made an important concession: it promised that, if the PLO clearly accepted Resolutions 242 and 338 and was prepared to negotiate with Israel and renounce terrorism, it would 'accept the fact' that an invitation be issued to the PLO to attend the prospective international conference. Arafat, though, refused to be seduced by this concession and demanded that the United States recognize the Palestinians' right to self-determination – a condition which was forcefully rejected by the US administration, since it was interpreted as a demand to recognize a Palestinian state. The end result was that King Husayn on 19 February publicly broke with the PLO and initiated a concerted campaign, which continued up to the end of 1987, to diminish the PLO's influence on the West Bank and to re-establish Jordan's traditional claim to the territory. The United States followed Jordan's example by cutting all links with the PLO and only accepting Jordanian and non-PLO members from the Occupied Territories as legitimate representatives of the Palestinian people.

The breakdown of the PLO–Jordanian *rapprochement* represented the final failure of Arafat's attempt to escape from the radical Syrian-dominated alliance and find a new base among the pro-Western moderate Arab axis. The end result was that Arafat had succeeded in making the PLO almost universally friendless. The PLO leadership had gained the fundamental distrust not only of the Soviet Union and the radical Arab states but also of the United States and its allies in the Arab world. In terms of securing a new base for the PLO in territory close to Israel, Arafat's policy had similarly failed to deliver. Expelled from Syria and Lebanon, and with Jordan denied as a potential base, the PLO was effectively excluded from all the states territorially contiguous with Israel – distant Tunis was a far from satisfactory compensation. Not unsurprisingly in these circumstances, Arafat's own authority within the Palestinian Resistance had become increasingly shaky. The majority of the factions of the PLO were dissatisfied with his leadership and, even more worryingly, leaders from the Occupied Territories were beginning to emerge who were willing to assert themselves independently from the exiled PLO.

It is clear that even prior to the eventual breakdown of the Amman Agreement, Arafat was contemplating a return to a closer relationship with the Soviet Union. During the final phase of PLO–US negotiations in Amman in February 1986, Arafat met with the Soviet ambassador to Jordan three times and gave him a full account of the American diplomatic *démarche* and the US proposals for an international conference.[2] As Arafat was later to admit, the Soviet ambassador had warned against the PLO placing trust in the US proposal for a conference and informed him that the Soviet Union had not been notified about this change in the American position. He suggested that this sudden American conversion to an international conference, to which it had been previously adamantly opposed, was a ruse to obtain the PLO's unilateral concession to recognize Israel without giving anything substantive in return.[3]

It is difficult to assess the impact of this Soviet assessment on Arafat's strategic decision-making. Soviet diplomats had also made clear to Arafat that, if the Jordanian–PLO dialogue was terminated, the PLO could hope to reforge its relations with the Soviet Union and that the Soviet Union would promote and sponsor the reunification of the Palestinian factions and a reconciliation with Syria.[4] For Arafat whose authority was already under considerable internal threat and who faced a US proposal which would potentially undermine his position even further, the Soviet counter-proposal must have appeared attractive. Although the Soviet proposal had its disadvantages, most notably by limiting Arafat's independent decision-making power and enforcing compromises with the leftist Palestinian factions and with Syria, it did offer the prospect of a reunified PLO under Arafat's consolidated and strength-ened leadership. In comparison, the US proposals for the initiation of a dialogue were far riskier. Arafat knew that he would be staking his political life if he accepted the US terms, since most of his closest colleagues, let alone his many critics, were convinced that the main diplomatic card held by the PLO – recognition of Israel – should only be surrendered for something substantive in return and, at the very least, for US recognition of Palestinian national rights.

However, if Arafat expected that the breakdown of the Jordanian dialogue would speedily result in a Soviet confirmation of his leader-ship, he was to be disappointed. Immediately prior to the 27th Con-gress of the CPSU in February 1986, Khalil al-Wazir tried to obtain an invitation for Arafat to lead the PLO delegation to the Congress.[5] The Soviet officials not only refused this request but insisted that the five-man PLO delegation, headed by Qaddumi, should include two representatives from the Syrian-sponsored PNSF and two representa-tives from the Democratic Alliance of the DFLP and the PCP.[6] It was a clear indication that Soviet acceptance of Arafat's leadership would be conditional on his regaining authority over the disaffected leftist Palestinian factions. Soviet reporting of the breakdown of the Amman Agreement also notably ignored the position of the PLO and the only mention of the Palestine Resistance effectively dismissed the PLO by stating that the Palestinian liberation struggle was now focused 'pri-marily on the West Bank, where the centre of the Palestine Resistance Movement has now shifted'.[7]

The Soviet Union's caution was driven both by a desire not to alienate Syria and by a continuing distrust of Arafat's intentions. Before con-templating any elevation in bilateral relations, Moscow wanted to be sure that Arafat and Fatah were genuinely committed to an internal reconciliation process with the other Palestinian factions. This process started with the Algerian initiative on 8 April by President Chadli Benjedid, who offered to convene a PNC for all the various Palestinian organizations to settle their differences and reunite the leadership. Benjedid had co-ordinated this move with the Soviet Union during his visit to Moscow in March, when he had been reassured by Soviet officials that the Fatah Central Committee had pledged to abrogate the Amman Agreement in the event that PLO unity was restored.[8]

Once the Algerian initiative had been announced, Gorbachev finally consented to meeting personally with Arafat on 18 April in East Berlin. The differences in the Soviet and Palestinian reporting of the visit revealed the stark contrast in the relative value that each side placed on the meeting. While the Soviet media gave only the most cursory and pass-ing reference to the talks, Palestinian broadcasts claimed it was a 'summit meeting', which had 'eliminated the problems surrounding Palestin-ian–Soviet relations in the previous stage. The mere convening of this summit meant that all these problems did not touch the essence of the relationship between the PLO and Moscow.'[9]

Gorbachev's meeting with Arafat was in fact far from a 'summit' and was short, lasting less than an hour, and perfunctory.[10] However, Gorbachev did give Soviet support to Arafat's leadership and prom-ised that the Soviet Union would work towards the reunification of the factions and a reconciliation with Syria.[11] But Gorbachev made it clear that there would be no immediate or unconditional Soviet stamp of approval for Arafat's leadership. Fatah would have to make significant concessions to the leftist factions, such as the annulment of the Amman Agreement and the resolutions of the 1984 17th PNC in Amman.[12] He was also adamant that there could be no major improvement in So-viet–PLO relations until the Algerian-sponsored reconciliation process had borne fruit.[13] It was only then that an invitation for Arafat to visit Moscow would be considered and that the Soviet Union would be in a position to promote the PLO's interests in an international conference. Until that time, the freeze in Soviet–PLO relations would remain essentially in place.

The Algerian initiative of 8 April was to be the start of a long and tortuous series of negotiations between Fatah and the other Palestinian factions which was eventually crowned with success a year later at the 18th Algiers PNC in April 1987. The first stage in the negotiations, mediated primarily by Algeria and South Yemen, was between Fatah and the Democratic Alliance of the DFLP and the PCP. The Demo-cratic Alliance had maintained a less hostile attitude to the Fatah lead-ership than the pro-Syrian factions and was more amenable to an agreement. A successful conclusion to the talks was reached in Prague on 6 September, when Fatah, the DFLP and the PCP issued a joint declaration which committed the PLO to independent participation at an international conference, the establishment of a collective leader-ship as envisaged in the 1984 Aden–Algiers Accord and, most import-antly, the affirmation that the Amman Agreement was 'no longer operative' and 'no longer constitutes a basis for the policy of the PLO'.[14]

The second and more difficult stage of the negotiations was to try to tempt the pro-Syrian factions of the PNSF to follow the example of the Democratic Alliance and reconcile themselves with the Fatah lead-ership. Syria was, as in the earlier attempts at reconciliation in 1984, the principal obstacle to such a reconciliation. Damascus continued to make demands, such as the convening of the PNC in Syria rather than Algeria, which were unacceptable to the Fatah leadership.[15] Given Syrian intransigence, Algerian and Yemeni mediators focused their attention on attempting to wean away the PFLP from the Syrian embrace. The PFLP was the only faction within the PNSF which had a significant base of support among the Palestinians and had maintained a degree of independence from Damascus. If the PFLP could be tempted into rejoining the PLO, the power of the PNSF and Syrian pretensions to leadership of the Palestine Resistance would be greatly undermined.

However, George Habash, the leader of the PFLP, was far more wary of Arafat and Fatah than the members of the Democratic Alliance. He was initially insistent that the Fatah leadership should give a more unambiguous commitment to political and organizational reforms than had been gained in the Prague Declaration. He argued that 'we will not accept general and vague formulations in this respect since we are not interested in returning to the language of 'yes' and "no".'[16] However, Habash's resistance to the call for a *rapprochement* with Fatah were to be progressively weakened in the latter part of 1986 as Palestinian refugee camps in Lebanon came under attack from Syrian-supported Shi'i forces. At a time when Syrian clients were actively engaged in the massacring of Palestinians in Lebanon, Habash could not afford to be perceived as a Syrian puppet. He thus agreed in November to enter talks with the Fatah leader, Khalil al-Wazir, and eventually on 12 April with Arafat. Habash's meeting with Arafat was the decisive turning point, representing his final break with Damascus and his return to the fold of the PLO. It cleared the final obstacle before the reconvening of the 18th PNC in Algiers on 20–6 April, which was named the 'national unity' session.

During the year-long negotiations between the different Palestinian factions, the Soviet Union, as Gorbachev promised in his April meeting with Arafat, remained officially cold and distant from the PLO. The Soviet media barely mentioned the reconciliation dialogue and continued to emphasize the damaging split in the Palestine Resistance Movement 'which engenders such extreme phenomena as, on the one hand, the tendency towards complicity found in bourgeois circles, and on the other, acts of terror as a manifestation of despair and political immaturity. Both discredit the liberation movement and hinder the search for a solution to the Palestinian problem.'[17] There was also hardly any indication provided in the Soviet media that this internal Palestinian split was in the process of being healed.[18] However, behind the scenes, the Soviet Union was taking an active part in the reconciliation process. It left most of the intra-factional mediation to Algeria but was more deeply involved in the attempts to forge a Syrian–PLO *rapprochement*, which was Moscow's most important strategic objective.

However, the PLO found the Soviet Union a far from ideal mediator since it continued to take a markedly pro-Syrian stance. This is illustrated in the minutes of an August 1986 meeting between delegates from Fatah, the DFLP and PCP and a Soviet delegation headed by Karen Brutents, the Deputy Head of the Central Committee International Department. Brutents argued that the Palestinian factions must reach an agreement in this 'difficult period' for otherwise the United States would impose a settlement at the expense of the Arabs and the Palestinians. He then affirmed that there could be no objective strengthening of the PLO's position unless it ended its conflict with Syria, since 'the Palestinians and the Syrians are in one trench'. But, he placed the onus of responsibility for the Syrian–PLO split on the Fatah leadership's mistaken policy over the Amman Agreement and that the 'easiest' path open to the PLO was 'to reach an agreement with Syria'. He recommended that Fatah should cease all propaganda attacks against Syria and put out its hand to the factions based in Damascus. Brutents concluded the session by stating that 'if Syria and the Palestinians work in collaboration with the Soviets, the American attempts to impose its control on the region are destined to failure.' Although the Palestinian delegates attempted to indicate that some, if not most, of the blame lay with Damascus, this did not find a favourable response from Brutents or the other members of the Soviet delegation.[19]

Even when it became clearer by the beginning of 1987 that Asad's opposition to a reconciliation between Fatah and the Syrian-backed factions was not to be easily overcome, the Soviet Union vacillated about whether to give its full diplomatic backing to the PLO's reconciliation efforts. It took considerable Palestinian pressure to convince the Soviet leadership to come to its support. Even a few weeks prior the PNC session, the Soviet Union demonstrated a singular unwillingness to contemplate such a course of action. In early April 1987, Arafat sent Sulayman al-Najjab, the Palestinian communist leader, to Moscow to ensure Soviet support for the PNC session scheduled for later in the month.[20] To his dismay, Najjab found that the Soviet officials were still undecided about their participation and asked for guarantees of the PNC's success in reforging a united PLO. Najjab replied that, as a communist, he was incapable of guaranteeing something which was dependent on the existing correlation of forces.[21]

In the end, however, the Soviet Union did decide to give its full backing to the approaching PNC session. Once this decision had been made, the Soviet diplomatic strategy had two main strands. First, the Soviet Union intensified efforts to secure a change of mind from Asad. In the event, Asad visited Moscow on 23–26 April at the same time as the Algiers PNC was in session. In a marathon seven and one-half hour session with Gorbachev, Asad was subjected to intense pressure to 'acquiesce to the new Palestinian status quo'.[22] The report on the Asad–Gorbachev meeting suggested that the Soviet leader had had some success since both leaders 'approved the efforts now being made by members of the Palestine Resistance Movement to rally their ranks and work out a united platform on a principled basis in the context of the overall settlement process and of preparations for an international conference.'[23] In Gorbachev's dinner speech given in honour of Asad he made crystal-clear Soviet support for the PLO by saying that 'naturally we saw a good sign in the current efforts to restore the unity of the PLO.'[24]

However, in his reply speech and also in the joint communiqué on the visit, Asad refused to give a public endorsement of the PLO and only agreed to the 'necessity of restoring the unity of the Palestine Resistance Movement on a principled, anti-imperialist basis'.[25] Even though Gorbachev did not ultimately succeed in changing Asad's antagonism to the PLO leadership, he did ensure that the Syrian leader would not show outright hostility to the Algiers PNC. Asad also promised that he would not punish Habash and the PFLP for their return to the PLO fold and that he would be more amenable to a reconciliation with Fatah. During the rest of 1987, Soviet pressure was to have some limited success as there emerged a small improvement in Syrian relations with the PLO.

The second strand of Soviet diplomatic activity was focused on ensuring the success of the Algiers PNC. It placed considerable diplomatic pressure on the various Palestinian factions, in particular the DFLP and PFLP, to maintain their commitment to unity. One sign of this Soviet diplomatic involvement was that the final agreement between Habash and Arafat was conspicuously signed in the presence of the Soviet ambassador to Algeria, Vasilii Taratuta.[26] At the PNC itself, the Soviet Union was represented by a high-level delegation.

However, Soviet reservations towards the PLO were not completely repressed by the success of the 18th PNC. Soviet reports stressed that the PNC represented only the first step towards unity and that there still remained the paramount need for improved relations with Syria and the Syrian-supported Palestinian organizations.[27] The continuing internal weaknesses of the Palestine Resistance Movement, with the loss of its Lebanese base and its relations with right-wing Arab states, were also not disguised.[28] Soviet commentators were furthermore sensitive to the Western criticisms that PLO reunification had only been bought at the price of political rejectionism, notably the PNC's explicit rejection of UN Resolution 242. One analyst, remarking on this perception of the PNC, defensively suggested that Israel and the West would see a very different picture if they 'give up discriminating against Palestinians, recognize their natural and inalienable rights and only then judge how responsible and realistic the Palestinian leadership's behaviour is. I for one have no doubt that the only reason the PLO is refusing to recognize Resolution 242 is the biased way in which it is being interpreted in Israel.'[29]

Nevertheless, the overall Soviet judgement on the Algiers PNC was favourable. Arafat's return to favour in Moscow was heralded by the confirmation that 'as a result of the elections which took place the authority of the PLO Executive Committee, led by Arafat, was completely restored and even increased.'[30] The election of the PCP leader, Sulayman al-Najjab, to the PLO Executive Committee was acclaimed as the just reward for the PCP's 'major role in organizing opposition to the expansionist policies of Tel Aviv and Washington and its contribution to efforts to overcome the schism'.[31] It was also noted that the PNC political programme gave full support to the Soviet proposals for an international conference. As a whole, the Soviet Union could be satisfied that the PLO had re-emerged as a broadly unified force, which could take its allotted position as an integral participant in the international conference so central to Soviet strategic objectives in the Middle East.

TOWARDS PLO RECOGNITION OF ISRAEL

The Soviet decision in 1987 to support the PLO's unification process, despite clear Syrian opposition, was a significant turning point. For the first time since the mid-1970s, the Soviet leadership demonstrated a willingness to promote relations with the PLO which were independent of, and not strictly subordinate to, the strategic alliance with Syria. In the following year, Soviet diplomatic energies were increasingly focused on encouraging reforms in the political programme of the PLO which culminated in November 1988 with the 19th PNC's proclamation of the state of Palestine with its implicit *de facto* recognition of

Israel. During this period of intense interaction between the Soviet Union and the PLO, Syrian relations assumed a secondary position in Soviet diplomatic priorities. As in the mid-1970s, the Soviet Union adopted a more sceptical and reserved stance towards the direction of Syria's policies while embracing more enthusiastically the PLO and its reformist political agenda.

The principal cause for this shift in Soviet attitudes was a growing disenchantment with Syrian rejectionism. While the Soviet Union had encouraged such an uncompromising Syrian stance in the Cold War atmosphere of the early 1980s, such obstructionism was less acceptable to Gorbachev's more accommodating Third World and Middle Eastern strategy. In the late 1980s, Gorbachev articulated this new vision of Soviet policy in terms of 'new thinking' (*novye myshleniye*) which sought to substitute the traditional Soviet Marxist-Leninist vocabulary of international class conflict with the more liberal internationalist language of a common destiny, global interdependence and the balancing of interests. Instead of the language of confrontation and zero-sum competition, 'new thinking' promoted constructiveness, collaboration and co-operation. In this new ideological framework, Syria's resolve to gain strategic parity with Israel and to seek a military, rather than a political, solution was viewed as anachronistic and ultimately self-defeating. In contrast, the PLO's movement towards recognition of Israel was considered to be constructive and a positive contribution to 'new thinking'.

It would be a mistake, though, to view 'new thinking' as emerging *ex nihilo* with Gorbachev's accession to power. In reality, 'new thinking' had its roots in a more sceptical assessment of Soviet activism in the Third World which pre-dated Gorbachev's rise to power.[32] Andropov's concerns over the dire state of the Soviet economy had led him to be less enthusiastic than his predecessors over the provision of aid to the Soviet Union's allies in the Third World. In his first major speech on the Third World, Andropov set out the limits of Soviet aid, stating that it could only be given 'to the extent of our ability' and that most of the responsibility for economic development in developing countries 'can only be the result of the work of their peoples and of a correct policy of their leadership.'[33] Connected with this more pragmatic economic approach was a growing ideological disillusionment with the promotion of Marxist-Leninist vanguard parties among Third World allies such as Angola, Afghanistan, Ethiopia and South Yemen. By the early 1980s, it was becoming increasingly clear that these regimes tended to be weak, narrowly based and heavily dependent on Soviet support to maintain their hold on power. In all these countries, there emerged indigenous opposition guerrilla movements, forcing the Soviet Union to assist in costly counter-insurgency wars.

Thus, prior to Gorbachev, pragmatic economic self-interest and a degree of ideological disenchantment had increasingly led Soviet officials to seek to promote a less ideologically driven policy towards the Third World. There was also a recognition that *détente* was not, as Brezhnev had argued, divisible and that improvement in Soviet relations with the West was dependent on a less aggressive Third World strategy. Karen Brutents, the influential Deputy Head of the Central Committee International Department, argued that some retrenchment of Soviet support for developing countries was inevitable 'while the arms race is progressing on such a gigantic scale and military expenditures are reaching astronomical proportions'.[34] Other commentators were to extend this analysis to argue that the re-establishment of *détente* would have to be the primary Soviet concern, overriding Soviet interests in the Third World.[35] It was an implicit admission that *détente* was a more important Soviet strategic interest than the advancement of revolution in the developing world.

Gorbachev's contribution was to promote these underlying currents in Soviet thinking so that they assumed an ideological supremacy in Soviet foreign policy. The promulgation of 'new thinking' involved a recognition that a new ideological approach was required if the distrust of the West and moderate Third World states was to be overcome.[36] The central thrust of 'new thinking' was to promote the common plight of mankind, with the corresponding assumption of an underlying mutuality of interests, in place of the traditional Marxist-Leninist conception of an elemental class struggle between socialism and capitalism. Gorbachev's foreign minister, Eduard Shevardnadze, struck a decisive blow in favour of 'new thinking' when he condemned as anti-Leninist the Brezhnevite conception of 'peaceful coexistence' as a specific form of class struggle.[37] The foreign policies that Shevardnadze pursued were presented as putting into practice the principles of 'new thinking' – promoting and consolidating the reality of global interdependence, finding a mutually acceptable balance of interests between parties in dispute and strengthening the role of multilateral institutions, like the United Nations, in place of traditional Great Power unilateralism.

Gorbachev's policies towards the Middle East increasingly reflected this more constructive and moderate approach in a number of areas. First, Moscow sought to escape from its over-dependence on radical Arab allies and to develop stronger political and economic ties with pro-Western Arab states. Thus, during 1985–6, diplomatic relations with Oman and the United Arab Emirates were established, relations with Saudi Arabia were improved, and Egypt and Jordan were given a far more favourable treatment by Moscow. More dramatic and ground-breaking, though, was the initiation, very tentative at first, of a dialogue with Israel. In August 1986, there was the first official meeting between Soviet and Israeli officials in nearly 20 years which, though failing to reach any substantive agreement, was a symbolically important step.

A second important initiative was Gorbachev's unveiling of a new Soviet peace plan for a settlement of the Arab–Israeli conflict in July 1986.[38] The substance of this new plan, with its central proposal of an international conference, did not differ in any radical manner from earlier Soviet thinking. However, the proposals did include two innovations. First, Gorbachev broke with the former insistence that only the Soviet Union and the United States would be co-chairmen of the conference. Instead it was proposed, as King Husayn and Mubarak had been suggesting for some time, that the conference should be chaired by the five Permanent Members of the UN Security Council. Second, the United Nations was itself given a more substantive role in the peace process with the suggestion that the five Permanent Members should work through the international organization to set up a preparatory committee to initiate negotiations for the convening of the desired international conference.

However, the strong element of continuity in this peace plan highlights the fact that the implementation of 'new thinking' to the Middle East was not as radical as its theoretical prescriptions might suggest. The core Soviet demands remained unchanged. Central to the plan was the convening of an international conference, which would be co-sponsored by the Soviet Union and would involve the participation of all parties to the dispute, including the PLO. Where there was significant change in approach was the greater acceptance of the need for flexibility and the accommodation of opposing viewpoints. Not only ties with moderate pro-Western Arab states were encouraged but even the taboo of Soviet relations with Israel was placed on the agenda. Gorbachev also went to great lengths to assure potential critics that the Soviet Union did not seek to impose its ideas and that the promotion of an international conference did not exclude earlier efforts through the preparatory committee 'to work jointly, through multilateral discussions and bilateral contacts and with flexibility and a constructive approach, to involve all the parties immediately concerned in business-like and serious negotiations'.[39]

In the Middle Eastern context, it is best to take 'new thinking' with a degree of scepticism. It certainly inaugurated a more constructive and positive approach in Soviet policy-making as compared to the transparently obstructionist strategy of the earlier part of the decade. However, Gorbachev's approach has clear historical parallels. Soviet strategy in the late 1980s can best be considered as an attempt to resurrect, and to improve upon, the more constructive and co-operative Soviet approach towards a settlement of the Arab–Israeli conflict which had last been promoted in the mid-1970s.

As in the mid-1970s, Soviet policies were driven by a resolve to demonstrate to the United States that superpower unilateralism was bound to fail and that it would only be through a comprehensive settlement, involving all parties including the Soviet Union, that a genuine and lasting peace could be secured. In both periods, the Soviet Union also sought to provide concrete evidence that it could be a balanced mediator and that its policies did not favour the radical elements in the region at the expense of the more moderate, pro-Western countries. Certainly, the historical parallels are not exact, since Gorbachev and Shevardnadze were willing to go further to demonstrate moderation and ideological neutrality than their predecessors Brezhnev and Gromyko. However, it should also be remembered that, in contrast to the mid-1970s, by the late 1980s the degree of US and Israel distrust of Soviet intentions was much greater and correspondingly more difficult to overcome.

Yet, irrespective of the degree to which 'new thinking' in the Middle East ought to be considered as distinctively new and radical, it was decidedly not to the liking of President Asad. Asad realized that, in terms of the new Soviet lexicon on foreign policy, his strategic priorities were dangerously close to being tarnished with the brush of 'old thinking'. Asad's resolve to gain strategic parity with Israel and his rejection of political compromise with Israel were increasingly at odds with Soviet ambitions to seek political rather than military solutions and to search for 'a balance of interests' between actors involved in regional conflicts.

This growing divergence in Soviet and Syrian strategies was barely disguised during Asad's visit to Moscow in April 1987. Not only was Asad under intense Soviet pressure to acquiesce to the PLO's rejuvenation at the Algiers PNC but Gorbachev insisted on developing the 'conceptual content of the work of the CPSU and the Soviet state in matters of foreign policy'. The Soviet leader argued that in the nuclear age 'we have to coexist with each other irrespective of whether we

like each other' and that only political means were available to resolve the Middle East conflict since 'the time for regional conflicts is
today already nearly over.' As a result, 'gambling on military force in
settling the conflict has become completely discredited.' Much as these
assertions were to Asad's disliking, they were only the opening shots
to Gorbachev's subsequent dramatic statement that the absence of diplomatic relations between Israel and the Soviet Union 'could not be
considered normal'. For Gorbachev to make this admission at a dinner
in honour of the most intransigent anti-Zionist Arab nationalist leader
was an unprecedented move, which openly confirmed that Soviet strategy in the Middle East would no longer be constrained by Arab
rejectionism.

However, while the precepts of 'new thinking' fostered a growing
Syrian–Soviet estrangement, it had an opposite effect on the Soviet
Union's relationship with the PLO. On 22–23 June 1987, a PLO Executive Committee delegation to Moscow was received with a warmth it
had not experienced since the Lebanon war. The delegation met
Shevardnadze and he unambiguously approved the decisions made at
the 18th PNC in Algiers and affirmed the Soviet Union's solidarity
with the 'struggle of the Palestinian people for its liberty and independence under the leadership of the PLO, its sole legitimate representative', and that the PLO must remain an 'effective and independent
factor in Near East affairs'.[40] The emphasis on 'independence' and the
clear support for the PLO leadership represented a qualitatively new
level of Soviet support for the PLO. Palestinian officials were quick to
seize upon this new approach, praising Gorbachev for dealing with the
PLO directly and not, as was formerly the case, as an indirect function
of Soviet relations with Arab states like Egypt and Syria.[41]

On the question of the PLO's relations to the rest of the Arab world,
there was a far more understanding Soviet stance. The PLO was given
Soviet support to improve its relations with the conservative regimes
of Jordan and Egypt. On the thorny question of PLO–Syrian relations,
the Soviet Union still argued that Arafat and Asad must resolve their
differences and that a PLO–Syrian alliance was essential for the success of an international conference. However, for the first time since
the mid-1970s, the Soviet Union did not place the onus of blame on
the PLO for the rupture in relations. Soviet officials agreed that the
PLO had shown flexibility and had offered its hand to Damascus but
that 'the response from Syria has so far been wanting'. They also confirmed that Asad's visit in April had been a stormy affair and that
there had been a number of disagreements. While the Syrian delegation

had focused on the goal of strategic parity, the Soviet Union had tried
to persuade Asad to improve his international position through mend-
ing relations with Iraq, Egypt, Jordan and the PLO. Syrian involvement in Lebanon and its support for Iran in the Iran–Iraq war had also
been the source of bitter disagreement between the two sides.[42]

The most significant sign of a Soviet–PLO *rapprochement* was that
the joint communiqué on the visit explicitly offered Arafat an invitation to visit Moscow as a head of a delegation. It was a clear indication that Moscow had regained its faith in Arafat's leadership after
over four years of estrangement. The PLO delegation was informed
that Arafat had not been invited earlier because of his feud with Asad
and the unpredictability of his diplomatic strategy. However, the success of the 18th PNC and the abrogation of the Amman Agreement
had 'changed things completely'.[43] Although Arafat was only to lead a
full PLO delegation to Moscow in April 1988, the Soviet Union confirmed their support for his leadership by inviting the Palestinian leader
to the celebrations for the 60th anniversary of the October 1917 Revolution in November 1987. During those celebrations, Arafat met with
Gorbachev and his visit was accorded a degree of publicity not given
to any other of the Arab leaders.[44]

By the end of 1987, therefore, the Soviet Union and the PLO had
defined the foundations for an enhanced relationship where the previous obstacles to close relations had been removed. Syria no longer
wielded a veto on the development of these relations, Arafat was confirmed as the authoritative leader of the PLO, and there was a joint
conviction that a Soviet–PLO alliance could act as the critical dynamic
factor in advancing both their strategic objectives in the Middle East.

As in the first year of the Carter administration in 1977, it was this
last consideration which provided the greatest impetus for the consolidation of Soviet–PLO relations. Both parties realized that it was in
their mutual interest to promote a closer and more intense relationship. The Soviet Union promoted PLO reforms on the basis that, if
successfully promoted through Soviet diplomacy, it would be the most
effective avenue for weakening US and Israeli opposition to Soviet
involvement in the peace process and to the idea of an international
conference. From the PLO's side, the benefits of Soviet sponsorship
were also clear. The Soviet Union was now dealing directly with the
PLO and was not allowing other Arab states to dictate policy. Moscow had also elevated the Palestinian aspect of the Arab–Israeli conflict as the central element in its plan and had confirmed that 'there
are no substantial differences between us and the PLO on the Soviet

proposals for a Middle East settlement.'[45] On the eve of the Washington US–Soviet Summit in December 1987, Arafat expressed his enthusiasm for the Soviet stance by noting that, 'for the first time we have a friend, the Soviet Union, which is using its weight to make the Middle East issue number two on the Summit agenda.'[46]

However, until the end of 1987 the Soviet Union and the PLO continued to suffer from an adamant and unchanging US refusal to permit their participation in the peace process. Despite Arafat's hopes, this was again confirmed at the US–Soviet summit when the United States restated its opposition to an international conference and its preference for direct talks under unilateral US mediation.[47] At this time, even the Arab states had strategic concerns which had a greater priority than the Arab–Israeli conflict. As Arafat was to discover at the Amman Arab Summit in November 1987, most Arab states were far more concerned about the course of the Iran–Iraq war than of the seemingly intractable state of the Arab–Israeli peace process. With such minimal international and regional concern over the Palestine question, there was little chance for the newly enhanced Soviet–PLO relationship to be effectively utilized.

It was the start of the Palestinian uprising or 'intifada' in December 1987 which finally changed the situation. Through the vast media coverage of the uprising, it was not just the Arab–Israeli conflict which was brought to the centre of regional and international attention but also the specifically Palestinian dimension of the dispute. For the Soviet Union, this development was particularly satisfying for two reasons. First, the Soviet Union viewed the uprising as a historical vindication of its long years of support for the Palestinian cause. The fact that the struggle was clearly being fought under the banner of the PLO was similarly presented as justification for the Soviet Union's close relations with the organization. Soviet media reports stated that the intifada had provided conclusive confirmation of the PLO's unassailable authoritative status as the legal representative of the Palestinian people.[48] As Gorbachev and King Husayn agreed at their meeting in December 1987, 'in all circumstances the Palestinian factor is the key element to a Near East settlement and that without the PLO it cannot be ensured.'[49] To emphasize the necessity of dealing with the PLO, the Soviet media provided expansive reporting on the activities of the organization and, in particular, portrayed Arafat as a statesman of international stature, who was deeply involved in the development of events on the West Bank and Gaza Strip.[50]

The second source of satisfaction for the Soviet Union was that the

upsurge in violence could be clearly presented as confirming the ultimate failure of the US-dominated search for separatist and partial agreements. Soviet reports insisted that such unilateral initiatives had failed
to address the central underlying sources of the conflict, most notably
the Jewish–Palestinian conflict. As such, the intifada confirmed that
the only practical and realistic path was to promote an international
conference which would necessarily have to include the PLO as the
representative of the Palestinian people.[51] In this regard, the Soviet
Union called for all parties, but especially the United States, to relin-
quish solutions based on 'old thinking', to reject the Cold War 'zero
sum game', and to engage in collective efforts with all interested parties, including the Soviet Union, to seek a comprehensive resolution
of the conflict.[52]

The United States did, to some extent, rise to the Soviet challenge.
Prior to a trip to the Middle East in February 1988, the US Secretary
of State, George Shultz, visited Moscow and informed the Soviet leadership of his new plan for a settlement, which included a renewed and
official US commitment to an international conference. Although the
proposed function of this conference was far removed from the authoritative, plenipotentiary status that was envisaged by the Soviet proposals, the Soviet Union did not explicitly condemn the US proposals.
The official Soviet position was non-committal and cautious, stating
that 'the chief criterion in evaluating the American proposals must be
to what degree it meets the task of achieving an all-encompassing and
durable Middle East settlement which takes into account the balance
of interests of all sides in the conflict.'[53] However, the Soviet media
also pointed out the perceived deficiencies of the Shultz plan, arguing
that it was a palliative measure and did not constitute a fundamental
solution and that it was essentially a continuation of the discredited
Camp David process.[54]

Nevertheless, the officially positive, if qualified, response to the Shultz
plan reflected the Soviet Union's overarching objective of persuading
the United States to move closer to the Soviet model of an international
conference. While demonstrating its constructive approach to Shultz's
proposals, the Soviet Union also focused on promoting its own peace
proposals, most notably through placing pressure on the PLO to make
an appropriate political response to the new regional and international
situation created by the intifada. As in the mid-1970s, the PLO assumed a central role in Soviet diplomatic endeavours. As in that earlier period, Soviet leaders and diplomats believed that the successful
persuasion of the PLO to adopt a more moderate political programme,

in particular by securing the PLO's recognition of Israel, could be presented to the United States as a convincing demonstration of the Soviet Union's co-operative stance and the potential benefits of US–Soviet collaboration.

It was in this heightened political context that Arafat finally visited Moscow in April 1988 as the head of a PLO delegation – his first official visit for over five years. The committed personal involvement of Gorbachev in the PLO visit was a sign of the importance now given to Soviet–PLO relations. In his dinner speech, Gorbachev set out the underlying Soviet objectives clearly:

> The Palestinians ... enjoy broad international support and therein lies the guarantee that the central issue for the Palestinian people, that of self-determination, will be resolved. *Like recognition of Israel and taking account of the state of its security interests*, the solution of that issue is an essential element for establishing peace and good-neighbourliness in the region on the basis of international law [emphasis added].[55]

The PLO leadership subsequently denounced as 'part of the psychological warfare being waged by our enemies' the widespread assumption in the Western media that Gorbachev had demanded the PLO's recognition of Israel.[56] Arafat explained the falsity of this interpretation by correctly noting that Gorbachev's statement had in fact been balanced between acceptance of Resolution 242 and recognition of the Palestinian right to self-determination, which means that 'they do not tell us only; they tell the other superpower.'[57]

Gorbachev's public call for recognition of Israel did, though, cause difficulties for the PLO leadership. The visit also highlighted that the Soviet position had become less forthrightly pro-Palestinian in other areas as well. During the visit, there was no direct support for a Palestinian state and only a commitment to Palestinian self-determination, with the proviso that the Palestinians themselves must decide how they might exercise that right. Similarly, there was no Soviet insistence that the Palestinians should be represented independently at an international conference, leaving open options for a pan-Arab or Jordanian–Palestinian delegation. It was furthermore noticeable that neither Gorbachev nor Shevardnadze referred to the PLO as the sole legitimate representative of the Palestinian people. After the visit it became common for Soviet announcements on the Middle East to refer to the PLO as the legitimate, omitting the sole, representative of the Palestinian people.[58]

Some Palestinian leaders did express concern that these developments signalled a weakening of Soviet support for the Palestinians and
that Moscow might be seeking a compromise with the United States.[59]
However, the PLO leadership was keen to ignore these doubts and
trumpet the visit as 'the most successful ever. For the first time, talks
were held with Gorbachev himself. In the past meetings were held
between brother Abu Ammar [Arafat] and the General Secretary, either
Brezhnev or Andropov. They were not official talks in the real sense
of the word. They were courtesy talks.'[60] In addition, despite their
reservations, the PLO leadership was influenced by Gorbachev's enthusiastic expectation that the 'popular uprising in the occupied territories has created a qualitatively new situation in terms of achieving a
settlement of the Arab–Israeli conflict' and that it was on this basis
that the PLO must seize this historic opportunity to advance the cause
of its people. Arafat and his colleagues were also attracted by the Soviet
argument that adopting a more moderate political stance would not
involve unilateral concessions but would be the final step forcing the
United States and Israel to recognize the Palestinians' right of self-
determination. As Mahmud Abbas recollected, the PLO responded favourably to Gorbachev's confirmation that he was 'optimistic about a solution'
and that the PLO had 'taken up clearer positions with regard to the
issue of international legitimacy'.[61]

However, the visit to Moscow did not in itself propel the PLO to
take the decisive steps towards recognition of Israel. A more important catalyst was King Husayn's decision in July 1988 to renounce Jordan's administrative and legal links to the West Bank. With the
undermining of the Jordanian option, the PLO realized that it had a
unique opportunity to 'take steps which would facilitate international
recognition, particularly American. This . . . can be achieved through
presenting an internationally acceptable political programme.'[62] In the
following months, there was an intense intra-PLO debate over the nature of the new political programme it should adopt. They were three
major proposals – the establishment of a government-in-exile; the proclamation of Palestinian independence and a Palestinian state; and the
adoption of a political programme which would include recognition of
Resolutions 242 and 228.

The Soviet contribution to this debate took place during a visit by
the PLO Executive Committee to Moscow on 10–11 October 1988. As
in the April visit, the Soviet Union adopted a flexible and ideologically neutral stance. As one of the Palestinian participants later noted,
the Soviet Union took a 'very relaxed' position towards the PLO's

suggested proposals.[63] They were not concerned about the timing of the PNC to decide upon these proposals. They were also not concerned over the idea of the proclamation of the state of Palestine. They did though stress that the critical element in the PLO's proposals was the adoption of a clear-cut political resolution, which would include recognition of Resolutions 242 and 338, albeit with the rider of recognition of the Palestinian right to self-determination. Their concern over the unilateral proclamation of a state was not on a point of principle but that it might be interpreted to contradict the political programme and that it would not gain support from the United States and the West, given the dubious international legality of proclaiming a state which was not yet in existence.[64]

However, once the Soviet Union was reassured that the PLO would commit themselves at the PNC to a political settlement of an international conference based on recognition of Resolutions 242 and 338, it promised to support all the proposed PNC resolutions in their entirety, including the proclamation of the state of Palestine. Soviet officials also exerted diplomatic pressure to convince the leftist Palestinian factions, especially the PFLP and DFLP, to submit to the PNC resolutions. In mid-October, Hawatmah was received in Moscow and was given stern advice not to disrupt the PLO consensus. For its part, the Soviet Union promised Hawatmah that it would give 'unqualified support for the proclamation of a Palestinian state and the launching of a provisional government'.[65] Hawatmah was extremely reluctant to change his opposition to the PNC resolutions and the Soviet officials could justly claim that it was their pressure that had secured his submission.[66] Habash and the PFLP was more resistant to pressure from the Soviet Union and only finally agreed to attend the PNC on the condition that the PFLP would be free to vote against the resolution recognizing Israel.

As the Soviet Union had promised to the PLO, it presented the proclamation of the state of Palestine and the political programme of the 19th PNC session in Algiers in November as 'really historic' and a 'turning point in the life of the Palestinian people'.[67] In the extensive reporting of the results of the PNC, the Soviet media constantly affirmed that the PLO was now adopting a responsible and realistic path.[68] However, the Soviet acclaim was tempered by a degree of caution. It was emphasized that the proclamation of the state of Palestine was founded on the legal basis of UN General Assembly Resolution 181, which had promoted both a Jewish state and an Arab state.[69] It was also stressed that the proclamation must be considered as part of a whole 'complex of decisions', which 'taken together are a major contribution to the process of a just political settlement in the Middle East.'[70] The Soviet ambivalence towards the establishment of the Palestinian state was subsequently to be confirmed when it only recognized the 'proclamation' of the state and not the state itself.[71] The Soviet spokesman was to qualify this recognition by saying that the Palestinian state had a 'political rather than a legal character'.[72]

The qualified nature of the Soviet support for the Palestinian state was partly a reflection of the Soviet Union's desire to do nothing which might be contradictory to international law. But, more importantly, it revealed that the central Soviet interest in the PNC decisions was the PLO's commitment to recognize Israel. This was the really dramatic breakthrough to which other aspects, like the proclamation of national sovereignty, were just secondary attributes. There was a clear sense of euphoria in Moscow that, after years of intense frustration at Palestinian intransigence, the PLO had finally crossed the Rubicon concerning UN Resolution 242. When the United States agreed in mid-December that the PLO had fulfilled the preconditions for a PLO–US dialogue, the Soviet Union was optimistic that at last the diplomatic process was moving in the direction of the international conference. The US decision was presented as a submission 'at last, of the long-established reality' and that 'the new situation opens up the possibility of Israel to reassess its stand and, abandoning the old stereotypes, to take the road of a joint search for constructive solutions'. As such, 'it opens up the possibility for a real breakthrough in the cause of settling the Near East conflict and convening with this end in view an international Near East conference.'[73]

THE RAPID RISE AND FALL OF A RELATIONSHIP

At the beginning of 1989, the Soviet Union clearly expected that the long years of promoting its peace proposals were finally on the verge of bearing fruit. The PLO decision to recognize Israel had overcome the main Arab obstacle to the Soviet peace plan. All the Arab parties to the dispute now officially accepted that peace could only be achieved through recognition of Israel on the basis of UN Resolutions 242 and 338. The PLO's decision in 1988 was also viewed as a historical vindication of Soviet policy-making in the region. From the Soviet perspective, 'new thinking' had not only identified and reformed the negative dimensions of Soviet foreign policy in the Middle East but had also highlighted and vindicated the positive and constructive elements of that policy. Soviet leaders and diplomats tirelessly argued that 'new thinking' had demonstrated the essential correctness and balanced nature of the longstanding Soviet peace proposals. It was argued that these proposals had not been advanced for the particular benefit of any one party but for the good of all. The Soviet Union and the Arab states, including now the PLO, had accepted this reality: it was clearly expected in Moscow that the inevitable logic was for the US and Israel to follow suit.

It was with this sense of expectation that Shevardnadze embarked on a wide-ranging tour of the Middle East in February 1989, visiting Syria, Jordan, Iraq, Iran and Egypt where he met both Arafat and the Israeli foreign minister, Moshe Arens. It was the first such tour by a Soviet foreign minister since Gromyko in the mid-1970s and reflected the Soviet Union's optimism for a breakthrough and its resolve to seek a lasting settlement of the conflict on the basis of the Soviet peace proposals. During the tour, Shevardnadze used every opportunity to acclaim the salience of new thinking and the value of its practical extension to the region. With some drama, he warned that the Middle East must learn the lessons of the history of East–West relations and 'not condemn themselves to repeating the path along which East–West nuclear rivalry developed. . . . If this happens, future archaeologists will find yet another layer of buried civilisation in the Near East.'[74] He stressed that 'traditional and – we'll be blunt – obsolete forms' must be reviewed in the same way, as the Soviet Union 'is reducing, even excluding it from the previously predominant ideological component.'[75] All countries and parties to the dispute must therefore act creatively, freed from the constraints of ideology, so as to seek a political settlement on the 'principle of an adjusted balance in the interest of all sides, be they the interest of the Arab states, the Palestinians or Israel'.[76]

On the substantive proposals for a Middle East settlement, Shevardnadze forcefully promoted the July 1986 plan for the establishment of a preparatory committee at the UN Security Council to start the process towards convening an international conference. He argued that there was an objective need to 'internationalize the search for a solution for the Near East settlement', given that the region has become 'a very serious obstacle to the further development of the disarmament process with which the majority of the peoples of the world link their hopes for a better future.' He also stressed that it was his 'distinct feeling' that not only the objective but also the subjective conditions for such a solution were present so that the situation was 'growing ripe for a 'breakthrough' in the task of setting up a full-scale dialogue on a Near East settlement in the context of an international conference.'[77]

When Shevardnadze expanded on the reasons for his optimism, they almost always focused on the PLO's decision to recognize Israel and renounce terrorism. The recurring theme of his visit was that 'the recent important steps taken by the PLO, which testify to the realism and constructive nature of its position' was the principal reason why 'a high degree of consensus has come about regarding the path to a Near Eastern settlement [which] lies through the convening an international conference with the participation of all the parties to the conflict, including the PLO.'[78] It was also as a result of the PLO's decision that the 'Arabs have done everything possible for the convening of the conference.'[79] Shevardnadze depicted the PLO as the party which had made a dramatic compromise and had thereby shown its commitment to finding a just solution on the basis of a balance of interests with Israel.

In his meeting with the Israeli foreign minister, Moshe Arens, Shevardnadze stressed that it was now the responsibility of Israel to make the appropriate response to the PLO. He argued that Israel no longer had 'even the pretext for refusing to enter into a dialogue with an organization recognized by the international community as the sole legitimate representative of the Palestinian people.'[80] When Arens refused to accept this strong Soviet advice, Shevardnadze blamed Israel as the principal obstacle to peace and 'expressed the hope that Israel has not yet spoken its last word regarding its participation in a conference and regarding talks with the PLO and that it will not oppose the view of the majority of countries in the world on this matter.'[81]

Although Shevardnadze's tour of the Middle East ended on this inconclusive note, the Soviet Union clearly expected that the dynamic for peace in the region would only be temporarily obstructed by Israeli intransigence. This expectation was reflected in the new-found intensity and harmony of the Soviet–PLO relationship. The Soviet Union viewed the PLO's recognition of Israel and its renunciation of terrorism as the historical vindication of its promotion of a comprehensive settlement of the Arab–Israeli conflict. For its part, the PLO was reassured that the Soviet Union was placing its full diplomatic and political might towards a resolution of the conflict which promoted and defended Palestinian rights. For both the Soviet Union and the PLO, there appeared to be a real historic opportunity for the two parties finally to be accepted as substantive and legitimate participants in the Middle East peace process.

The reality, though, was to be cruelly disappointing. During 1989, the new Bush administration accepted Israeli reservations over the inclusion of the Soviet Union in the peace process and promoted the traditional approach of American-dominated bilateral negotiations between Israel and the Palestinians.[82] As the United States continued its traditional unilateralist approach, the Soviet Union's diplomatic energies became increasingly diverted away from the Middle East to more urgent and immediate challenges. From 1989 onwards, these focused on the disintegration of the Soviet empire in Eastern Europe and the growing internal and political problems within the Soviet Union. As a consequence, the Soviet Union had neither the energy nor the will to seek to obstruct the US initiative or even to promote its own alternative path to a settlement.

The effective loss of Soviet power in the Middle East was to be graphically displayed during the Gulf War when Moscow supported the US-led military campaign against Iraq and failed to find an alternative peaceful resolution to the crisis, despite the energetic efforts of Gorbachev's special envoy, Evgenii Primakov. As a mark of gratitude for Soviet compliance during the Gulf War, the Bush administration finally agreed to the long-held Soviet demand for joint collaboration in the diplomatic search for a Middle East settlement and the convening of an international conference. It should, in theory, have been the Soviet Union's crowning glory when it acted as co-chairman with the United States at the convening of the Madrid Middle East Peace Conference on 30 October to 1 November 1991. However, it was generally recognized that the Soviet Union had only been accorded this privilege in respect to its past rather than its present influence and power. It was only because the Soviet Union presented not even a marginal threat to US dominance of the Middle East peace process that it was accorded this strictly symbolic presence. In reality, by the time the Soviet Union formally ceased to exist at the end of 1991, its power and influence in the Middle East was almost nonexistent.

For the PLO, the failure of the much acclaimed Soviet 'new thinking' to fulfil its promised ambitions was a major strategic blow. The PLO leadership had correctly analysed that 'new thinking' had involved a rejection of the traditional Soviet ideological commitment to promoting and supporting radicalism and progressive national liberation movements. However, the PLO had failed to realize that the roots of 'new thinking' lay not only in the loss of Soviet ideological fervour but also in the reality of the decline of Soviet power and influence. In an important sense, the idealism and liberal internationalism of 'new thinking' was driven as much by the Soviet Union's self-interested resolve to maintain its superpower status as by an ideological conversion from earlier obstructionist and competitive policies. In this more cynical light, 'new thinking' was at least partly a device to obscure the reality of the Soviet Union's decline as a Great Power.

The manner in which the type of liberal internationalism at the foundations of 'new thinking' ultimately rests on national self-interest was tellingly exposed by E. H. Carr in his famous realist critique of the liberal internationalism of the inter-war period. Carr argued that the principal assumption of liberal internationalism of 'the doctrine of the harmony of interests . . . is the natural assumption of a prosperous and privileged class, whose members have a dominant voice in a community and are therefore naturally prone to identify its interest with their own.'[83] Although it would be a mistake to view 'new thinking' purely in this self-interested light, it does indicate an important influence on the evolution of Soviet foreign policy during the Gorbachev period. It is of particular relevance to the Middle East where, as has been argued above, the core Soviet national interest in an international conference remained constant and where 'new thinking' sought to present this objective as an interest common to all parties rather than just to the Soviet Union and its allies. However, when the United States and Israel refused to accept this 'commonality' of their interests and rejected any participation by the Soviet Union or its ally the PLO, the idealistic prescriptions of 'new thinking' could no longer mask the powerlessness of the Soviet Union to counter the US assertion of hegemonic power in the region.

During 1989, the PLO finally realized that 'new thinking' had turned out to be a paper tiger. Up to 1989, the PLO had continued to place its faith in Soviet sponsorship, despite the clear evidence of a decline of Soviet ideological commitment to the Palestinian cause, expecting that the Soviet Union would continue to act as a countervailing 'balance' against US hegemony in the region. However, as it became clear during the latter part of 1989 that the Soviet Union lacked the power to act in this countervailing capacity, the value that the PLO placed on its relationship with the Soviet Union was critically undermined. The sense of disillusion, even betrayal, by the Soviet Union was a bitter source of resentment for the PLO. From their perspective, the Soviet Union had not only presented a false picture of its potential influence but had also reneged on its promises to protect the Palestinians from the dictates of the United States and Israel.

During 1989 and the early part of 1989, Arafat tried to accommodate his unruly organization to the reality of US dominance. Despite strong internal pressures, he had adopted a constructive stance towards the US attempt, strongly supported by Egypt, to initiate an Israeli–Palestinian dialogue. Towards the end of 1989, the effort seemed to be on the verge of success as the PLO accepted a joint American–Egyptian proposal for talks between Israel and a PLO-designated group of Palestinians. However, this peace initiative was to fatally undermined during the first half of 1990. The Israeli prime minister, Yitzhak Shamir, delayed giving a clear response to the so-called Baker Plan and then, under the increasing US pressure, his government literally disintegrated, leading to political paralysis and the eventual election in June of the most right-wing government in Israeli history. With the momentum for peace stalled, the rejectionist elements in the PLO gained the ascendance. On 30 May, an armed group from the Iraqi-sponsored Abu al-Abbas PLF faction attempted an abortive strike on the Israeli coast near Tel Aviv. When Arafat refused to condemn the attack, the Bush administration suspended the US–PLO dialogue.

In these difficult circumstances, Arafat did not turn to the Soviet Union, which might have been his reflex reaction in earlier times. The Soviet Union had in fact consistently supported the US and Egyptian attempts at forging an Israeli–Palestinian dialogue and, in a message the Soviet Union sent to Arafat after the breakdown of the US–PLO dialogue, Arafat was reportedly urged to adopt a 'rational policy' and eschew counter-productive terrorist acts.[84] Arafat was under no illusion that the Soviet Union would be interested in reforging a relationship with a PLO determined to follow a more militant and rejectionist path.

Instead, Arafat made the fateful decision to tie the PLO's flag to Iraq and to support the increasingly belligerent pan-Arab stance taken by the Iraqi President, Saddam Husayn. At the Baghdad Summit in May 1990, Arafat ignored the Soviet advice for moderation and fully aligned the PLO with Saddam Husayn's anti-Western campaign by agreeing that 'the fierce campaign against fraternal Iraq is led by Israel and its Western imperialist backers.'[85] Arafat's return to 'old thinking', with its emphasis on the imperialist and Zionist threat, made the Soviet–PLO relationship even colder and more distant than it had been before. When the Soviet Union supported the anti-Iraq coalition, the PLO's faith in the Soviet Union deteriorated to an even lower level.

There was a brief upsurge in PLO hopes when Shevardnadze resigned in November 1990 and Gorbachev's personal envoy, the renowned orientalist Yevgeny Primakov, began searching for a political solution, but these were dispelled when the Soviet Union finally gave its backing to the US-dominated military campaign against Iraq.[86] In the aftermath of the war, the Soviet Union had no desire to compromise its new-found role as co-sponsor of the Middle East peace process by reforging relations with a PLO which had become so internationally discredited as a result of its implicit support for Iraq. It was perhaps a fitting symbol of the depth of the decline of the Soviet–PLO relationship that the PLO foreign minister, Faruq Qaddumi, joined the select band of Arab pariah leaders, along with Saddam Husayn and Mu'ammar Gaddafi, in welcoming the overthrow of the 'renegade' Gorbachev in the August 1991 coup in Moscow.[87]

The factor, though, which overshadowed all other aspects of the PLO's relationship with the Soviet Union, and which proved to be the most damaging to bilateral relations, was the issue of the emigration of Soviet Jews. In the first four years of Gorbachev's period in power, the Soviet Union had gradually developed a more liberal policy towards Jewish emigration. Yet, even so, the numbers permitted to leave in this period were limited, not reaching the levels reached in the 1970s, and most of the emigrants went to the United States and not to Israel. However, in early 1989, the floodgates to Jewish emigration were opened after the Soviet Union committed itself to the full implementation of the Helsinki Final Accords. In October of that year, the ensuing flood of emigrants was forced to make its way to Israel after the United States imposed strict quotas on the numbers it would accept. By early 1990, Soviet Jews were entering Israel at a rate of ten thousand a month with projections that up to three-quarters of a million would finally make their home in Israel.

For the PLO, this immigration of Soviet Jews into Israel was considered an existential threat to the whole Palestinian nation. Much of the PLO's strategic thinking had been based on the premise that Israel would eventually have to sue for peace given the growing demographic threat posed by the faster birth-rate of Arab Palestinians to Jews. The influx of Soviet Jews had radically undermined this premise, changing the balance in favour of the Jewish population and, most threateningly, emboldening those elements in Israeli society which supported the retention of the occupied territories and the consolidation of a Greater Israel. In January 1990, the PLO's worst fears were seemingly confirmed by the alleged statement from the Israeli prime minister, Yitzhak Shamir, that a 'big Israel' was now needed in order to settle the Soviet Jews.[88] This was widely considered by most Palestinians to mean that Israel had decisively opted for the annexation of the West Bank and Gaza Strip.

The fact that the Soviet Union had calmly allowed this situation to develop infuriated the PLO. Practically all the bilateral discussions from 1989 to 1991 were dominated by this issue with the PLO demanding the Soviet authorities stem the flow of emigrants into Israel. But the PLO's pleas fell on deaf ears with Soviet officials reiterating that it was an internal matter related to the application of international and Soviet law. It was true that there were forceful statements from Moscow about Israel's settlement of Soviet Jews in the Occupied Territories but the implied threats to stop or restrict the flow never materialized. The only concession that the Soviet Union made to the PLO and the Arabs generally was not to allow direct flights to Israel from the Soviet Union. But this did little to diminish the deep disillusionment and even hostility of the PLO leadership with the Soviet Union. For the PLO, it was the bitterest of ironies that their much-heralded 'strategic ally' had ended up being the ultimate cause of one of the greatest strategic threats to the very existence of the Palestinian nation.

Conclusion

Since the disintegration of the Soviet Union in 1991, the Arab–Israeli peace process has made significant advances. Although the elimination of the Soviet–US superpower confrontation contributed to this progress, a more immediate catalyst was the comprehensive defeat of Iraq in the Gulf War of 1990–1. In the aftermath of the liberation of Kuwait, the United States exerted substantial diplomatic and political efforts to persuade and cajole Israel and the Arab states to return to the negotiating table. The culmination of these efforts, promoted energetically by the US Secretary of State James Baker, was the Madrid Middle East Peace Conference in October 1991 where Israel and the principal Arab states committed themselves to an ongoing peace process. At the conference, a number of bilateral and multilateral Israeli–Arab negotiating bodies were established to promote a full and comprehensive solution of the fundamental causes of the Arab–Israeli conflict.

Inevitably, given the accumulation of distrust and the intractable nature of the conflict, the Madrid framework for peace has produced some disappointing results. Despite intense diplomatic activity and innumerable negotiating rounds, little substantive progress has been made in forging a peace between Israel and Syria. Syria's suspicious and cautious approach to the peace process has been highlighted by its refusal to participate in the multilateral talks. These suspicions have only been accentuated by the accession to power of the Likud government under Benjamin Netanyahu in Israel in May 1996, which resulted in increased military tensions between Israel and Syria. More generally in the Arab world, the election of the Likud government, given the party's historic attachment to a Greater Israel, has been perceived as a threat to the future progress of the peace process.

However, despite the failure on the Syrian–Israeli front, a number of significant historic successes have been reached in securing peace between Israel and its other Arab enemies. In October 1994, King Husayn of Jordan joined Egypt in signing a full peace with Israel. However, Jordan has enjoyed a semi-peace with Israel for many years and the far more dramatic development was the agreement reached in July 1993 between Israel and the PLO, which was secretly negotiated in Oslo outside of the official Washington channels, and which set out a phased programme for a settlement between Israel and the Palestinians. Although the ensuing negotiations have faced numerous obstacles and have resulted in a number of delays, there have been concrete successes with Israel withdrawing from the Gaza Strip and from most of the Palestinian towns of the West Bank and transferring authority to the PLO-led Palestinian Authority (PA). The momentum has also been maintained with the change in the Israeli government, as Netanyahu, albeit reluctantly, acceded to the Israeli withdrawal from most of Hebron in late 1996. In general, as a result of these diplomatic breakthroughs, Israel in the mid-1990s enjoyed a degree of peace with its neighbours almost inconceivable a decade earlier.

As regards the Russian contribution to these developments, Moscow has only played a marginal and relatively insignificant role. Ironically, it was during the final days of the Soviet Union's existence that Moscow was finally granted its longstanding demand to be a co-sponsor with the United States to the international peace conference in Madrid. The Soviet response to this inclusion was to overturn some of its most notorious policies in the Middle East, most notably by joining the United States in reversing the infamous UN 'Zionism is racism' resolution and by agreeing to re-establish diplomatic relations with Israel which had been severed in the aftermath of the 1967 war. But, despite these indications of Soviet goodwill, the US concession of offering Soviet co-chairmanship of the conference was driven more by the reality of Soviet weakness than any accommodation to the Soviet Union's traditional policy objectives in the Middle East.

With the collapse of the Soviet Union and the accession of President Yeltsin, Russia has continued to play a low-key and even-handed role in the post-Madrid peace process which has rarely deviated from providing support to the US-dominated diplomatic drive for a settlement. Indeed, the most distinctive feature of post-Soviet Russian policy has been the strengthening of Russia's relationship with Israel and the consolidation of bilateral political, economic and cultural ties. As a consequence, little effort has been expended in re-establishing close relations with the PLO or the newly formed Palestinian Authority. Although both conservative nationalist and communist critics of Yeltsin's foreign policy have predictably condemned the perceived submission to US hegemony in the Middle East, there has been surprisingly little criticism of the economic and political benefits of closer relations with Israel.[1]

The economic and political weakness of post-Soviet Russia has undoubtedly been a major factor behind Russia's lack of activism in the peace process. Russian diplomats have conceded that Russia has 'not invested a copeck' into the peace process and that Russia's high profile depends on past, rather than present, prestige which has been gained through the many years of traditional engagement in the region.[2] However, Yeltsin's Russia has also eschewed any substantive ideological commitment to adopting an assertive diplomatic position towards the Arab–Israeli conflict. Russia has not only rejected the Marxist-Leninist ideological imperatives which propelled Khrushchev to project Soviet power into the Arab world but also the liberal internationalism of the late Gorbachev period which similarly justified a global role for Soviet diplomatic activity. Without such an ideological commitment, and without in any case the economic and political resources to sustain such a commitment, Russia has been willing to submit to US leadership in the search for an Arab–Israeli settlement.

Yet, although ideological interests play a lesser role in post-Soviet Russia, it would be a mistake to assume that Moscow has lost its interest in power projection and in protecting its national interests in the Middle East. However, in redefining these interests, Russia has returned to an understanding of its core national interests which has a closer connection to Tsarist Russian than Soviet conceptions. Instead of projecting a global role, Russian diplomatic and strategic priorities have focused on regions contiguous to Russian territory. In the Middle East, this involves a return to according strategic priority to Central Asia and the 'northern tier' countries such as Turkey, Iran and Afghanistan. In this region, Russia has forcefully promoted its independent policies and has been willing to resist US disapproval, most notably over the burgeoning Russian–Iranian strategic relationship. In the Arab world, though, Russia has not been so active since it has not felt its core national interests as under threat. As a consequence, Russian engagement in the Arab–Israeli peace process has tended to play a subordinate role to the Russian drive for economic advantage, particularly in the area of arms sales. In the diplomatic and political fields, Russia has little appetite or will to disturb US regional dominance.

THE SOVIET LEGACY TO THE PEACE PROCESS

The evidence is, therefore, that in the period since the Soviet–PLO relationship disintegrated in 1989–90, the Soviet Union and its successor state, Russia, have not played a substantive role in the peace process. In seeking to make a historical assessment of the Soviet legacy and contribution to the Arab–Israeli peace process, one question which naturally arises is whether the absence of the countervailing and obstructive power of the Soviet Union has been a significant cause for the progress that has been made since the 1991 Madrid Conference. In other words, has the disintegration of the Soviet Union been a major catalyst for the historic agreements made between Israel and its traditional enemies, most notably with Israel's closest neighbour – the Palestinians?

There are two broad answers to this question which can be taken to represent opposing positions in assessing the Soviet legacy. One approach argues that Soviet Union was always an obstructive and destabilizing force in the Middle East and that peace in the region was continually undermined by Soviet support for Arab extremism and rejectionism. As such, the progress made since 1991 in the peace process represents a vindication of this representation of the highly negative nature of Soviet policy-making. By and large, during the Cold War the Israeli and US leadership subscribed to this assessment of Soviet strategy in the Middle East, which strengthened and justified their refusal to include the Soviet Union in any substantive role in the peace process. In February 1987, the US Secretary of State, George Shultz, offered a good example of this negative critique of Soviet actions:

> Look what they do. They encourage the PLO to turn even more radical and rejectionist. They align themselves with the worst terrorists and tyrants in the region. They refuse to re-establish relations with Israel. Their treatment of Jews and the practice of the Jewish religion is not acceptable by any standard, let alone the Universal Declaration of Human Rights and the Helsinki Final Act, to which they are bound by their own signature.[3]

The alternative view, representing the opposing viewpoint, argues that far from facilitating a peace settlement the disengagement of Soviet power from the Middle East has left the region defenceless against US and Israeli hegemonic control and the imposition of an unjust and illegitimate peace. This is a view which has particular appeal to many Arab intellectuals who have interpreted the collapse of the Soviet Union as directly strengthening Israel and ensuring the unchallenged dominance of US military, political and economic power.[4] On this analysis, the progress made in the peace process is viewed more as a capitulation to US–Israeli demands rather than the just and equitable peace earnestly sought by the Soviet Union and its Arab allies during the Cold War. The most well-known Palestinian intellectual, Edward Said, who has also been the most trenchant critic of the PLO agreements made in Oslo, has argued along these lines asserting that, with the end of the Cold War, 'American rejectionism *vis-à-vis* Arab national goals has been reinforced as Arab aims have either been significantly reduced or, as was the case with the PLO's position in Oslo, openly subordinated to Israel.'[5]

The evidence and conclusions provided in this book suggest that neither of these two opposing views captures the true underlying dynamics and the complex nature of the Soviet approach to the Arab–Israeli conflict. As seen through the prism of the Soviet relationship with the PLO, the Soviet Union had a complex set of ideological and strategic interests which resulted in policies and actions which could, at times, be a positive contribution to the peace process and, at other times, be a significant barrier to progress. The Soviet historical legacy to the peace process is not, therefore, a strictly black-and-white issue and both the constructive and obstructive aspects must be given their due consideration.

On the constructive side of the ledger, the Soviet Union's consistent refusal to accept the PLO's rejectionist political programme as legitimate was a significant contribution to the evolution of a more moderate PLO stance. In the early period of the PLO's existence, Moscow even refused to have any dealings with the organization, rejecting as ideologically unacceptable the objective of the Palestinian guerrilla groups to 'liquidate' Israel. When the Soviet–PLO relationship was cautiously initiated in 1968, the Soviet Union strongly advocated that the PLO should recognize Israel and accept Resolutions 242 and 338. Over the next two decades, Soviet leaders and officials tirelessly sought to influence the PLO towards a more moderate stance towards Israel. Soviet advice to the PLO also emphasized the inadmissibility of the use of terrorism, the limitations of guerrilla warfare, and the need to promote a clearly defined political programme and to build a mass base in the West Bank and Gaza Strip.

Although the PLO consistently ignored these Soviet admonitions, the Soviet Union was nevertheless a significant catalyst for the gradual moderation of the PLO's political stance. In the 1970s, it was in Moscow that the PLO made the first official confirmation of its willingness to attend the Geneva Conference and its commitment to the political objective of the creation of Palestinian state. In two periods in particular, in 1977 and in 1987–8, the Soviet Union placed considerable diplomatic pressure to secure PLO concessions. In 1977, this was rewarded by the PLO's acceptance of the US–Soviet Joint Statement and by its commitment to a process of *de facto* mutual recognition between Israel and the PLO, if and when both parties sat together at the reconvened Geneva Conference. In 1988, the historic PLO decision to recognize

Israel, which was again influenced by Soviet diplomatic pressure, was particularly satisfying for the Soviet Union. As Arab and Palestinian communists acclaimed, the PLO decision represented a historic vindication of the communist position on the Arab–Israeli conflict and the ultimate failure of Arab nationalist rejectionism.

However, the Soviet Union's willingness to act as a constructive partner for peace had distinct and well-defined limits and the obstructive and negative elements in Soviet strategic thinking must also be recognized. Ultimately, the key prize that the Soviet Union sought from adopting a constructive and positive stance was US recognition of the Soviet Union's equal status in a Great Power settlement of the conflict. When, however, the Soviet Union felt that the United States was reneging on commitments to co-operation and was pursuing a unilateralist diplomatic strategy, as for example during the Camp David process, the Soviet leadership felt under no obligation to sustain a constructive diplomatic stance. Instead, Soviet strategy shifted towards an obstructionist position which was willing to utilize the most radical and rejectionist elements within the Arab world to undermine US and Israeli regional objectives.

For the Fatah leadership of the PLO, it was in the early 1980s that the impact of Soviet obstructionism proved to be most damaging. In the aftermath of the 1982 Lebanon War, Arafat sought to enhance the PLO's relations with King Husayn of Jordan as an avenue for initiating a dialogue with the United States. From the very start, the Soviet Union was unremittingly hostile to Arafat's diplomatic strategy and forged a powerful coalition in opposition to the Fatah leader, which brought together Syria and a number of disaffected Palestinian leftist factions under Soviet patronage. The eventual failure of the Amman Accord of 1985 was, to a considerable degree, a consequence of this uncompromising Soviet opposition. The Soviet Union and Syria successfully ensured that Arafat's political authority, weakened by wide-scale internal dissent and conflict, was never sufficiently strong to make the necessary concessions required for stimulating a positive US response.

More broadly, the PLO also suffered from its association with an external power which was perceived to be acting in such an obstructionist manner. As evidence of Soviet rejectionism became clear during the 1980s, the US only increased its determination to exclude Moscow from any substantive role in the peace process even with Gorbachev's 'new thinking'. Undoubtedly, American perceptions of the PLO were adversely influenced by the organization's close strategic relationship with the Soviet Union. Analogously, the Soviet Union's poor relations with Israel were also ultimately damaging to PLO's interests. As Soviet officials were to admit in the late 1980s, the decision to break diplomatic relations with Israel after the 1967 war was a major strategic mistake. It meant that the Soviet Union had no direct access to, or influence on, Tel Aviv and ensured that Israel regarded Soviet diplomatic activity with considerable suspicion. For the PLO, it meant that the Soviet Union could never offer a full mediatory role, which ultimately could only be provided by the United States. Soviet ideological hostility to Zionism similarly acted both to undermine Israeli trust and to strengthen the PLO's rejectionist posture towards Israel. Overall, as PLO officials now admit, the Soviet influence was damaging in that it discouraged earlier and more intensive Palestinian contacts with Israelis and Americans.

However, there was an internal logic to the Soviet–PLO relationship which acted to overcome the intrinsic limitations of their alliance. The Soviet Union and the PLO were ultimately driven into each other's arms by a mutual sense of vulnerability and a joint perception of their relative marginalization in the Arab–Israeli peace process. The PLO suffered from being a non-state actor whose legitimacy was explicitly denied both by the United States and Israel. Without the support of the Soviet Union, the PLO leadership believed that it had no realistic opportunity of being included in the peace process on politically acceptable terms. For the Soviet Union, the relationship with the PLO was driven by Moscow's relative political and diplomatic weakness in the superpower regional competition with the United States, reflecting in particular Moscow's poor or nonexistent relations with two key confrontation states – Israel and Egypt. Soviet possession of the Palestinian card was a critical element in supporting the claim that the Soviet Union was a necessary and essential participant in the peace process. The Soviet Union rightly argued, if only for self-interested reasons, that there could be no comprehensive settlement of the Arab–Israeli conflict without a resolution of the Jewish–Palestinian conflict.

In a sense, the Soviet–PLO relationship sought to mirror the strategic US–Israeli alliance. However, it was far from a comparable relationship. The US–Israeli relationship was an alliance of the strongest powers in the region who had it in their power to deliver a peace. Israel controlled the land which was the key bargaining chip in the negotiations and the United States was the only external power to have a significant influence on Israeli decision-making. In contrast, the Soviet–PLO relationship was an alliance of the weak. The Soviet Union had no influence over Israel and had fluctuating relations with the Arab confrontation states. Moreover, most Arab states agreed with Sadat that the US had 99 per cent of the cards in the peace process. The PLO's position was even more fragile, confronting an Israeli enemy which refused to recognize its existence and a number of supposedly friendly Arab states which regularly sought the PLO's destruction or expulsion. Given their intrinsic weakness, the Soviet Union and the PLO had no independent power to promote or consolidate the peace process, which was primarily the prerogative of the United States and Israel.

However, the Soviet Union and the PLO were not completely powerless. Although they had little ability unilaterally to advance the peace process, they had the power to obstruct a comprehensive settlement which ignored their interests. As the Oslo Accords finally demonstrated, an Israeli–Palestinian settlement necessarily must involve the PLO. From the Rabat Summit in 1974 onwards, the PLO was popularly recognized by the vast majority of Palestinians as their true representative and, as a consequence, other potential claimants like King Husayn of Jordan lacked the legitimacy to make concessions on the Palestinians' behalf. For its part, the Soviet Union asserted its own pretensions to participation in the peace process by regularly succeeding in undermining unilateral US–Israeli attempts to forge a comprehensive peace, most notably demonstrated by the Soviet campaign in 1982–3 to obstruct US–Israeli strategic ambitions in Lebanon. The Soviet Union's negative power lay in the fact that it could always mobilize a sufficiently powerful coalition of Arab rejectionist forces to obstruct any US drive for a comprehensive peace.

However, the fact that, under certain conditions, the Soviet Union had a predisposition towards playing a constructive regional role also meant that Moscow had, at least potentially, the power and influence to bring its recalcitrant allies, in particular the PLO, to the negotiating table. As was demonstrated in the periods of 1977 and 1987–8, the Soviet Union could act in a highly constructive manner if it felt that its interests were being respected by the United States. Whether the failure of the United States ever to call Moscow's bluff and fully to co-operate with the Soviet Union was a missed opportunity for peace is clearly an unanswerable counterfactual question. Perhaps, as Kissinger regularly argued, the Soviet Union would only ever have been an obstructive actor who would have encouraged the Arabs to adopt political demands unacceptable to Israel. However, the reality was that for over twenty years the Soviet Union and the PLO could always ensure that a comprehensive settlement would not be reached. As such, during the period of the Cold War the participation of both the Soviet Union and the PLO was a necessary, if not sufficient, condition for the realization of a full Arab–Israeli settlement. Given the evidence provided in this book of the constructive elements in Soviet policy-making towards the PLO, such a risk would have been worth taking.

Notes

INTRODUCTION

1. Elizabeth Monroe, *Britain's Moment in the Middle East, 1914–1956* (London, Chatto & Windus, 1963).

CHAPTER 1 FRAMEWORK OF SOVIET ENGAGEMENT IN THE ARAB–ISRAELI CONFLICT

1. David Gilliard, *The Struggle for Asia 1828–1914: A Study in British and Russian Imperialism* (London: Oxford University Press, 1958).
2. Derek Hopwood, 'Soviet Policy in the Middle East', in Gustav Stein and Udo Steinbach (eds), *The Contemporary Middle Eastern Scene (Basic Issues and Trends)* (Opladen: Leske Verlag & Budrich, 1979), p. 12.
3. Fedor M. Dostoevskii, *Dnevnik pisatel'ia za 1877* (Paris: YMCA-Press, n.d.), p. 97.
4. Ibid., p. 89; see also see Derek Hopwood, *The Russian Presence in Syria and Palestine, 1843–1914: Church and Politics in the Near East* (Oxford: Clarendon Press, 1969), p. 78.
5. George Antonius, *The Arab Awakening: The Study of the Arab National Movement* (London: Hamish Hamilton, 1938).
6. Hopwood, *The Russian Presence in Syria and Palestine*, p. 134.
7. *The USSR and the Middle East: Problems of Peace and Security, 1947–1971* (Moscow: Novosti Press Agency, 1972), p. 64.
8. V. I. Lenin, *The National Liberation Movement in the East* (Moscow: Progress, 1952), p. 263.
9. F. Alestin, *Palestina v petle sionizma. Prestupniki. Zhertvy. Svideteli. Sud'i* (Moscow: Iuridicheskaia literatura, 1988), p. 280.
10. Ibid., p. 284.
11. For a full study of the PCP, see Musa Budeiri, *The Palestine Communist Party, 1919–1948: Arab and Jew in the Struggle for Internationalism* (London: Ithaca Press, 1979).
12. Jane Degras (ed.), *The Communist International 1919–1943*, Vol. 1 (London: Frank Cass, 1956), p. 144.
13. Budeiri, *The Palestine Communist Party*, p. 7.
14. Ibid., pp. 19–68; and Joel Beinen, 'The Palestine Communist Party 1919–1948', *MERIP* Middle East Report, 15 (March 1977), pp. 8–9.
15. Yaacov Ro'i, 'Soviet–Israeli Relations, 1947–1954', in Michael Confino and Shimon Shamir (eds), *The USSR and the Middle East* (Jerusalem: Israel Universities Press, 1973), p. 123.
16. Yaacov Ro'i, *Soviet Decision Making in Practice: The USSR and Israel 1947–1954* (New Brunswick, NJ: Transaction Books, 1980), pp. 16–17.
17. V. B. Lutskii, *Palestinskaia problema* (Moscow: Nauka, 1946), p. 13.

18. Michael J. Cohen, *Palestine and the Great Powers 1945–1948* (Princeton, NJ: Princeton University Press, 1982), p. 260.
19. Quoted in Yaacov Ro'i, *Soviet Decision Making*, p. 253.
20. 'Palestine and the United Nations', *New Times*, 24 (June 1948), pp. 1–2.
21. Yaacov Ro'i, *Soviet Decision Making*, p. 144.
22. For discussion of this issue, see Arnold Krammer, 'Soviet Motives in the Partition of Palestine, 1947–1948', *Journal of Palestine Studies*, 2:2 (Winter 1973), pp. 102–19; Yaacov Ro'i, *Soviet Decision Making*, pp. 44–5, pp. 211–12 and pp. 279–80; Arthur Jay Klinghoffer with Judith Apter, *Israel and the Soviet Union: Alienation or Reconciliation?* (Boulder, Colo.: Westview Press, 1985), p. 14; and Avigdor Dagan, *Moscow and Jerusalem: Twenty Years of Relations between Israel and the Soviet Union* (London: Abelard-Schumann, 1970). All these accounts dismiss the idea that Stalin or the Soviet Union supported the creation of the state of Israel on the expectation that it would become a pro-Soviet socialist state.
23. *The USSR and the Middle East*, p. 46.
24. Quoted in Yaacov Ro'i, *From Encroachment to Involvement: A Documentary Study of Soviet Policy in the Middle East 1945–1973* (New York: Transaction Books, 1974), p. 38.
25. D. Prokof'ev, 'Rozhdenie krizisa', *Aziia i Afrika segodnia*, 1 (January 1988), pp. 16–20.
26. E. D. Dmitriev, *Palestinskiia tragediia* (Moscow: Mezhdunarodye otnosheniia, 1986), p. 21.
27. For the response of Soviet Jews to the creation of the state of Israel, see Yehoshua A. Gilboa, 'The 1948 Zionist Wave in Moscow', *Soviet Jewish Affairs*, 2 (1971), pp. 35–9.
28. Jonathon Frankel, *The Soviet Regime and Anti-Zionism: An Analysis* (Jerusalem: Hebrew University of Jerusalem, 1984), pp. 15–22.
29. This is confirmed in Robert Conquest, *Stalin: Breaker of Nations* (London: Weidenfeld & Nicolson, 1991), pp. 290–1. For a fuller account, see Gennadi Kostyrenko, *Out of the Red Shadows: Anti-Semitism in Stalin's Russia* (New York: Prometheus Books, 1995).
30. For an example of the Soviet academic debate over these competing definitions of Zionism, see E. L. Solmar, 'Document: Protocols of the Anti-Zionists', *Soviet Jewish Affairs*, 8:2 (1978), pp. 57–66.
31. Y. Primakov, *Anatomy of the Middle East Conflict* (Moscow: Nauka, 1979), p. 145.
32. For a more extended analysis, see Uri Ra'anan, *The USSR and the Third World: Case Studies in Soviet Foreign Policy* (Cambridge, Mass.: MIT Press, 1969), pp. 13–172: and Oles M. Smolansky, *The Soviet Union and the Arab East under Khrushchev* (Lewisburg, Va.: Bucknell University Press, 1974), pp. 23–33.
33. Quoted in Roger E. Kanet (ed.), *The Soviet Union and the Developing Nations* (Baltimore, Md.: John Hopkins University Press, 1974), p. 29. See also Mark N. Katz, *The Third World in Soviet Military Thought* (Baltimore, Md.: John Hopkins University Press, 1982), pp. 13–36; and Raymond L. Garthoff, *Soviet Military Policy: A Historical Analysis* (New York: Praeger, 1966).
34. Quoted in Yaacov Ro'i, *From Encroachment to Involvement*, p. 156.

35. Text of messages in *Pravda*, 6 November 1956.
36. Quoted in Oded Eran, *The 'Mezhdunarodniki': An Assessment of Professional Expertise in the Making of Foreign Policy* (Tel Aviv: Turtledove Press, 1979), p. 186.
37. There is a comprehensive analysis of the ensuing debate over this issue in Jerry F. Hough, *The Struggle for the Third World: Soviet Debates and American Options* (Washington, DC: Brookings Institution, 1986), pp. 142–83; Oded Eran, *The 'Mezhdunarodniki'*; Neil Malcolm, 'Soviet Decisionmaking in the Middle East', in Peter Shearman and Phil Williams (eds), *The Superpowers: Central America and the Middle East* (London: Brassey's Defence Publishers, 1988); and Uri Ra'anan, 'Moscow and the Third World', *Problems of Communism*, 14:1 (January–February 1965), pp. 22–31.
38. Georgii Mirskii, 'The U.A.R. Reforms', *New Times*, 18 (May 1964), pp. 6–9. See also R. Avakov and G. Mirskii, 'Klassovaia struktura v slaborazvitykh stranakh', *Mirovaia ekonomika i mezhdunarodnye otnosheniia* (hereafter MEiMO), 4 (April 1962), pp. 68–82; and G. Mirskii, 'Tvorcheskii marksizm i problemy natsional'no-osvoboditel'nykh revolutsii', *MEiMO*, 2 (February 1963), pp. 63–8.
39. Robert O. Freedman, *Moscow and the Middle East: Soviet Policy Since the Invasion of Afghanistan* (Cambridge: Cambridge University Press, 1991), p. 2. For a similar analysis, see Alvin Z. Rubinstein, *Moscow's Third World Strategy* (Princeton, NJ: Princeton University Press, 1988), p. 34.
40. Galia Golan, *Yom Kippur and After: The Soviet Union and the Middle East Crisis* (Cambridge: Cambridge University Press, 1977), p. 10.
41. Efrain Karsh, *Soviet Policy Towards Syria since 1970* (London: Macmillan, 1991).
42. See Leonard Schapiro, 'The International Department of the CPSU: Key to Soviet Policy', *International Journal*, Winter 1976–7.
43. It was well known that the surest way to upset Gromyko was to start a conversation on the Middle East peace process. To encourage a more emollient mood, it was best to discuss his two great loves – the United Nations and hunting. See Alexei Vasiliev, *Russian Policy in the Middle East: From Messianism to Pragmatism* (Reading, Pa.: Ithaca Press, 1993), p. 231.
44. E. D. Pyrlyn, *Palestinskaia problema – Vazhneishii faktor blizhnevostochnogo uregulirovaniia* (Moscow: Nauka, 1978), p. 4.
45. Interview with Vitalii Naumkin in Moscow, 28 January 1991.
46. George W. Breslauer, 'Militants, Moderates, and Centrists: Soviet Perspectives on the Arab–Israeli Conflict, 1971–87', in George W. Breslauer, *Soviet Strategy in the Middle East* (London: Unwin Hyman, 1990).
47. The five commentators are V. Kudriatsev, *Izvestiia* correspondent; P. Demchenko, *Pravda* correspondent; I. Beliaev, *Literaturnaia gazeta* correspondent; A. Bovin, political observer for *Izvestiia*; and E. Primakov, Director of the Oriental Institute.

CHAPTER 2 TOWARDS A RELUCTANT RELATIONSHIP: 1964-70

1. Malcolm H. Kerr, *The Arab Cold War: A Study of Ideology in Politics* (Oxford: Oxford University Press, 1975).
2. For a fuller analysis of Nasir's strategy in this period, see Moshe Shemesh, *The Palestinian Entity 1959-1974: Arab Politics and the PLO* (London: Frank Cass, 1988), pp. 2-8 and 37-40; Malcolm Kerr, *The Arab Cold War*, pp. 97-125; and Daniel Dishon (ed.) *The Middle East Record 1967* (Tel Aviv: Shiloah Center, 1974), pp. 107-10.
3. Georgii Mirskii, 'Basic Trends in the Middle East', *New Times*, 6 (February 1965), pp. 6-7. For further reporting on the Arab Summits, see *Izvestiia*, 26 January 1964, on the Cairo Summit; *Pravda*, 16 September 1964, on the Alexandria Summit; and *Izvestiia*, 19 September 1965, on the Casablanca Summit.
4. Pavel Demchenko, 'Arab Differentiation', *New Times*, 34 (August 1966), pp. 5-6.
5. Farid Seiful'-Muliukov, 'The Casablanca Summit Conference', *New Times*, 39 (September 1965), pp. 14-16. For the Israeli journalist's reply, see 'Comments of an Israeli Journalist', *New Times*, 46 (November 1965), pp. 24-5.
6. Ahmad Shuqayri, *Min al-qimma ila al-hazima* (Beirut: n.p., 1971), pp. 214-19.
7. Ibid., p. 217.
8. R. G. Landa, 'Osvoboditel'naia bor'ba apabov Palestiny (1948-1967)', *Narody Azii i Afriki*, 1 (1976), p. 11.
9. Ibid., p. 13; and see the Soviet response to Shuqayri's resignation after the 1967 war in *Pravda*, 28 December 1967; and *Radio Moscow in Chinese* in *BBC Summary of World Broadcasts: Part 1 - The USSR*, hereinafter *SWB-USSR*, 15 January 1968.
10. Reported in *Ma'ariv* (Tel Aviv), 20 October 1968; from the Aryeh Yodfat Collection at the Moshe Dayan Centre, Tel Aviv.
11. Quoted in Moshe Shemesh, *The Palestinian Entity*, p. 66.
12. See Stephen T. Hosmer and Thomas W. Wolfe, *Soviet Policy and Practice Towards Third World Conflicts* (Lexington, Mass.: Lexington Books, 1983), pp. 27-38: and Robert O. Freedman, *Soviet Policy Towards the Middle East since 1970* (New York: Praeger, 1975), pp. 17-34.
13. Ilana Kass, *Soviet Involvement in the Middle East* (Boulder, Colo.: Westview Press, 1978), p. 31.
14. For example, see Iurii Bochkarev, 'Washington's New Tactics', *New Times*, 27 (July 1966), pp. 4-6.
15. *Krasnaia zvezda*, 25 May 1967.
16. *Pravda*, 12 February 1967. Palestinian commentators also noted the increased Soviet attention on the Palestinian issue, as seen in Salah Dabagh, *Al-ittihad al-sofieti wa-qadiyyat Filastin* (Beirut: PLO Research Centre, 1968), pp. 67-70.
17. See Kosygin's speech in Cairo in *Pravda*, 18 May 1966.
18. Such Soviet ambiguity can be seen in Moscow's support both for the Israeli Communist Party's acceptance of the 1949 armistice lines and the Arab communist parties' adherence to the 1947 partition lines. See Joel

Beinin, *Was the Red Flag Flying There? Marxist Politics and the Arab–Israeli Conflict in Egypt and Israel, 1948–1965* (London: I. B. Tauris, 1990), pp. 124–5 and p. 143.

19. Yaacov Ro'i, *From Encroachment to Involvement*, p. 441; Moshe Sneh, 'The Soviet–Egyptian "Solution" to the "Israel Problem"', *International Problems*, 7:1–2 (May 1969), pp. 24–5; and Aryeh Yodfat, 'USSR Proposals', p. 26.
20. See the condemnation of the terrorist attacks by the leader of the ICP in M. Vilner, 'Present developments in Israel', *World Marxist Review*, 10:4 (April 1967), pp. 23–6.
21. A Soviet note to Israel of 9 November 1966, as quoted in Aryeh Y. Yodfat, 'USSR Proposals to Regulate the Middle East Crisis', *International Problems*, 10:3–4 (December 1971), p. 25. For similar claims, see *Sovetskaia Rossia*, 21 May 1966; and *Izvestiia*, 8 May 1966.
22. Arnold Horelick, 'Soviet Policy in the Middle East, Part One: Policy from 1955 to 1972', in Paul Hammond and Sidney Alexander (eds), *Political Dynamics in the Middle East* (New York: American Elsevier, 1972), p. 582.
23. Diplomatic note to Israel, as reported in *Izvestiia*, 10 June 1967.
24. Quoted in Ministerstvo inostrannykh del SSSR, *SSSR i blizhnevostochnoe uregulirovanie 1967–1988: Dokumenty i materialy* (Moscow: Politizdat, 1989), p. 38. For further articles expressing fear of a renewed war, see *Izvestiia*, 5 September 1967; *Za rubezhom*, 39 (1967), p. 15; and *Radio Moscow* in *SWB–USSR*, 24 September 1967.
25. For example, see 'Za pravoe delo arabskykh narodov', *Azia i Afrika segodnia*, 10 (October 1967), p. 1; V. Kudriavtsev, 'The Middle East Knot', *International Affairs* (Moscow), 9 (September 1967), p. 32; and G. Mirskii, 'Israeli Agression and Arab Unity', *New Times*, 28 (July 1967), p. 5.
26. *Pravda*, 27 July 1967; and *Radio Moscow* in *SWB–USSR*, 2 August 1967.
27. 'The Fight Goes On', *New Times*, 27 (July 1967), p. 3.
28. Hashim S. H. Behbehani, *China's Foreign Policy in the Arab World 1955–1975* (London: Kegan Paul International, 1981), p. 61.
29. L. Sheiden, 'Imperialisticheskii zagovor na Blizhnem Vostoke', *Kommunist*, 11 (July 1967), p. 116.
30. *Radio Moscow in Chinese* in *SWB–USSR*, 15 January 1968.
31. Lawrence L. Whetten, *The Canal War: Four Power Conflict in the Middle East* (Cambridge, Mass.: MIT Press, 1974), p. 47 and p. 54.
32. Full details of plan in *CCCP i blizhnevostochnoe uregulirovanie*, pp. 87–91. For insistence on Arab recognition of Israel in its pre-1967 borders, see Viktor Laptev, 'Middle East Divide', *New Times*, 6 (February 1970), pp. 4–6.
33. Mohamed Heikal, *Sphinx and Commissar: The Rise and Fall of Soviet Influence in the Middle East* (London: Collins, 1978), p. 195.
34. William B. Quandt, *Decades of Decision: American Policy towards the Arab–Israeli Conflict 1967–1976* (Berkeley: University of California Press, 1977), p. 87.
35. Henry Kissinger, *White House Years* (Boston: Little, Brown, 1979), pp. 354–5.
36. Ibid., p. 99.
37. Lawrence Whetten, *The Canal War*, p. 104.

38. Mohamed Heikal, *The Road to Ramadan* (London: Collins, 1975), pp. 86–7.
39. *Radio Moscow* in *SWB–USSR*, 9 August 1968. See also *Pravda*, 16 January 1968; and *Izvestiia*, 1 October 1968.
40. M. Kremnev, 'Israeli Aggressors Miscalculate', *New Times*, 13 (April 1968), p. 11.
41. *Za rubezhom*, 9–15 August 1968.
42. Georgii Mirskii, 'Israel: Illusions and Miscalculations', *New Times*, 39 (October 1968), p. 7.
43. *Pravda*, 26 September 1968; G. Mirskii, 'Arabskie narody prodaljaiut bor'bu', *MEiMO*, 3 (March 1968), p. 122; and G. Mirskii, 'Rebirth of the Arab World', *New Times*, 25 (June 1969), p. 11.
44. Fahmi Salfiti, 'The Situation in Jordan and Communist Activities', *World Marxist Review*, 11:11–12 (November–December 1968), pp. 43–6. See also Georges Batal, Ajmad Rashad and Mohamed Harmal, 'Vital Tasks of the Arab National Liberation Movement', *World Marxist Review*, 11:9 (September 1968), pp. 26–30.
45. *Sovetskaia Rossiia*, 15 April 1969.
46. Ibid; interview with R. Ulianovskii in *Al-Ahram* (Cairo), 4 June 1969; and Dmitrii Volskii, 'Middle East Schemes of China', *New Times*, 3 (January 1969), pp. 6–8.
47. *Al-Hayat* (Beirut), 5 May 1969.
48. *Radio Voice of Fatah* in *BBC Summary of World Broadcasts: Part 4 – The Middle East* (hereinafter *SWB–ME*), 10 April 1969; and ibid., 23 September 1969.
49. *Trud*, 21 October 1969. For further statements on the elevation to national liberation status, see Prime Minister Kosygin in *Pravda*, 11 December 1969; and V. Rumiantsev, 'Arabskii Vostok na novom puti', *Kommunist*, 16 (November 1969), p. 97.
50. *Radio Moscow* in *SWB–USSR*, 3 February 1970.
51. *Pravda*, 12 June 1970; and Dmitrii Volskii, 'The Middle East Ten Years After', *New Times*, 23 (June 1970), pp. 10–11.
52. I. Belaev, 'The Downed Phantoms and Peace Prospects', *New Times*, 32 (August 1970), p. 5.
53. For a favourable account of Soviet–Jordanian relations, see A. Zubekhin and T. Zumbadze, 'Jordan', *International Affairs* (Moscow), 12 (December 1969), pp. 95–6.
54. P. Demchenko, 'Stiffening Rebuff', *New Times*, 27 (July 1970), pp. 8–9.
55. *Radio Moscow* in *SWB–USSR*, 18 September 1970.
56. Dmitrii Volskii and A. Usvatov, 'Events in Jordan', *New Times*, 39 (September 1970), pp. 4–5.
57. V. P. Ladeikin and E. D. Dmitriev, *Put' k miru na Blizhnem Vostoke* (Moscow: Mezhdunarodnye otnosheniia, 1974), p. 63.
58. *Radio Moscow* in *SWB–USSR*, 19 September 1970.
59. For evidence of the USSR urging 'utmost restraint' on Egypt during the crisis, see Mohamed Heikal, *Road to Ramadan*, pp. 98–100.
60. William B. Quandt, *Decade of Decisions*, p. 115.
61. *Pravda*, 24 September 1970.
62. William B. Quandt, *Decade of Decisions*, pp. 123–7.

CHAPTER 3   THE RELATIONSHIP BLOSSOMS: 1971-6

1. Henry Kissinger, *Years of Upheaval* (Boston: Little, Brown, 1982), p. 299.
2. Victor Israelyan, *Inside the Kremlin During the Yom Kippur War* (University Park, Pa.: Pennsylvania State University Press, 1995), p. 3.
3. V. Aleksandrov, 'Blizhnii Vostok; neobkhodim spravedlivyi mir', *Azia i Afrika segodnia*, 2 (February 1974), pp. 8–10; *Pravda*, 30 November 1973; and G. Mirskii, 'The Middle East: New Factors', *New Times*, 48 (November 1973), pp. 18–19.
4. *Shu'un Filastiniyya*, No. 13 (September 1972), pp. 244–5.
5. A notable example of such Palestinian enthusiasm can be seen in the Palestinian poet, Mahmud Darwish, 'Azif al-kaman 'ala al-jamjama', *Shu'un Filastiniyya*, 25 (September 1973), p. 4. For the Palestinian expectation that a Soviet–Palestinian relationship was being formed to mirror the US–Israeli alliance, see *Filastin al-Thawra* (Beirut), 16 August 1972.
6. *New York Times*, 18 September 1972; *Daily Telegraph*, 28 September 1972; and *Al-Nahar* (Beirut), 29 August 1972.
7. *Pravda*, 26 June 1973. See the effusive Palestinian praise for this in *Radio Voice of Palestine*, in *SWB–ME*, 6 August 1973.
8. *Al-Muharrir*, 31 October 1973; *Le Monde*, 31 October 1973; and *Times*, 1 November 1973.
9. *Times*, 17 February 1971; and *Egyptian Gazette*, 17 February 1971.
10. *Radio Amman* in *SWB–ME*, 29 August 1972.
11. *Al-Muharrir* (Beirut), 13 August 1973.
12. The conditional nature of Soviet support can be seen in its continuing criticisms of the PLO's lack of unity, its extremist slogans and its lack of a mass base of support. For example, see *Sovetskaia Rosiia*, 7 August 1973; and *Pravda*, 27 November 1973.
13. *Pravda*, 29 August 1972.
14. Naji 'Alush, 'Al-ahzab al-shuyu'iyya al-'arabiyya wa'l-qadiyya al-filastiniyya b'ad adwan 1967', *Shu'un Filastiniyya*, 4 (September 1971), p. 161–2; Naim Ashhab, 'Colonialist Policy of Israeli Aggressors', *World Marxist Review*, 16:8 (August 1973), pp. 31–2; and *Christian Science Monitor*, 19 March 1973.
15. The whole exchange is reported in *Afrique-Asie*, 10–23 December 1973.
16. Ibid., p. 13.
17. *Journal of Palestine Studies*, 3:3 (Spring 1974), p. 201.
18. For Habash's attacks, see *Al-Nahar*, 18 August 1974; and *Al-Hadaf* (Beirut), 3 August 1974. For the Soviet response, see *Literaturnaia gazeta*, 14 August 1974.
19. *INA* in *SWB–ME*, 26 November 1973; and *Journal of Palestine Studies*, 3:3 (Spring 1974), p. 199.
20. *Radio Voice of Palestine* in *SWB–ME*, 29 November 1973.
21. See Kissinger's surprise at this in Kissinger, *Years of Upheaval*, pp. 756.
22. Quoted in Ministerstvo inostrannykh del SSSR, *SSSR i blizhnevostochnoe uregulirovanie 1967–1988: Dokumenty i materialy* (Moscow: Politizdat, 1989), p. 186.
23. Ibid., p. 180.

24. Kissinger, *Years of Upheaval*, pp. 670–1.
25. *Pravda*, 17 March 1974.
26. *Izvestiia*, 1 April 1974; and A. Ulanskii, 'USSR and Syria: Solidarity and Cooperation', *New Times*, 16 (April 1974), p. 6.
27. William B. Quandt, *Decade of Decisions: American Policy Toward the Arab–Israeli Conflict, 1967–1976* (Berkeley: University of California Press, 1977), p. 236.
28. Brezhnev interview with French journalists in *Radio Moscow in Arabic* in *SWB–USSR*, 13 March 1974; *Pravda*, 27 March 1974; and *Radio Moscow in Arabic* in *SWB–USSR*, 25 May 1974.
29. *Izvestiia*, 21 March 1974; *Pravda*, 23 March 1974; and *Radio Moscow* in *SWB–USSR*, 28 March 1974.
30. *Pravda*, 19 May 1974; and 'The Aggressors Crimes', *New Times*, 21 (May 1974), p. 19.
31. *Pravda*, 19 December 1973.
32. Interview with Sulayman al-Najjab, 17 June 1992.
33. *Radio Moscow in Arabic* in *SWB–USSR*, 2 June 1974.
34. *Shu'un Filastiniyya*, 32 (April 1974), p. 181.
35. For the text of the Political Programme agreed at the PNC, see Jorgen S. Nielsen (ed.), *International Documents on Palestine 1974* (Beirut: Institute of Palestine Studies, 1977), pp. 449–50.
36. Viktor Bukharkov, 'Palestine National Council Session', *New Times*, 25 (June 1974), p. 13.
37. *Izvestiia*, 29 July 1974.
38. *Pravda*, 4 August 1974.
39. Ibid. The Soviet Union also committed itself during this visit to the establishment of a PLO representation in Moscow but this was only set up two years later in June 1976.
40. *Neues Deutschland* (East Berlin), 10 August 1974. For the Palestinian reaction, see *Shu'un Filastiniyya*, 37 (September 1974), p. 187.
41. *Pravda*, 9 September 1974.
42. *SSSR i blizhnevostochnoe uregulirovanie*, p. 201.
43. *Pravda*, 31 October 1974; *Radio Peace and Progress* in *SWB–USSR*, 31 October 1974; and Dmitrii Volskii, 'After the Rabat Summit', *New Times*, 45 (November 1974), pp. 10–11.
44. *SSSR i blizhnevostochnoe uregulirovanie*, pp. 202–7.
45. *Pravda*, 13 November 1974.
46. The concept of a paradigm shift comes from T. S. Kuhn, *The Structure of Scientific Revolutions* (Chicago: Chicago University Press, 1970).
47. This document can be found in 'Special Document: The Soviet Attitude to the Palestine Problem: From the Records of the Syrian Communist Party 1971–2', *Journal of Palestine Studies*, 2:1 (Autumn 1972), pp. 187–202.
48. For the full text of the 1974 Brezhnev peace proposals, see *SSSR i blizhnevostochnoe uregulirovanie*, pp. 207–8.
49. Gerald R. Ford, *A Time to Heal* (New York: Harper & Row and Reader's Digest, 1979), p. 303.
50. *Pravda*, 11 November 1976.
51. *Izvestiia*, 2 December 1975.

52. Andrei Gromyko, 'Programma mira v deistvii', *Kommunist*, 14 (September 1975), p. 9.
53. Jorgen S. Nielsen (ed.), *International Documents on Palestine 1976* (Beirut: Institute of Palestine Studies, 1978), p. 149.
54. *Radio Moscow in Arabic* in *SWB–USSR*, 27 January 1976; and Yurii Potomov, 'The Middle East: Aggressors' Exposed', *New Times*, 6 (February 1976), pp. 12–13.
55. For an extensive analysis of the Brookings Report, see *Journal of Palestine Studies*, 6:2 (Winter 1977), pp. 195–205.
56. In early April, two Soviet representatives visited Israel; see *The Times*, 12 April 1975; and *New York Times*, 12 April 1975.
57. *Pravda*, 24 April 1975.
58. See speech by Fahmi in *Radio Cairo Voice of the Arabs*, in *SWB–ME*, 19 April 1975.
59. *Al-Jaridah* (Beirut), 3 May 1975.
60. *Al-Nahar*, 30 April 1975.
61. *Shu'un Filastiniyya*, 46 (June 1975), p. 239; Arafat in *WAFA* in *SWB–ME*, 9 May 1975.
62. *Pravda*, 6 May 1975; *Radio Moscow in Arabic* in *SWB–USSR*, 5 May 1975; E. Dmitriev, 'Za mirnoe uregulirovanie na Blizhnem Vostoke', *Azia i Afrika segodnia*, 6 (June 1975), pp. 7–8.
63. *Radio Peace and Progress*, 12 May 1975.
64. E. D. Pyrlin, 'Palestinskoe natsional'no-osvoboditel'noe dvizhenie i blizhnevostochnoe uregulirovanie', *Sovetskoe gosudarstvo i pravo*, 10 (October 1977), pp. 95–6. Pyrlin was to become an influential advocate of the Palestinian cause, later writing books and articles on the Palestine question sponsored by the Central Committee under the pseudonym E. D. Dmitriev. See, for example, E. D. Dmitriev, *Palestinskii uzel* (Moscow: mezhdunarodnye otnosheniia, 1978).

CHAPTER 4   THE LEBANESE CIVIL WAR

1. *Pravda*, 9 July 1975; *Radio Moscow in Arabic* in *SWB–USSR*, 26 May 1975; and 'Crisis in Lebanon', *New Times*, 22 (May 1975), p. 17.
2. *Radio Moscow in Arabic* in *SWB–USSR*, 6 September 1975.
3. Michael C. Hudson, *The Precarious Republic: Political Modernization in Lebanon* (New York: Random House, 1968); Kamal S. Salibi, *Crossroads to Civil War: Lebanon, 1958–1976* (London: Ithaca Press, 1976); and Roger Owen (ed.), *Essays on the Crisis in Lebanon* (London: Ithaca Press, 1976).
4. The first mentions of a 'civil war' occurred in *Pravda*, 9 September 1975; *Izvestiia*, 11 September 1975; and *Radio Moscow in Arabic* in *SWB–USSR*, 22 September 1975.
5. *Pravda*, 28 October 1975.
6. *Radio Moscow in Arabic* in *SWB–USSR*, 6 September 1975; *Pravda*, 5 October 1975; and O. Ol'chushin, 'Livan: Dni ispytanii', *Aziia i Afrika segodnia*, 9 (September 1976), pp. 15–16.
7. *Radio Peace and Progress* in *SWB–USSR*, 2 August 1975; and O. Ol'chushin, 'Livan: Dni ispytanii', *Aziia i Afrika segodnia*, 9 (September 1975),

p. 16. In December, Soviet reporting also de-emphasized the Palestinian aspect of the conflict, suggesting it was a localized 'internal-political' affair. See *Izvestiia*, 4 December 1975; and *Pravda*, 30 December 1975.

8. *Radio Moscow* in *SWB–USSR*, 24 October 1975. For Asad's assertion of the same inter-linking of Syrian–Lebanese security concerns, see Radio Damascus in *SWB–ME*, 20 July 1976.

9. Efraim Karsh, *The Soviet Union and Syria: The Asad Years* (London: Routledge for the Royal Institute of International Affairs, 1988), p. 12.

10. *Radio Moscow* in *SWB–USSR*, 24 October 1975.

11. *Radio Moscow* in *SWB–USSR*, 24 October 1975.

12. *Izvestiia*, 17 February 1976; *Pravda*, 17 February 1976; and 'Political Reform Programme', *New Times*, 8 (February 1976), pp. 7–8.

13. *Radio Damascus* in *SWB–ME*, 20 July 1976.

14. V. Nikolaev, 'Trying Days for Lebanon', *New Times*, 16 (April 1976), p. 10.

15. *Pravda*, 18 March 1976; *Pravda*, 25 April 1976; and *Pravda*, 29 May 1976.

16. Radio Peace and Progress in *SWB–USSR*, 28 May 1976.

17. *Radio Moscow in Arabic* in *SWB–USSR*, 15 May 1976.

18. *Pravda*, 4 April 1976; and *Radio Peace and Progress* in *SWB–USSR*, 13 May 1976.

19. *Pravda*, 3 June 1976.

20. *Pravda*, 6 June 1976; *Tass*, 7 June 1976; *Izvestiia*, 7 June 1976.

21. Karsh, *The Soviet Union and Syria*, p. 33.

22. *Radio Voice of Palestine* in *SWB–ME*, 1 June 1976. See also Salah Khalaf's appeal in *Radio Voice of Palestine* in *SWB–ME*, 1 June 1976 and 4 June 1976.

23. *WAFA* in *SWB–ME*, 10 June 1976.

24. *Radio Voice of Palestine* in *SWB–ME*, 13 June 1976; and *Ruz al-Yusuf* (Beirut), 26 July 1976.

25. *Pravda*, 25 June 1976; *Pravda*, 27 June 1976.

26. *Pravda*, 10 July 1976.

27. *Pravda*, 11, 12, 13, 15 July 1976; *Krasnaia zvezda*, 13, 14, 15 July 1976. *Izvestiia* took a less hostile stance, perhaps reflecting differences of opinion in the Soviet leadership, and even failed to publish on 15 June, when the other papers included their most strident criticisms of Syria.

28. *Pravda*, 16 July 1976.

29. *Al-Safir* (Beirut), 15 July 1976; *Financial Times*, 9 August 1976. Salah Khalaf (Abu Iyad) also claimed that Asad had personally showed him documents proving Soviet hold-ups of the supply of spare arms; in Abu Iyad with Eric Rouleau, *My Home, My Land* (London: Times Books, 1981), p. 200.

30. *Le Monde*, 20 July 1976. The letter was authenticated by Naif Hawatmah in *Le Monde*, 28 July 1976. See also *Jerusalem Post*, 8 August 1976; and *WAFA* in *SWB–ME*, 12 July 1976.

31. *Pravda*, 3 August 1976.

32. *Pravda*, 4, 5 August 1976; *Izvestiia*, 7 August 1976.

33. *Pravda* articles signed by 'Observer' are generally thought to reflect the thinking of the Politburo.

34. *Pravda*, 27 August 1976.
35. The Soviet peace plan was announced in *Pravda*, 2 October 1976.
36. *Pravda*, 18 September 1976.
37. *Radio Beirut* in *SWB–ME*, 21, 22 September 1976.
38. *Pravda*, 25 September 1976.
39. Salah Khalaf in *Radio Beirut* in *SWB–ME*, 26 September 1976; and *Monday Morning* (Beirut), 27 October 1976.
40. *Radio Moscow in Arabic* in *SWB–USSR*, 30 September 1976.
41. *Pravda*, 18 October 1976.
42. *Pravda*, 20 October 1976.
43. *Pravda*, 16, 19 November 1976.
44. Galia Golan and Itamar Rabinovich, 'The Soviet Union and Syria: The Limits of Co-operation', in Yaacov Ro'i, *The Limits to Power: Soviet Policy in the Middle East* (London: Croom Helm, 1979), p. 227.
45. Karsh, *The Soviet Union and Syria*, p. 30.
46. Baruch Gurevitz, 'The Soviet Union and the Palestinian Organizations', in Ro'i, *The Limits to Power*, p. 267.
47. Ibid. p. 268; and Ilana Kass, *The Lebanon Civil War, 1975–1976: A Case of Crisis Management* (Jerusalem: The Hebrew University, 1979), p. 53.
48. Galia Golan, *The Soviet Union and the Palestine Liberation Organization: An Uneasy Alliance* (New York: Praeger, 1980), p. 187.
49. Karsh, *The Soviet Union and Syria*, p. 34.
50. Adeed Dawisha, *Syria and the Lebanese Crisis* (London: Macmillan, 1980).
51. Article in *Izvestiia* reported in *Tass* in *SWB–USSR*, 29 July 1976.
52. *Radio Moscow in Arabic* in *SWB–USSR*, 29 July 1976.
53. *Radio Peace and Progress* in *SWB–USSR*, 2 October 1976.
54. *Pravda*, 17 October 1976.
55. *Pravda*, 19 October 1976.
56. *Radio Beirut* in *SWB–ME*, 26 September 1976.
57. *Observer*, 22 August 1976.

CHAPTER 5   AN OPPORTUNITY MISSED: 1977–80

1. See the additions to the basic Soviet peace plan as set out on 28 April 1976 and 2 October 1976 in *Pravda*, 29 April 1976 and *Pravda*, 2 October 1976.
2. Ministerstvo inostrannykh del SSSR, *SSSR i blizhnevoctochnoe uregulirovanie 1967–1988: Dokumenty i materialy* (Moscow: Politizdat, 1989), pp. 256–7.
3. *Radio Israel* in *SWB–ME*, 23 March 1977.
4. Address by Marshall D. Shumann, Special Adviser to the Secretary of State on Soviet Affairs, 4 October 1979, quoted in Abraham Ben-Zvi, *The American Approach to Superpower Collaboration in the Middle East, 1973–1986* (Tel Aviv: Jerusalem Post and Westview Press, 1986), p. 44.
5. For an extensive analysis of the Brookings Report, see *Journal of Palestine Studies*, 6:2 (Winter 1977), pp. 195–205.
6. For a sympathetic evaluation of the Brookings report, see E. M. Primakov, *Anatomiia blizhnevostochnogo konflikta* (Moscow: Mysl', 1978), p. 280.

7. Cyrus Vance, *Hard Choices: Critical Years in America's Foreign Policy* (New York : Simon & Schuster, 1983), p. 164.
8. *Weekly Compilation of Presidential Documents* (henceforth *WCPD*), 21 March 1977.
9. William B. Quandt, *Camp David: Peacemaking and Politics* (Washington, DC: The Brookings Institution, 1986), p. 43.
10. Raymond L. Garthoff, *Detente and Confrontation: American–Soviet Relations from Nixon to Reagan* (Washington, DC: Brookings Institution, 1985), p. 588.
11. Note Asad's interview in *Time* magazine in January 1977 that 'the refusal of the PLO will not cause any paralysis in the movement of the Arab states concerned.'
12. *Pravda*, 27 January 1977; *Radio Peace and Progress* in *SWB–USSR*, 11 January 1977; and E. Dmitriev, 'Way to a Peaceful Settlement', *International Affairs* (Moscow), 3 (March 1977), p. 52.
13. *Pravda*, 24 March 1977; *Izvestiia*, 30 March 1977; and Oleg Alov, 'Groundwork for a Middle East Peace', *New Times*, 16 (April 1977), p. 4.
14. *Radio Peace and Progress* in *SWB–USSR*, 11 January 1977.
15. For an analysis of the political decisions of the 13th PNC, see *Journal of Palestine Studies*, 6:4 (Summer 1977), pp. 150–6.
16. *Pravda*, 23 March 1977; *Tass* in *SWB–USSR*, 4 April 1977; and Viktor Bukharkov, 'The Palestinians' Stand', *New Times*, 15 (April 1977), pp. 10–11.
17. Aleksandr Bovin in *Tass* in *SWB–USSR*, 13 April 1977.
18. *Pravda*, 8 April 1977.
19. *International Herald Tribune*, 7 April 1977; *Radio Voice of Palestine* in *SWB–ME*, 8 April 1977; and *Al-Dustur* (Amman), 25 April 1977.
20. *Shu'un Filastiniyya*, 67 (June 1977), p. 38.
21. Qaddumi in ibid.; Muhsin in *Akhbar al-Yawm* (Cairo), 23 April 1977; and Hawatmah in *Al-Siyassa* (Kuwait), 7 May 1977.
22. *Journal of Palestine Studies*, 6:4 (Summer 1977), p. 184.
23. *Le Monde*, 14 April 1977.
24. *Guardian*, 30 March 1977.
25. This was not a new position as Mahmud Abbas (Abu Mazin) had stated in *Radio Amman* in *SWB–ME*, 4 January 1977.
26. *Agence France Presse*, 4 May 1977.
27. *Financial Times*, *Guardian* and *New York Times*, 10 May 1977. The US State Department verified this leaked report.
28. *Financial Times*, 13 May 1977.
29. *New York Times*, *Egyptian Gazette* and *Guardian*, 6 May 1977.
30. *Radio Voice of Palestine* in *SWB–ME*, 14 May 1977; and *Al-Watan* (Kuwait), 21 May 1977.
31. *Christian Science Monitor*, 5 September 1977; and *Shu'un Filastiniyya*, 71 (October 1977), p. 196.
32. Qaddumi in *Radio Voice of Palestine* in *SWB–ME*, 15 September 1977; and Khalid al-Hasan in *Monday Morning*, 12 September 1977.
33. *Pravda*, 1 September 1977.
34. Ibid. See also Arafat's statement in *Radio Moscow in Arabic* in *SWB–USSR*, 30 August 1977.

35. Meir Vilner, the leader of Rakah, confirmed this in *Radio Israel*, 17 September 1977.
36. Cyrus Vance, *Hard Choices*, p. 188.
37. *Radio Voice of Palestine* in *SWB–ME*, 19 August 1977; *Al-Nahar*, 24 August 1977; *New York Times*, 25 August 1977; and *Al-Mustaqbal*, 10 and 13 September 1977.
38. *Radio Voice of Palestine* in *SWB–ME*, 19 August 1977.
39. The joint statement was published in *Pravda*, 2 October 1977.
40. Brzezinski, *Power and Principle*, p. 108; and Quandt, *Camp David*, p. 120 and p. 133.
41. Zbigniew Brzezinski, François Duchene, and Kiichi Saeki, 'Peace in an International Framework', *Foreign Policy*, 19 (Summer 1975), p. 16.
42. *Time*, 8 August 1977.
43. *WCPD*, 29 September 1977.
44. For Soviet thinking along these lines, see Igor Blishchenko, 'The Rights of Palestinians', *New Times*, 4 (January 1978), pp. 20–1; *Radio Peace and Progress* in *SWB–USSR*, 17 July 1977; and O. Alov, 'For a Middle East Settlement', *International Affairs* (Moscow), 1 (January 1978), pp. 94–5.
45. *Christian Science Monitor*, 5 September 1977.
46. Jimmy Carter, *Keeping Faith: Memoirs of a President* (New York: Bantam Books, 1982), p. 293.
47. Ibid.
48. Ismail Fahmi, *Negotiating for Peace in the Middle East* (London: Croom Helm, 1983), p. 235.
49. Vance, *Hard Choices*, p. 192.
50. For PLO support, see Qaddumi in *Pravda*, 3 October 1977; Mahmud Abbas in *WAFA* in *SWB–ME*, 2 October 1977; Habash in *Al-Nahar*, 2 October 1977.
51. Sa'id Kamil in *Radio Tunis* in *SWB–ME*, 13 November 1977.
52. Quandt, *Camp David*, p. 130.
53. E. M. Primakov, *Istoriia odnogo sgovora* (Moscow: Politizdat, 1985), p. 138; R. V. Borisov, *SShA: blizhnevostochnaia politika v 70-e gody* (Moscow: Nauka, 1982), pp. 173–7; and I. Zviagelskaia, 'Blizhnevostochnye al'ternativy', *Aziia i Afrika segodnia*, 2 (February 1982), p. 15.
54. *Izvestiia*, 19 October 1977; *Radio Moscow in English for North America* in *SWB–USSR*, 5 November 1977; and Dmitrii Volskii, 'Taking up a Point', *New Times*, 44 (October 1977), pp. 30–1.
55. Oleg Alov, 'The Objective: Geneva', *New Times*, No. 44 (October 1977), pp. 8–9.
56. *Arab Report and Record*, 23–4 (1–31 December 1977).
57. *Paris Match*, 29 December 1977.
58. *Pravda* and *Krasnaia Zvezda*, 28 December 1978.
59. *Pravda*, 24 December 1977.
60. *Izvestiia*, 26 December 1977.
61. *Radio Moscow in Arabic* in *SWB–USSR*, 8 December 1977.
62. *Le Monde*, 12 May 1978.
63. *KUNA* in *SWB–ME*, 9 June 1979.
64. *Radio Voice of Palestine* in *SWB–ME*, 23 October 1981.

65. *Radio Voice of Palestine* in *SWB–ME*, 18 January 1979.
66. *Pravda*, 2 November 1978.
67. *Pravda*, 30 November 1978.
68. *Radio Moscow in Arabic* in *SWB–USSR*, 6 December 1978.
69. *Radio Voice of Palestine* in *SWB–ME*, 28 November 1978.
70. Quoted in Raphael Israeli, *PLO in Lebanon: Selected Documents* (London: Weidenfeld & Nicolson, 1983), pp. 50–1 and p. 54.
71. *Time*, 15 January 1979.
72. *Pravda*, 7 October 1978.
73. Patrick Seale, *Asad of Syria: The Struggle for The Middle East* (London: I. B. Tauris, 1980), p. 311; and Efraim Karsh, *The Soviet Union and Syria: The Asad Years* (London: Routledge for the Royal Institute of International Affairs, 1988), p. 49.
74. Minirsterstvo inostrannykh del SSSR, *SSSR i blizhnevostochnoe uregulirovanie, 1967–1988: Dokumenty i materialy* (Moscow: Politizdat, 1989, pp. 296–300).
75. *Radio Peace and Progress* in *SWB–USSR*, 4 February 1982. For other reports on Syria's leading role, see 'Middle East Fuse', *New Times*, 14 (April 1980), p. 1; O. Fomin, 'Arab Unity and the Middle East Settlement', *International Affairs* (Moscow), 6 (1981), pp. 29–38; and O. M. Gorbatov and L. Y. Cherkasskii, *Bor'ba SSSR za obespechenie prochnogo i spravedlivogo mira na Blizhnem Vostoke, 1967–1980* (Moscow: Nauka, 1980), p. 235.
76. Victor Bukharkov, 'The Palestine Movement Shapes its Course', *New Times*, 52 (December 1976), p. 26.
77. E. D. Dmitriev, *Palestinskii uzel* (Moscow, Mezhdunarodnye otnosheniia, 1978), p. 65; R. G. Landa, 'Iz istorii Palestinskogo dvizheniia coprotivleniia (1967–1971)', *Narody Azii i Afriki*, 4 (1976), pp. 23–4.
78. Habash in *Tass* in *SWB–USSR*, 8 February 1980; and *Izvestiia*, 13 February 1980. For Hawatmah's visit and support for the Soviet move, see *Izvestiia*, 19 February 1980; *Pravda*, 12 March 1980; and Na'if Hawatmah, 'Sorvat' plany amerikanskogo imperializma', *Azia i Afrika segodnia*, 5 (May 1980), p. 25.
79. *MENA* in *SWB–ME*, 17 January 1980.
80. *Tass* in *SWB–USSR*, 6 February 1980.
81. Hawatmah criticized the participation of 'part of the Palestine Resistance' in Islamabad in Na'if Hawatmah, 'Ma huwa al-matlub li-ta'ziz al-whada al-wataniyya al-filastiniyya', *Shu'un Filastiniyya*, 103 (June 1980), p. 11.
82. The PFLP and DFLP were joined in their criticisms by other smaller factions. See the joint statement by the PFLP, DFLP, PLF, PPSF, ALF and PFLP-GC in *New York Times*, 25 May 1978.
83. *Reuter*, 24 May 1978.
84. Faiq Warrad, 'National and Class Aspects of the Arab Liberation Movement', *World Marxist Review*, 22:2 (February 1978), p. 70.
85. See the leftist Palestinian debate on this issue between Majid Abu Sharar (Fatah), Abu Ali Mustafa (PFLP), Yasir Abd Rabbu (DFLP), Muhammad Khalifa (Sa'iqa) and Arabi Awad (JCP), 'Qadiyyat al-nidal al-watani fi'l-diffa al-gharbiyya wa'l-qita' ghaza', *Shu'un Filastiniyya*, 118 (September 1981), pp. 45–71 and 119 (October 1981), pp. 22–52. See also Emile

Sahliyeh, *In Search of Leadership: West Bank Politics since 1967* (Washington, DC: The Brookings Institution, 1988), pp. 98–102.

86. See, for example, Naim al-Ashhab, 'The Battle for National Existence', *World Marxist Review*, 24:12 (December 1980), p. 76.

87. Christopher Andrew and Oleg Gordievskii, *KGB: The Inside Story of Its Foreign Operations From Lenin to Gorbachev* (London: Sceptre, 1991), p. 551.

88. Andrew Gowers and Tony Walker, *Beyond the Myth: Yasser Arafat and the Palestinian Resistance* (London: W. H. Allen, 1990), pp. 191–3; and John and Janet Wallach, *Arafat: In the Eyes of the Beholder* (London: Heinemann, 1991), pp. 404–9.

89. *Radio Moscow in Arabic* in *SWB–USSR*, 29 July 1981; and *Izvestiia*, 22 August 1981.

90. E. D. Dmitriev, *Palestinskaia tragediia* (Moscow: Mezhdunarodnye otnosheniia, 1986), p. 100.

91. Andrew and Gordievskii, *KGB*, p. 551.

CHAPTER 6   THE RELATIONSHIP DETERIORATES: 1981–5

1. The warnings given to this effect by Evgenii Primakov and Igor Beliaev are noted in Rashid Khalidi, *Under Siege: PLO Decisionmaking During the 1982 War* (New York: Columbia University Press, 1986), p. 194.

2. *Pravda*, 26 April 1982.

3. *Financial Times*, 18, 28 October 1981; *Radio Voice of Palestine* in *SWB–ME*, 20 October 1981. Arafat also stated that he had informed the Soviet leadership on Israel's use of 'hyper-modern weapons' in *Radio Moscow in Arabic* in *SWB–USSR*, 21 October 1981.

4. Salah Khalaf in *Radio Voice of Palestine* in *SWB–ME*, 6. January and 7 February 1982.

5. Khalid al-Hasan in *Al-Khalij* (Abu Dhabi), 7 January 1982.

6. Khalidi, *Under Siege*, p. 195; *New York Times*, 13 February 1980; *Times*, 21 February 1982.

7. For example, see the Soviet–PLO joint communiqué in *Pravda*, 19 November 1979; and the Soviet–Syrian joint communiqués in *Pravda*, 7 October 1978 and *Pravda*, 19 October 1979.

8. Raphael Israeli (ed.), *PLO in Lebanon: Selected Documents* (London: Weidenfeld & Nicolson, 1983), p. 53.

9. The Soviet ambassador to Lebanon, Sarvar Soldatov, made this point in *Radio Beirut* in *SWB–ME*, 16 May 1981.

10. For example, the Soviet Union emphasized this point to a Fatah delegation in August 1978, see *Radio Voice of Palestine* in *SWB–ME*, 3 August 1978. For the linkage of the Syrian–PRM positions, see E. M. Primakov, 'A Dead-End Middle East Settlement', *International Affairs* (Moscow), 2 (February 1979), pp. 38–46; and the report on the Soviet-sponsored International Conference of Solidarity with Syria and the PLO in June 1981 in L. Zhegalov, 'The Damascus Conference', *New Times*, 27 (July 1981), p. 9.

11. Khalidi, *Under Siege*, pp. 34–5.

12. *Pravda*, 3 August 1982. See also messages in *Pravda*, 9 July 1982; and *Financial Times*, 21 September 1982.
13. *Daily Telegraph*, 3 August 1982.
14. Khalidi, *Under Siege*, p. 165.
15. Mahmud Abbas, *Radio Voice of Palestine* in *SWB–ME*, 16 March 1984; and Yasir Abd Rabbu, *Radio Moscow in Arabic* in *SWB–USSR*, 28 June 1982.
16. *Radio Voice of Palestine* in *SWB–ME*, 17 July 1982. For other criticisms by Khalaf, see *Radio Monte Carlo* in *SWB–ME*, 18 June 1982; and *Le Monde*, 23 June 1982.
17. *Reuter*, 26 June 1982.
18. Karen Dawisha, 'The USSR in the Middle East: Superpower in Eclipse?', *Foreign Affairs*, 61:2 (Winter 1982–3), pp. 438–52; and Galia Golan, 'The Soviet Union and the Israeli Action in Lebanon', *International Affairs* (London), 59:1 (Winter 1982–3), pp. 7–16.
19. *Guardian*, 5 July 1982.
20. Khalidi, *Under Siege*, p. 210.
21. Zamiatin, Head of CPSU Information Section, in *Soviet Television* in *SWB–USSR*, 3 July 1982; and V. Shelepin, 'Lacerated but Unvanquished', *New Times*, 25 (June 1982), pp. 12–13.
22. *Pravda*, 6 July 1982; *Radio Moscow in Arabic* in *SWB–USSR*, 27 August 1982; and Vitalii Kobysh, Head of a section of the Central Committee International Information Department, *Soviet Television* in *SWB–USSR*, 25 September 1982.
23. Primakov on *Soviet Television* in *SWB–USSR*, 11 June 1982; *Radio Moscow in Arabic* in *SWB–USSR*, 28 June 1982; Karen Brutents, 'Livanskaia tragediia', *SShA: ekonomika, politika, ideologiia*, 9 (September 1982), p. 8.
24. *Budapest Television* in *SWB–USSR*, 16 September 1982.
25. Brutents on *Soviet Television* in *SWB–USSR*, 24 April 1982.
26. For the text of the plan, see Yehuda Lukacs (ed.), *The Israeli–Palestinian Conflict: A Documentary Record, 1967–1990* (Cambridge: Cambridge University Press, 1992), pp. 72–8.
27. Ibid., pp. 478–9.
28. *Frankfurter Allgemeine Zeitung*, 11 November 1982.
29. Oleg Fomin, 'Stop the Aggressor, Ensure Peace', *New Times*, 39 (September 1982), p. 8. See also *Pravda*, 17 September 1982; and *Tass* in *SWB–USSR*, 11 November 1982.
30. Vadim Zagladin in *Budapest Television* in *SWB–USSR*, 16 September 1982. See also *Radio Moscow in Arabic* in *SWB–USSR*, 17 December 1982.
31. King Hussein interview in 'Panorama', *BBC Television* in *SWB–ME*, 13 September 1982.
32. Qaddumi in *Guardian*, 3 September 1982; Mahmud Abbas in *Radio Voice of Palestine* in *SWB–ME*, 12 February 1982.
33. *Radio Amman* in *SWB–ME*, 14 December 1982.
34. Mahmud al-Labadi in *Radio Cairo* in *SWB–ME*, 12 October 1982.
35. Efraim Karsh, *The Soviet Union and Syria: The Asad Years* (London: Routledge for the Royal Institute of *International Affairs*, 1988), p. 73.

36. *Pravda*, 31 March 1983.
37. *Jerusalem Post*, 16 April 1983.
38. *Tishrin*, 18 September 1982.
39. *Wall Street Journal*, 14 April 1983.
40. Interview with King Husayn in *Radio Amman* in *SWB–ME*, 10 January 1983.
41. *KUNA* in *SWB–ME*, 7 January 1983.
42. Interview with Aleksandr Golytsin in London on 15 May 1990. Golytsin was present at the Andropov–PLO discussions.
43. This idea of mutual recognition, which had been central to the Soviet–PLO negotiations during 1977, was further confirmed in a Rakah–PCP joint communiqué in Moscow on 23 December 1982, the text of which can be found in *Journal of Palestine Studies*, 12:2 (Winter 1983), p. 235.
44. *Pravda*, 14 January 1983.
45. *Radio Moscow in Arabic* in *SWB–USSR*, 14 January 1983.
46. *Al-Nahar*, 14 January 1983; A. Notin and A. Alekseev, 'Samoopredelenie arabskogo naroda Palestiny: predposylki i realii', *Azia i Arika segognia*, 6 (June 1983), p. 13; and M. Zeinalov, 'The Palestinians Chart their Course', *New Times*, 3 (January 1983), p. 13;
47. Faiq Warrad, 'A New Development in the Balance of Strength in the Middle East', *World Marxist Review*, 27:5 (May 1983), pp. 25–6.
48. *Pravda*, 14 January 1983.
49. For the text of the final PNC statement, see *Middle East Contemporary Survey*, Vol. 7, 1982–3, p. 320.
50. Salah Khalaf in *KUNA* in *SWB–ME*, 23 February 1983.
51. *New York Times*, 11 April 1983.
52. *Tass* in *SWB–USSR*, 11 April 1984.
53. Dmitrii Volskii, 'Cover for Blackmail', *New Times*, 18 (May 1983), p. 15.
54. *Pravda*, 5, 19, 20, February 1983; and *Izvestiia*, 2 January 1983.
55. *Pravda*, 3 March 1983; and *Radio Moscow in Arabic* in *SWB–USSR*, 25 March 1983.
56. *Christian Science Monitor*, 12 April 1983.
57. William B. Quandt, 'US Policy Toward the Arab–Israeli Conflict', in William B. Quandt (ed.), *The Middle East: Ten Years after Camp David* (Washington DC: The Brookings Institution, 1988), p. 367.
58. King Husayn on *Amman Television* in *SWB–ME*, 16 May 1983.
59. King Hussein on *Amman Television* in *SWB–ME*, 15 March 1984.
60. E. D. Dmitriev, *Palestinskii uzel* (Moscow: Mezhdunarodnye otnosheniia, 1978), p. 65. See also previous chapter for discussion of the Soviet position towards Fatah.
61. *Radio Moscow* in *SWB–USSR*, 17 July 1983.
62. *Pravda*, 26 June 1983; and *Literaturnaia gazeta*, 6 July 1983.
63. *Al-Kifah al-Arabi* (Beirut), 30 May 1983. The PLO leadership was also convinced that Moscow indirectly supported the dissidents – letter from Mahmud Abbas from Tunis, 15 July 1992.
64. *International Herald Tribune*, 8 June 1983; *Times*, 6 June 1983; *KUNA* in *SWB–ME*, 24 June 1983.
65. *Pravda*, 27 June 1983; *Radio Moscow* in *SWB–USSR*, 5 August 1983; and Primakov on *Soviet Televison* in *SWB–USSR*, 30 July 1983.

66. See the joint DFLP–PFLP programme, published on 16 October 1983, as reported in *Middle East Contemporary Survey*, Vol. 8, 1983–4, pp. 199–203.
67. Patrick Seale, *Asad: The Struggle for the Middle East* (London: I. B. Tauris, 1988), p. 411.
68. *Radio Monte Carlo* in *SWB–ME*, 21 January 1983. For Syrian refusal to pass on the arms, see *Times*, 27 May 1983.
69. *Tanjug* in *SWB–USSR*, 7 June 1983. The DFLP confirmed after its visit in July that this had been the Soviet advice – see *Radio Moscow in Arabic* in *SWB–USSR*, 5 July 1983.
70. *Times*, 6 June 1983. Arafat reported that Andropov had sent six messages in *Le Monde*, 27 July 1983.
71. *Radio Havana* in *SWB–ME*, 28 June 1983; *International Herald Tribune*, 12 July 1983; and *Radio Voice of Palestine* in *SWB–ME*, 11 July 1983.
72. *WAFA* in *SWB–ME*, 3 July 1983; and *International Herald Tribune*, 4 July 1983.
73. *Pravda*, 14 July 1983.
74. *Tass* in *SWB–USSR*, 5 November 1983.
75. Boris Ponomarev, 'Sovremennaia obstanovka i rol' demokraticheskoi pechati', *Kommunist*, 17 (November 1983), p. 13.
76. *Pravda*, 19 November 1983; 'The Root of the Problem', *New Times*, 29 (July 1983), p. 1; and A. Ustogov and V. Gurev, 'American Threat to the Arab Peoples', *International Affairs* (Moscow), 10 (October 1983), p. 129.
77. *Pravda*, 19 November 1983.
78. *Pravda*, 14 July 1983; and *Pravda*, 24 November 1983.
79. Ibid.
80. *Al-Khalij*, 18 December 1983.
81. *Pravda*, 13, 19 November 1983.
82. *International Herald Tribune*, 12 September 1983; and *Guardian*, 19 August 1983.
83. *Frankfurter Allgemeine Zeitung*, 24 October 1983.
84. *Radio Moscow* in *SWB–USSR*, 23 November 1983; and *Izvestiia*, 1 January 1983.
85. *Radio Moscow* in *SWB–USSR*, 28 November 1983.
86. Dmitrii Volskii, 'The Inter-Palestinian Conflict', *New Times*, 49 (December 1983), p. 15.
87. Aleksandr Bovin on *Soviet Television* in *SWB–USSR*, 25 February 1984.
88. *Radio Moscow in Arabic* in *SWB–USSR*, 11 January 1984; *Pravda*, 14 January 1984; and O. Kovtunovich and V. Nosenko, 'Blizhnii Vostok: silovaia politika imperializma v deistvii', *MEiMO*, 4 (April 1984), p. 62.
89. Ministerstvo inostrannykh del SSSR, *SSSR i blizhnevostochnoe uregulirovanie, 1967–1988: dokumenty i materialy* (Moscow: Politizdat, 1989), pp. 368–71.
90. Larry C. Napper, 'The Arab Autumn of 1984: A Case Study of Soviet Middle East Diplomacy', *The Middle East Journal*, 39:4 (Fall 1985), p. 738.
91. *International Herald Tribune*, 18 October 1984; Arafat in *Ruz Al-Yusuf*,

19 November 1984; and *Al-Watan Al-Arabi*, 9 November 1984.
92. MID, *SSSR i blizhnevostochoe uregulirovanie*, p. 370.
93. *Radio Voice of Palestine* in *SWB–ME*, 11 February 1983; *Radio Voice of Palestine* in *SWB–ME*, 16 March 1983; and *Afrique-Asie*, 12–25 March 1983.
94. *QNA* in *SWB–ME*, 3 July 1984; and Arafat in *Radio Voice of Palestine* in *SWB–ME*, 18 June 1983.
95. The first mention of Arafat came in *Izvestiia*, 26 August 1984.
96. *Pravda*, 8 October 1984. For Palestinian reaction, see KUNA in SWB–ME, 7 October 1984; and *Radio Voice of Palestine* in *SWB–ME*, 7 October 1984.
97. Dmitrii Volskii, 'Diplomats or Generals', *New Times*, 32 (August 1984), p. 9; *Pravda*, 9 August 1984; and *Izvestiia*, 14 October 1984.
98. *Izvestiia*, 25 April 1984; *Izvestiia*, 14 July 1984; and *Pravda*, 15 July 1984.
99. *Afrique-Asie*, 18 June 1984; *Christian Science Monitor*, 20 April 1984; and letter from Mahmud Abbas from Tunis, 15 July 1992.
100. *Pravda*, 14 March 1984.
101. *Pravda*, 23 November 1984; and *Soviet Television* in *SWB–USSR*, 23 November 1983.
102. *Pravda*, 1 January 1985.
103. *MENA* in *SWB–ME*, 23 January 1983. See also Arafat in *Le Monde*, 23 November 1984.
104. Letter from Mahmud Abbas from Tunis, 15 July 1992; Interview with Sulayman al-Najjab in Tunis, 17 June 1992.
105. *Tass* in *SWB–USSR*, 23 November 1984.
106. Letter from Mahmud Abbas from Tunis, 17 July 1992.
107. *Tass* in *SWB–USSR*, 11 January 1985.
108. For the text of the Amman Accord , see Lukacs, *Israeli–Palestinian Conflict*, pp. 488–9. The principal thrust of the agreement was for a joint Palestinian–Jordanian delegation to participate at an International Conference with the five Permanent Members of the UN Security Council to obtain Palestinian self-determination within a confederated Jordanian–Palestinian state.
109. O. Fomin, 'Palestinian Rights: Two Lines', *New Times*, 12 (March 1985), p. 22. See also *Tass* in *SWB–USSR*, 19 February 1985; and *Pravda*, 27 February and 8 March 1985.
110. Primakov in *Izvestiia*, 28 October 1985; and Beliaev in *Radio Moscow in Arabic* in *SWB–USSR*, 29 July 1985.
111. *Soviet Television* in *SWB–USSR*, 24 February 1984.
112. *Radio Moscow in Arabic* in *SWB–USSR*, 29 July 1985.
113. *Al-Hawadith*, 1 March 1985.
114. King Husayn on *Amman Television* in *SWB–ME*, 19 February 1985. For the retrospective substantive criticisms of the Amman Agreement, see *Govoriat fakty (Seriia 'mezhdunarodnaia' otvechaet na voprosy po problemam blizhnevostochnogo uregulirovaniia)* (Moscow: Znanie, 1986), pp. 37–9.
115. Interview with Sulayman al-Najjab in Tunis, 17 June 1992.
116. O. Fomin, 'The Casablanca Summit', *New Times*, 34 (August 1985),

p. 10; O. Fomin 'The Murphy Shuttle', *New Times*, 35 (August 1985), pp. 7–8; and Leonid Zamiatin on *Soviet Television* in *SWB–USSR*, 25 August 1985.

117. For report on PCP visit, see *Radio Moscow in Arabic* in *SWB–USSR*, 23 May 1985; for al-Sa'iqa, see *Izvestiia*, 30 October 1985; for PFLP, see *Tass* in *SWB–USSR*, 23 October 1985; and for the DFLP visit, see Radio Peace and Progress in *SWB–USSR*, 12 November 1985.

118. *Radio Voice of Palestine* in *SWB–ME*, 3 September 1985.

119. *New York Times*, 8 September 1985.

120. *Pravda*, 29 November 1985.

121. Khalid al-Hasan in *Radio Monte Carlo* in *SWB–ME*, 22 November 1985; and Arafat in *Third World Quarterly*, 8:2 (April 1986), p. 407.

122. Salah Khalaf in *KUNA* in *SWB–ME*, 31 December 1985.

123. E. D. Dmitriev, *Palestinskii uzel* (Moscow: Mezhdunarodye otnosheniia, 1978), p. 57 and p. 134.

124. E. D. Dmitriev, *Palestinskaia tragediia* (Moscow: Mezhdunarodnye otnosheniia, 1986), p. 85.

125. Ibid., p. 146.

126. E. Dmitriev, 'Palestinskaia dvizhenie soprotivleniia – na novykh rubezhakh', *MEiMO*, 8 (August 1987), p. 59.

CHAPTER 7   THE FINAL RISE AND FALL OF A RELATIONSHIP: 1986–91

1. The extent of US distrust of the Soviet presence in the Middle East in the mid-1980s can be seen in George Shultz's speech to the American–Israeli Public Affairs Committee in February 1987 where he condemned the Soviet Union for 'aligning themselves with the worst terrorists and tyrants in the region'. As quoted in Yehuda Lukacs (ed.), *The Israeli–Palestinian Conflict: A Documentary Record* (Cambridge: Cambridge University Press, 1992), p. 88.

2. *Washington Post*, 10 February 1986; *International Herald Tribune*, 12 February 1986; and *Al-Ittihad*, 8 February 1986.

3. *Radio Voice of Palestine* in *SWB–ME*, 20 February 1986.

4. *Toronto Star*, 13 January 1986; and *International Herald Tribune*, 18 January 1986.

5. *Radio Voice of Palestine* in *SWB–ME*, 22 February 1986.

6. *Frankfurter Allgemeine Zeitung*, 12 April 1986. For the composition of the delegation, see *Pravda*, 25 February 1986.

7. Dmitrii Volskii and Pavel Davydov, 'A Threat Not Only to the Arabs – That's Clearly Seen from Damascus', *New Times*, 4 (February 1986), p. 15.

8. Fatah Central Committee members, Mahmud Abbas and Rafiq al-Natshah, had made this pledge as reported in *Al-Riyadh*, 27 May 1986.

9. *Radio Voice of Palestine* in *SWB–ME*, 19 April 1986; PLO Central Committe praise for meeting in *Radio Voice of Palestine* in *SWB–ME*, 1 May 1986; and Salah Khalaf in *MENA* in *SWB–ME*, 19 May 1986.

10. *Daily Telegraph*, 8 May 1986.

11. Letter from Mahmud Abbas from Tunis, 15 July 1992.

12. *Al-Qabas*, 22 April 1986.
13. *Daily Telegraph*, 8 May 1986.
14. "Prague Declaration" as quoted in *Journal of Palestine Studies*, 16:2 (Winter 1987), pp. 211–13.
15. *KUNA* in *SWB–ME*, 30 May 1986.
16. *Al-Khalij*, 20 August 1986.
17. *Pravda*, 11 August 1986.
18. V. Avakov, 'K vozobnovleniiu izrail'sko-egipetskogo dialoga', *MEiMO*, 12 (December 1986), p. 117; and *Pravda*, 1 and 16 December 1986.
19. 'The Minutes of a Meeting on 5/8/1986 in the Central Committee Headquarters between a Delegation of Abu Mazin – Yasir Abd Rabbu – and Na'im al-Ashhab – with Comrade Brutents – Deputy Head of International Relations Department of the Soviet Communist Party' (in Arabic).
20. *Pravda*, 1 April 1987.
21. Interview with Sulayman al-Najjab in Tunis, 17 June 1992.
22. *Times*, 27 April 1987.
23. *Radio Moscow* in *SWB–USSR*, 24 April 1987.
24. Ibid.
25. *Pravda*, 27 April 1987.
26. *New York Times*, 27 April 1987.
27. *Pravda*, 28 April 1987; *Radio Moscow* in *SWB–USSR*, 28 April 1987; and *Izvestiia*, 6 June 1987.
28. G. Guchetl' and I. Zviagel'skaia, 'Arabskii mir: poiski putei k konsolidatsii', *Aziia i Afrika segodnia*, 4 (April 1988), p. 12.
29. Aleksandr Zotov, 'Is Long-Awaited Settlement in Sight', *New Times*, 22 (June 1987), p. 15.
30. *Radio Moscow* in *SWB–USSR*, 28 April 1987; *Tass* in *SWB–USSR*, 26 April 1987; and Evgenii Bolonov, 'PLO Unity Restored', *New Times*, 10 (March 1987), pp. 9–10.
31. *Izvestiia*, 25 April 1987.
32. For more extensive studies on this discussion, see Elizabeth Valkenier, 'Revolutionary Change in the Third World: Recent Soviet Reassessments', *World Politics*, 38:3 (April 1986), pp. 415–34; Francis Fukuyama, *Moscow's Post-Brezhnev Reassessment of the Third World* (Santa Monica, Calif.: Rand Corporation, 1986); and Jerry F. Hough, *The Struggle for the Third World: Soviet Debates and American Options* (Washington, DC: The Brookings Institution, 1986).
33. 'Rech' General'nogo Sekretariia Ts.K KPSS tovarishcha Yu. V. Andropova', *Kommunist*, 9 (June 1983).
34. Karen Brutents, 'Dvizhenie neprisoedineniia v sovremennom mire', *MEiMO*, 5 (May 1984), p. 33.
35. For example, see Aleksandr Bovin in *Izvestiia*, 12 November 1984.
36. For a more extended analyses on Gorbachev's new thinking, see Margot Light, 'New Political Thinking', *Coexistence*, 24 (1987), pp. 233–43; Robert Levgold, 'The Revolution in Soviet Foreign Policy', *Foreign Affairs*, 68:1 (1989), pp. 82–98; and Stephen Sestanovich, 'Gorbachev's Foreign Policy: A diplomacy of Decline', *Problems of Communism*, 37:1 (January–February 1988), pp 1–15.
37. Speech of E. A. Shevardnadze, in *Vestnik ministerstva inostrannykh del*

SSSR, 15 August 1988, p. 33.

38. *Tass* in *SWB–USSR*, 11 July 1986.
39. *Radio Moscow* in *SWB–USSR*, 10 February 1987.
40. *Pravda*, 25 June 1987.
41. Hani al-Hasan in *Frankfurter Allgemeine Zeitung*, 9 July 1987; Arafat in *Financial Times*, 7 September 1987; and PLO Executive Committee statement in *Radio Voice of Palestine* in *SWB–ME*, 4 July 1987.
42. A full analysis of the PLO delegation visit can be found in 'Mubahathat al-wafd al-filastiny fi Musku', *Al-Taqrir* (Abu Dhabi), 3:10 (1987), pp. 1–3.
43. Ibid.
44. *Tass* in *SWB–USSR*, 4 November 1987; *Izvestiia*, 7 November 1987; and *Pravda*, 5 November 1987.
45. Aleksandr Zotov, 'Palestine: Forty Years of Tragedy', *New Times*, 48 (December 1987), pp. 18–21.
46. *Radio Voice of Lebanon* in *SWB–ME*, 3 December 1987.
47. Primakov in *Radio Israel* in *SWB–ME*, 10, 11 December 1987.
48. *Pravda*, 23 March 1988; and *Literaturnaia gazeta*, 29 March 1988.
49. *Radio Moscow* in *SWB–USSR*, 22 December 1987.
50. Interview with Arafat in *Literaturnaia gazeta*, 27 January 1988; *Sovetskaia Rossiia*, 20 January 1988; and *Radio Moscow* in *SWB–USSR*, 16 January 1988.
51. Message from Gorbachev to Arafat in *Pravda*, 17 December 1987; *Pravda*, 20 December 1987; and Dmitrii Zgerskii, 'Two Approaches', *New Times*, 3 (January 1988), p. 9.
52. *Komsomol'skaia pravda*, 2 March 1988.
53. Shevardnadze in *Pravda*, 19 March 1988.
54. *Pravda*, 13 February 1988; *Tass* in *SWB–USSR*, 6 March 1988; and Evgennii Korshunov, 'Separate Deals Again', *New Times*, 10 (October 1988), p. 8.
55. *Radio Moscow* in *SWB–USSR*, 9 April 1988.
56. Salah Khalaf in *Radio Voice of Palestine* in *SWB–ME*, 28 April 1988. See also Yasir Abd Rabbu in *Radio Monte Carlo* in *SWB–ME*, 20 May 1988; and PLO denial in *International Herald Tribune*, 12 April 1988.
57. *Radio Monte Carlo* in *SWB–ME*, 11 March 1988.
58. For example, see Soviet–Egyptian Joint Communiqué in *Pravda*, 22 May 1988.
59. Hani al-Hasan in *Radio Monte Carlo* in *SWB–ME*, 20 May 1988; and Salah Khalaf in *Al-Usbu' Al-Arabi*, 15 August 1988.
60. *Radio Voice of Palestine* in *SWB–ME*, 28 April 1988.
61. Letter from Mahmud Abbas, 15 July 1992.
62. Salah Khalaf in *MENA* in *SWB–ME*, 12 August 1988.
63. Letter from Mahmud Abbas from Tunis, 15 July 1992.
64. Abdullah al-Hurani in *Al-Anba'*, 15 October 1988; *INA* in *SWB–ME*, 15 October 1988; and *MENA* in *SWB–ME*, 15 October 1988. See also *Le Monde*, 14 October 1988.
65. *WAKH* in *SWB–ME*, 16 October 1988.
66. Interview with Deputy Foreign Minister Vladimir Petrovskii in *Al-Hawadith*, 21 October 1988; and with Foreign Ministry Head of Middle East Section Vladimir Poliakov in *Le Quotidien de Paris*, 13 October 1988.

67. *Tass* in *SWB–USSR*, 15 November 1988; and Aleksandr Zotov, 'A Bid for Statehood', *New Times*, 48 (November 1988), p. 15.
68. For example, see *Izvestiia*, 18, 20, 27 November 1988; *Pravda*, 21 November 1988; and *Krasnaia Zvezda*, 29 November 1988.
69. Pavel Demchenko, 'Revolutsiia kamnei', *Azia i Afrika segodnia*, 1 (January 1989), p. 11; and Zotov, 'A Bid for Statehood', p. 15.
70. *Pravda*, 19 November 1988.
71. Ibid.
72. *Krasnaia Zvezda*, 25 November 1988.
73. *Tass* in *SWB–USSR*, 17 December 1988.
74. *Izvestiia*, 24 February 1989.
75. Talks with Ismat Abd al-Majid in *Tass* in *SWB–USSR*, 20 February 1988.
76. Ibid.
77. Speech in Egypt in *Tass* in *SWB–USSR*, 23 February 1989.
78. Talks with Moshe Arens, *Radio Moscow* in *SWB–USSR*, 22 February 1988.
79. Talks in Amman, *Tass* in *SWB–USSR*, 19 February 1989.
80. Speech in Egypt, *Tass* in *SWB–USSR*, 23 February 1988.
81. Meeting with Arens, *Radio Moscow* in *SWB–USSR*, 22 February 1989. See also Shevardnadze's review of his visit in *Pravda*, 2 March 1989.
82. See US Secretary of State, James Baker, address to the American–Israeli Public Affairs Committee on 22 May 1989 in Lukacs, *The Israeli–Palestinian Conflict*, pp. 123–8.
83. E. H. Carr, *The Twenty Years Crisis: 1919–1939* (London: Macmillan, 1939), p. 80.
84. *Radio Amman* in *SWB–ME*, 7 July 1991.
85. Arafat Speech at Baghdad Summit in *Radio Republic of Iraq* in *SWB–ME*, 28 May 1990.
86. *International Herald Tribune*, 22 December 1990.
87. *Middle East International*, No. 407, 30 August 1991, p. 3.
88. *International Herald Tribune*, 16 January 1990.

CONCLUSIONS

1. See Richard K. Hermann, 'Russian Policy in the Middle East: Strategic Change and Tactical Considerations', *Middle East Journal*, 48:3 (Summer 1994), pp. 464–5.
2. *ITAR-TASS*, 23 March 1995.
3. Quoted in Yehuda Lukacs (ed.), *The Israeli–Palestinian Conflict: A Documentary Record* (Cambridge: Cambridge University Press, 1992), p. 88.
4. For an excellent analysis of Arab strategic thinking since the end of the Cold War, see Ibrahim A. Karawan, 'Arab Dilemmas in the 1990s: Breaking Taboos and Searching for Signposts', *Middle East Journal*, 48:3 (Summer 1994), p. 435.
5. Edward Said, *Peace and its Discontents: Gaza–Jericho 1993–5* (London: Vintage, 1995), p. 87.

Bibliography

PRIMARY SOURCES

Soviet and East European newspapers and journals

Aziia i Afrika segodnia
International Affairs (Moscow)
Izvestiia
Kommunist
Komsomol'skaia pravda
Krasnaia zvezda
Literaturnaia gazeta
Mirovaia ekonomika i mezhdunarodnye otnosheniia
Narody Azii i Afriki
Neues Deutschland (East Berlin)
New Times
Pravda
Sovetskoe gosudarstvo i pravo
Sovetskaia Rossiia
SShA: ekonomika, politika, ideologiia
Tass
Trud
World Marxist Review (Prague)
Za rubezhom

Arabic newspapers and journals

Al-Ahram (Cairo)
Akhbar al-Yawm (Cairo)
Al-Dustur (Amman)
Filastin al-Thawra (Beirut and, after 1982, Nicosia)
Al-Hadaf (Beirut and, after 1982, Damascus)
Al-Hawadith (Beirut)
Al-Hayat (Beirut)
Al-Hurriya (Beirut and, after 1982, Nicosia)
Al-Ittihad (Abu Dhabi)
Al-Khalij (Abu Dhabi)
Al-Kifah al-'Arabi (Beirut)
Al-Muharrir (Beirut and Paris)
Al-Nahar (Beirut)
Al-Nahar al-'Arabi wa'l-Duwali (Paris and Zurich)
Al-Qabas (Kuwait)
Al-Safir (Beirut)
Al-Sayyad (Beirut)

Shu'un Filastiniyya (Beirut and, after 1982, Nicosia)
Al-Siyassa (Kuwait)
Al-Taqrir (Abu Dhabi)
Tishrin (Damascus)
Al-Usbu' al-'Arabi (Beirut)
Al-Watan (Kuwait)
Ruz al-Yusuf (Beirut)

Newspapers and journals in other languages

Afrique-Asie
Agence France Presse
Arab Report and Record
Christian Science Monitor
Egyptian Gazette
Financial Times
Frankfurter Allgemeine Zeitung
Guardian
Israel & Palestine (Paris)
Jerusalem Post
Jeune Afrique
Le Figaro
Le Monde
Le Quotidien de Paris
Middle East International
Monday Morning (Beirut)
New York Times
Observer
Paris Match
Times
Toronto Star
Wall Street Journal

Radio and television broadcasts

BBC Summary of World Broadcasts: Part 1 – The USSR
BBC Summary of World Broadcasts: Part 4 – The Middle East

Collections of documents; annual reports

Al-kitab al-sanawi li'l-qadiya al-filastiniyya (Beirut: Institute of Palestine Studies, yearly from 1965–76)
Al-watha'iq al-filastiniyya al-'arabiyya (Beirut: Institute of Palestine Studies, yearly from 1965–76)
Daniel Dishon (ed.) *Middle East Record* (Tel Aviv: Shiloah Center, annually 1967–70)
International Documents on Palestine (Beirut: Institute of Palestine Studies and Kuwait University, yearly from 1965–81)
Lukacs, Yehuda, *The Israeli–Palestinian Conflict: A Documentary Record,*

1967–1990 (Cambridge: Cambridge University Press, 1992)
Middle East Contemporary Survey (Tel Aviv: Shiloah Center, annually 1976–88)
Ministerstvo inostrannykh del SSSR, *SSSR i blizhnevostochnoe uregulirovanie, 1967–1988: dokumenty i materialy* (Moscow: Politizdat, 1989)
Ro'i, Yaacov, *From Encroachment to Involvement: A Documentary Study of Soviet Policy in the Middle East, 1945–1973* (New York: Transaction Books, 1974)
The USSR and the Middle East: Problems of Peace and Security, 1947–1971 (Moscow: Novosti Press Agency, 1972)

Memoirs

Abu Iyad with Eric Rouleau, *My Home, My Land* (New York: Times Books, 1981)
Brzezinski, Zbigniew, *Power and Principle: Memoirs of the National Security Adviser, 1977–1981* (London: Weidenfeld & Nicolson, 1983)
Carter, Jimmy, *Keeping Faith: Memoirs of a President* (New York: Bantam Books, 1982)
Dayan, Moshe, *Breakthrough: A Personal Account of the Egypt–Israel Peace Negotiations* (New York: Alfred A. Knopf, 1981)
Fahmi, Ismail, *Negotiating For Peace in the Middle East* (London: Croom Helm, 1983)
Ford, Gerald R., *Time to Heal* (New York: Harper & Row and Reader's Digest, 1979)
Gromyko, Andrei, *Memories* (London: Hutchinson, 1989)
Haig, Alexander M., *Caveat: Realism, Reagan, and Foreign Policy* (New York: Macmillan, 1984)
Heikal, Mohammed, *The Cairo Documents* (New York: Doubleday, 1973)
——, *The Road to Ramadan* (London: Collins, 1975)
——, *Sphinx and Commissar: The Rise and Fall of Soviet Influence in the Middle East* (London: Collins, 1978)
Kissinger, Henry, *The White House Years* (Boston: Little, Brown, 1979)
——, *Years of Upheaval* (Boston: Little, Brown, 1982)
Shuqayri, Ahmad, *Min al-qimma ila al-hazima* (Beirut: n.p., 1971)
Vance, Cyrus, *Hard Choices: Critical Years in America's Foreign Policy* (New York: Simon & Schuster, 1983)

Interviews

Mahmud Abbas (Abu Mazin), PLO Executive Committee Member, Letter from Tunis, 15 July 1992
Viktor Bukharkov, Head of Arab Section of the Soviet Afro-Asian Solidarity Committee, Moscow, 8 January 1991
Aleksandr Golytsin, Counsellor to the Soviet Embassy in London, London, 15 May 1990
Abd al-Latif Abu Hijlih (Abu Ja'far), Deputy Head of the Political Department of the PLO, Tunis, 19 June 1992
Tigran Karakhanov, Deputy Head of the Arab Section of the USSR Foreign Ministry, Moscow, 15 January 1991

Marai' Abd al-Rahman (Abu Faris), General Secretary of Palestine Committee for NGOs, Tunis, 20 and 27 June 1992
Sulayman al-Najjab, PLO Executive Committee Member and PCP Politburo Member, Tunis, 17 June 1992
Vitalii Naumkin, Head of Arab Section of Oriental Institute of the Academy of Sciences, Moscow, 28 January 1991
Andrei Zakharov, Head of Arab Section of the CPSU Central Committee International Department, Moscow, 29 January 1991

SECONDARY SOURCES

Books and articles in Russian

Alestin, F., *Palestina v petle sionizma. Prestupniki. Zhertvy. Svideteli. Sud'i* (Moscow: Iuridicheskaia literatura, 1988)
——, *Antikommunizm i antisovetizm professiia sionistov* (Moscow: Politizdat, 1971)
Baryshev, A. P., *Blizhnii Vostok: problemy mira na rubezhe 80-x godov* (Moscow: Znanie, 1979)
——, *SSSR v bor'be za spravedlivoe blizhnevostochnoe uregulirovanie* (Moscow: Znanie, 1985)
Blizhnevostochnyi konflikt i pozitsiia Sovetskogo Soiuza (iiun' 1967 goda-iiun' 1974 g.) (Moscow: Novosti Press Agency, 1974)
Bol'shakov, V. V., *Sionizm na sluzhbe antikommunizma* (Moscow: Politizdat, 1972)
Borisov, R. V., *SShA: blizhnevostochnaia politika v 70-e gody* (Moscow: Nauka, 1982)
Brutents, K., *Osvobodiesia strany v 70-e gody* (Moscow: Politizdat, 1979)
Dadiani, L. R., *Ideologiia i praktika mezhdunarodnogo sionizma* (Moscow: Politizdat, 1978)
Dmitriev, E. D., *Palestinskii uzel* (Moscow: Mezdunarodnye otnosheniia, 1978)
——, *Palestinskaia tragediia* (Moscow: Mezhdunarodnye otnosheniia, 1986)
——, 'Palestinskoe dvizhenie soprotivleniia – na novykh rubezhakh', MEiMO, 8 (1987)
Evseeva, E. A. (ed.), *Sionizm – pravda i vymysly* (4 vols; Moscow: Nauka, 1978, 1980, 1983 and 1987)
Gorbatov, O. M. and Cherkasskii, L. Y., *Bor'ba SSSR za obespechenie prochnogo i spravedlivogo mira na Blizhnem Vostoke 1967–1980* (Moscow: Nauka, 1980)
Govoriat fakty (Seriia "mezhdunarodnaia" otvechaet na voprosy po problemam blizhnevostochnogo uregulirovaniia) (Moscow: Znanie, 1986)
Kiselev, V. I., *Palestinskaia problema i blizhnevostochnyi krizis* (Kiev: Politizdat, 1983)
——, *Palestinskaia problema v mezhdunarodnykh otnosheniiakh* (Moscow: Nauka, 1988)
Korneev, L. A., *Klassovaia sushchnost' sionizma* (Kiev: Politizdat, 1982)
Ladeikin, V.P., *Istochnik opasnogo krizisa* (Moscow: Politizdat, 1973)
——, and Dmitriev, E. D., *Put' k miru na Blizhnem Vostoke* (Moscow: Mezdunarodnye otnosheniia, 1974)

208 *Bibliography*

Landa, R. G., 'Osvoboditel'naia bor'ba arabov Palestiny (1948–1967)', *Narody Azii i Afriki*, 1 (1976)
——, 'Iz istorii Palestinskogo dvizheniia soprotivleniia (1967–1971)' *Narody Azii i Afriki*, 4 (1976)
——, 'Sovremennyi etap bor'by Palestinskogo dvizheniia soprotivleniia (1971–1976)', *Narody Azii i Afriki*, 5 (1976)
Lebedev, E. A. (ed.), *Noveishchaia istoriia arabskykh stran Azii 1917–1985* (Moscow: Nauka, 1988)
Losev, S. A., and Tysovskii, Y. K., *Blizhnevostochnyi krizis: neft' i politika* (Moscow: Mezhdunarodnye otnosheniia, 1980)
Lutskii, V. B., *Palestinskaia problema* (Moscow: Nauka, 1946)
Medvedko, L. I., *K vostoku i zapadu ot Suetsa* (Moscow: Politizdat, 1980)
——, *Etot blizhnii buriashchii Vostok* (Moscow: Politizdat, 1985)
Mikhailov, F. M., *U politicheskoi karty mira* (Moscow: Znanie, 1985)
Nesuk, N. D., Poliuk, S. P. and Ksendzyk, N. N., *Mezhdunarodnaia solidarnost' s bor'boi arabskikh narodov za spravedlivyi mir na Blizhnem Vostoke, 1967–1988* (Kiev: Naukogo dumka, 1989)
Osipov, A. I., *SShA i arabskie strany: 70-e gody – nachalo 80-x godov* (Moscow: Nauka, 1980)
Primakov, E. M., *Anatomiia blizhnevostochnogo konflikta* (Moscow: Mysl' 1978)
——, *Istoriia odnogo sgovora* (Moscow: Politizdat, 1986)
Pyrlin, E. D., *Palestinskaia problema – vazhneishii faktor blizhnevostochnogo uregulirovaniia* (Moscow: Nauka, 1978)
——, 'Palestinskoe natsional'no-osvoboditel'noe dvizhenie i blizhnevostochnoe uregulirovanie', *Sovetskoe gosudarstvo i pravo*, 10 (1977)
Tolkunov, L., *Blizhnii Vostok: ot voiny k peregovoram* (Moscow: Novosti Press Agency, 1974)
Zakharov, A. M. and Fomin, O. I., *Kemp Devid: Politika, obrechennaia na proval* (Moscow: Mezhdunarodnye otnosheniia, 1982)
Zviagel'skaia, I. D., *"Konfliktnaia politika": SShA na Blizhnem i Srednom Vostoke* (Moscow: Nauka, 1990)

Books and articles in Arabic

Abbas, Mahmud, *Bayna al-tahlil wa'l-taqlil* (Beirut: Dar al-Quds, 1982)
Abu Aun, Rif'at, 'Al-ittihad al-sofieti wa'l-thawra al-filastiniyya, 1925–1975', *Shu'un Filastiniyya*, 41–42 (September 1975)
Abu Sharar, Majid, Abu Ali Mustafa, Yasir Abd Rabbu, Muhammad Khalifa, and Arabi Awad, 'Qadiyyat al-nidal al-watani fi'l-diffa al-gharbiyya wal-qita' ghaza', *Shu'un Filastiniyya*, 118 (September 1981) and 119 (October 1981)
Alush, Naji, 'Al-ahzab al-shuyu'iyya wa-'arabiyya wa'l-qadiyya al-filastiniyya ba'd adwan 1967', *Shu'un Filastiniyya*, 4 (September 1971)
Amar, Muhammad, 'Al-ittihad al-sofieti wal-sira' al-arabi al-isra'ili: Mahlula lil-fahm wa da'wa lil-fi'l', *Mustaqbal al-Arab*, 118 (December 1988)
Awad, Arabi, 'Hawla al-wahda al-wataniyya al-filastinniya', *Shu'un Filastiniyya*, 94 (September 1979)
Dabagh, Salah, *Al-ittihad al-sofieti wa-qadiyyat Filastin* (Beirut: PLO Research Centre, 1968)

Darwish, Mahmud, 'Azif al-kaman 'ala al-jamjama', *Shu'un Filastiniyya*, 25 (September 1973)

English, Cynthia, 'Mawqif al-ittihad al-sofieti min al-qadiyya al-filastiniyya wa-munazzamat al-tahrir, 1947–1982', *Shu'un Filastiniyya*, 148–9 (July–August 1985)

Haidari, Nabil, 'Munazzamat al-tahrir al-filastiniyya fi'l-sharq al-awsat', *Shu'un Filastiniyya*, 187 (January 1988)

Hawatmah, Na'if, 'Ma huwa al-matlub li-ta'ziz al-wahda al-wataniyya al-filastiniyya', *Shu'un Filastiniyya*, 103 (June 1980)

Al-Khatib, Isheq, 'Ala hamish al-alaqat al-sofietiyya-filastiniyya al-muqawama 'ala al-tariq al-sa'b', *Shu'un Filastiniyya*, 37 (September 1974)

'Mubahathat al-wafd al-filistani fi Musku', *Al-Taqrir*, 3:10 (1987)

Shafiq, Munir, 'Munaqasha ma' al-hizb al-shuyu'iyya al-urduni', *Shu'un Filastinyya*, 13 (September 1972)

Al-Sharif, Mahir, *Al-shuyu'iyun wa qadiyyat al-nidal al-watani al-rahin* (Damascus: Center of Socialist Research and Study in the Arab World, 1988)

Books and articles in English

Abu Khalil, Assad, 'Internal Contradictions in the PFLP: Decision Making and Policy Orientation', *Middle East Journal*, 41:3 (Summer 1987)

Abu-Lughod, Ibrahim, 'Flexible Militancy: Report on the Sixteenth Palestine National Council', *Journal of Palestine Studies*, 12:4 (Summer 1983)

Ajami, Fuad, *The Arab Predicament* (Cambridge: Cambridge University Press, 1981)

Andrew, Christopher and Oleg Gordievsky, *KGB: The Inside Story of its Operations from Lenin to Gorbachev* (London: Sceptre, 1991)

Aruri, Naseer, 'The PLO and the Jordan Option', *Third World Quarterly*, 7:4 (October 1985)

Bailer, Seweryn and Joan Afferica, 'Reagan and Russia', *Foreign Affairs*, 61:2 (Winter 1982–3)

Ball, George, *Error and Betrayal in Lebanon: An Analysis of Israel's Invasion of Lebanon and the Implications for US–Israeli Relations* (Washington DC: Foundation for Middle East Peace, 1984)

Bar-Simon-Tov, Yaacov, *The Israeli–Egyptian War of Attrition, 1969–1970* (New York: Columbia University Press, 1980)

Behbehani, Hashim S. H., *China's Foreign Policy in the Arab World, 1955–1975: Three Case Studies* (London: Kegan Paul International, 1981)

Beinin, Joel, 'The Palestine Communist Party, 1919-1948', *MERIP*, 15 (March 1977)

——, *Was the Red Flag Flying There?: Marxist Politics and the Arab–Israeli Conflict in Egypt and Israel, 1948–1965* (London: I. B. Tauris, 1990)

Ben-Zvi, Avraham, *The American Approach to Superpower Collaboration in the Middle East 1973–1986* (Tel Aviv: Jaffee Center for Strategic Studies, 1986)

Breslauer, George W., *Soviet Strategy in the Middle East* (Boston: Unwin Hyman, 1990)

Brynen, Rex, *Sanctuary and Survival: The PLO in Lebanon* (Boulder, Colo.: Westview Press, 1990)

Brzezinski, Zbigniew, François Duchene and Kiichi Saeki, 'Peace in an International Framework', *Foreign Policy*, 19 (Summer 1975)

Budeiri, Musa, *The Palestine Communist Party, 1919–1948: Arab and Jew in the Struggle for Internationalism* (London: Ithaca Press, 1979)

Cobban, Helena, *The PLO: People, Power and Politics* (Cambridge: Cambridge University Press, 1984)

Cohen, Michael J., *Palestine and the Great Powers 1945–1948* (Princeton, NJ: Princeton University Press, 1982)

Cohen, Raymond, 'Israel and the Soviet–American Statement of October 1 1977: The Limits of Patron–Client Influence', *Orbis*, 22 (Fall 1978)

Confino, Michael and Shimon Shamir (eds), *The USSR and the Middle East* (Tel Aviv: Israel Universities Press, 1973)

Conquest, Robert, *Stalin: Breaker of Nations* (London: Weidenfeld & Nicolson, 1991)

Cooley, John K., *Green March, Black September: The Story of the Palestinian Arabs* (London: Frank Cass, 1973)

——, 'The Shifting Sands of Arab Communism', *Problems of Communism*, 24: 2 (March–April 1975)

Dawisha, Adeed and Karen Dawisha (eds), *The Soviet Union in the Arab World* (London: Heinemann for the Royal Institute of International Affairs, 1982)

——, *Syria and the Lebanese Crisis* (London: Macmillan, 1980)

Dawisha, Karen, *Soviet Foreign Policy Towards Egypt* (London: Macmillan Press, 1979)

——, 'The Soviet Union and the Middle East: Strategy at the Crossroads', *World Today*, 5 (March 1979)

——, 'The USSR and the Middle East: A Superpower in Eclipse', *Foreign Affairs*, 61:2 (Winter 1982–3)

Deeb, Marius, *The Lebanese Civil War* (New York: Praeger, 1980)

Degras, Jane (ed.), *The Communist International 1919–1943* (3 vols; London: Frank Cass, 1956)

Eran, Oded, *The "Mezhdunarodniki": An Assessment of Professional Expertise in the Making of Soviet Foreign Policy* (Tel Aviv: Turtledove Press, 1979)

Evron, Yair, *War and Intervention in Lebanon: The Israeli-Syrian Deterrence Dialogue* (London: Croom Helm, 1987)

Frankel, Jonathan, *The Soviet Regime and Anti-Zionism: An Analysis* (Jerusalem: Hebrew University, 1984)

Freedman, Robert O., *Moscow and the Middle East: Soviet Policy Since the Invasion of Afghanistan* (Cambridge: Cambridge University Press, 1991)

——, *Soviet Policy Toward the Middle East Since 1970* (New York: Praeger, 1975)

Fukuyama, Francis, *Moscow's Post-Brezhnev Reassessment of the Third World* (Santa Monica, Calif.: Rand Corporation, 1986)

——, 'Nuclear Shadowboxing: Soviet Intervention in the Middle East', *Orbis*, 25:3 (Fall 1981)

Garfinkle, Adam, *Israel and Jordan in the Shadow of War: Functional Ties and Futile Diplomacy in a Small Place* (London: Macmillan, 1992)

——, 'Sources of al-Fatah Mutiny', *Orbis*, 27:3 (Fall 1983)

Garthoff, Raymond, *Detente and Confrontation: American–Soviet Relations from Nixon to Reagan* (Washington, DC: Brookings Institution, 1985)

——, *Soviet Military Policy: A Historical Analysis* (New York: Praeger, 1966)

George, Alexander, *Prevention* (Boulder, Colo.: Westview Press, 1983)

Gilboa, Yehoshua A., 'The 1948 Zionist Wave in Moscow', *Soviet Jewish Affairs*, 2 (1971)

Gilliard, David, *The Struggle for Asia, 1828–1914: A Study in British and Russian Imperialism* (London: Oxford University Press, 1958)

Golan, Galia, *Moscow and the Middle East: New Thinking on Regional Conflict* (London: Pinter Publishers for the Royal Institute of International Affairs, 1992)

——, 'The Soviet Union and the Israeli Action in Lebanon', *International Affairs* (London), 59:1 (Winter 1982–3)

——, *The Soviet Union and National Liberation Movements in the Third World* (London: Unwin & Hyman, 1988)

——, *The Soviet Union and the Palestine Liberation Organization: An Uneasy Alliance* (New York: Praeger, 1980)

——, 'The Soviet Union and the PLO since the War in Lebanon' *Middle East Journal*, 40:2 (Spring 1986)

——, *Yom Kippur and After: The Soviet Union and the Middle East Crisis* (Cambridge: Cambridge University Press, 1977)

Goodman, Melvin A. and Carolyn McGiffert Ekedahl, 'Gorbachev's "New Directions" in the Middle East', *Middle East Journal*, 42:4 (Autumn 1988)

Gorbachev, Mikhail, *Perestroika, New Thinking for Our Country and the World* (London: Collins, 1987)

Gowers, Andrew and Tony Walker, *Behind the Myth: Yasser Arafat and the Palestinian Revolution* (London: W. H. Allen, 1990)

Gresh, Alain, 'Communistes et nationalistes au Proche-Orient: le cas palestinien depuis 1948', *Communisme*, 6 (1984)

——, *The PLO: The Struggle Within* (London: Zed Books, 1988)

Halliday, Fred, 'The Arc of Crisis and the New Cold War', *MERIP* Middle East Report, 11:8–9 (October–December 1981)

——, *Cold War, Third World: An Essay on Soviet–American Relations* (London: Hutchinson Radius, 1989)

——, *The Making of the Second Cold War* (London: Verso, 1983)

Hammond, Paul Y. and Sidney S. Alexander (eds), *Political Dynamics in the Middle East* (New York: American Elsevier, 1972)

Hopwood, Derek, *The Russian Presence in Syria and Palestine, 1843–1914: Church and Politics in the Near East* (Oxford: Clarendon Press, 1969)

——, 'Soviet Policy in the Middle East', in Gustav Stein and Udo Steinbach (eds), *The Contemporary Middle Eastern Scene (Basic Issues and Trends)* (Opladen: Leske Verlag & Budrich, 1979)

Hosmer, Stephen T. and Thomas W. Wolfe, *Soviet Policy and Practice Towards Third World Countries* (Lexington, Mass.: Lexington Books, 1983)

Hough Jerry F., *The Struggle for the Third World: Soviet Debates and American Options* (Washington, DC: The Brookings Institution, 1986)

Hudson, Michael, 'The Palestinian Factor in the Lebanese Civil War', Middle East Journal, 32 (Summer 1978)

——, *The Precarious Republic: Political Modernization in Lebanon* (New York: Random House, 1968)

212 *Bibliography*

Irwin, Zachary, 'The USSR and Israel', *Problems of Communism*, 36:1 (January–February 1987)

Israeli, Raphael, *The PLO in Lebanon: Selected Documents* (London: Weidenfeld & Nicolson, 1983)

Kanet, Roger E. (ed.), *The Soviet Union and the Developing Nations* (Baltimore, Md.: John Hopkins University Press, 1974)

Karsh, Efraim, *The Cautious Bear: Soviet Military Engagement in the Middle East* (Tel Aviv: Jaffee Center for Strategic Studies, 1985)

——, *The Soviet Union and Syria: The Asad Years* (London: Routledge for the Royal Institute of International Affairs, 1988)

Kass, Ilana, *The Lebanon Civil War, 1975–1976: A Case of Crisis Management* (Jerusalem: The Hebrew University, 1979)

——, *Soviet Involvement in the Middle East: Policy Formulation, 1966–1973* (Boulder, Colo.: Westview Press, 1978)

Katz, Mark, *The Third World in Soviet Military Thinking* (Baltimore, Md.: John Hopkins University Press, 1986)

Kerr, Malcolm H., *The Arab Cold War: A Study of Ideology in Politics* (Oxford: Oxford University Press, 1975)

Khalidi, Rashid, 'Arab Views of the Soviet Role in the Middle East', *Middle East Journal*, 39:4 (Autumn 1985)

——, *Soviet Middle East Policy in the Wake of Camp David* (Beirut: Institute for Palestine Studies, 1979)

——, *The Soviet Union and the Middle East in the 1980's* (Beirut: Institute for Palestine Studies, 1980)

——, *Under Siege: PLO Decisionmaking During the 1982 War* (New York: Columbia University Press, 1986)

Kitrinos, Robert W., 'International Department of the CPSU', *Problems of Communism*, 33:5 (September–October 1984)

Klinghoffer, Arthur J. with Judith Apter, *Israel and the Soviet Union: Alienation or Reconciliation?* (Boulder, Colo.: Westview Press, 1985)

Korey, William, 'The Soviet Public Anti-Zionist Committee: An Analysis', in Robert O Freedman (ed.), *Soviet Jewry in the 1980s* (Durham: Durham University Press, 1989)

Krammer, Arnold, 'Soviet Motives in the Partition of Palestine', *Palestine Studies*, 2:2 (Winter 1973)

Lacquer, Walter, *The Road to War 1967* (London: Weidenfeld & Nicolson, 1968)

——, *The Soviet Union and the Middle East* (New York: Praeger, 1959)

——, *The Struggle for the Middle East: The Soviet Union and the Middle East, 1958–1968* (London: Routledge & Kegan Paul, 1969)

Lenin, Vladimir I., *The National Liberation Movement in the East* (Moscow: Progress, 1952)

Levgold, Robert, 'The Revolution in Soviet Foreign Policy', *Foreign Affairs*, 68:1 (1989)

Light, Margot, 'New Political Thinking', *Coexistence* 24 (1987)

——, 'Soviet Policy in the Third World', *International Affairs* (London) 67:2 (Spring 1991)

Lynch, Allen, *The Soviet Study of International Relations* (Cambridge: Cambridge University Press, 1987)

MccGwire, Michael, 'The Middle East and Soviet Military Strategy', *MERIP*, 151 (March–April 1988)
——, *Military Objectives in Soviet Foreign Policy* (Washington, DC: The Brookings Institution, 1987)
Maoz, Moshe, *Palestinian Leadership on the West Bank: The Changing Role of the Arab Mayors under Jordan and Israel* (London: Frank Cass, 1984)
Menon, Rajan, *Soviet Power and the Third World: Aspects of Theory and Practice* (New Haven, Conn.: Yale University Press, 1986)
Merari, Ariel and Shlomi Elad, *The International Dimension of Palestinian Terrorism* (Tel Aviv: Jaffee Center for Strategic Studies, 1986)
Miller, David Aaron, 'Jordan and the Arab–Israeli Conflict: The Hashemite Dimension', *Orbis*, 29:4 (Winter 1986)
——, *The PLO: The Politics of Survival* (New York: Praeger, 1983)
Mishal, Shaul, *The PLO under Arafat: Between Gun and Olive* (New Haven, Conn.: Yale University Press, 1986)
Napper, Larry C., 'The Arab Autumn of 1984: A Case Study of Soviet Middle East Policy', *Middle East Journal*, 39:4 (Fall 1985)
O'Neill, Bard E., *Armed Struggle in Palestine: An Analysis Of the Palestinian Guerrilla Movement* (Boulder, Colo.: Westview Press, 1978)
Owen, Roger (ed.), *Essays on the Crisis in Lebanon* (London: Ithaca Press, 1976)
Pennar, Jean, *The USSR and the Arabs: The Ideological Dimension, 1917–1972* (New York: Crane Russack, 1973)
Quandt, William B., *Camp David: Peacemaking and Politics* (Washington, DC: The Brookings Institution, 1986)
——, *Decade of Decisions: American Policy Toward the Arab–Israeli Conflict, 1967–1976* (Berkeley: University of California Press, 1979)
—— (ed.), *The Middle East: Ten Years after Camp David* (Washington, DC: The Brookings Institution, 1988)
——, Fuad Jabber and Ann Mosely Lesch, *The Politics of Palestinian Nationalism* (Berkeley: University of California Press, 1973)
——, 'Soviet Policy in the October 1973 Middle East War I', *International Affairs* (London), 53:3 (July 1977)
——, 'Soviet Policy in the October 1973 Middle East War II', *International Affairs* (London), 53:4 (October 1977)
Ra'anan, Uri, 'Moscow and the Third World', *Problems of Communism*, 14:1 (January–February 1965)
——, *The USSR and the Third World: Case Studies in Soviet Foreign Policy* (Cambridge, Mass.: MIT Press, 1969)
——, 'The USSR and the Middle East: Some Reflections on the Soviet Decision-Making Process', *Orbis*, 17:3 (Fall 1973)
Rabinovich, Itamar, *The War for Lebanon, 1970–1983* (Ithaca, NY: Cornell University Press, 1984)
Ro'i, Yaacov (ed.), *The Limits to Power: Soviet Policy in the Middle East* (London: Croom Helm, 1979)
——, *Soviet Decision-Making in Practice: The USSR and Israel, 1947–1954* (New Brunswick, NJ: Transaction Books, 1980)
—— (ed.), *The USSR and the Muslim World* (London: Allen & Unwin, 1984)
Rubinstein, Alvin, *Moscow's Third World Strategy* (Princeton, NJ: Princeton University Press, 1988)

——, *Red Star on the Nile: The Soviet-Egyptian Influence relationship Since the June War* (Princeton, NJ: Princeton University Press, 1977)

—— (ed.), *Soviet and Chinese Influence in the Third World* (New York: Praeger, 1975)

Sahliyeh, Emile F., *The PLO After the Lebanon War* (Boulder, Colo.: Westview Press, 1986)

——, *In Search of Leadership: West Bank Politics Since 1967* (Washington, DC: The Brookings Institution, 1988)

Salibi, Kamal S., *Crossroads to Civil War: Lebanon, 1958–1976* (London: Ithaca Press, 1976)

Sayigh, Yezid, 'Palestinian Military Performance in the 1982 War', *Journal of Palestine Studies*, 13:1 (Fall 1983)

——, 'Struggle Within, Struggle Without: The Transformation of PLO Politics since 1982', *International Affairs* (London) 65:2 (Spring 1989)

Schapiro, Leonard, 'The Soviet Union and the PLO', *Survey*, 23:3 (Summer 1977–8)

Scherer, John L., 'A Note on Soviet Jewish Emigration: 1971–1984', *Soviet Jewish Affairs*, 15:2 (1985)

Schichor, Yitzhak, *The Middle East in China's Foreign Policy, 1949–1977* (Cambridge: Cambridge University Press, 1979)

Schiff, Zetev, and Ehud Ya'ari, *Israel's Lebanon War* (New York: Simon & Schuster, 1984)

——, *Intifada: The Palestinian Uprising – Israel's Third Front* (New York: Simon & Schuster, 1989)

Scholch, Alexander (ed.), *Palestinians over the Green Line: Studies on the Relations between Palestinians on Both Sides of the 1949 Armistice Line since 1967* (London: Ithaca Press, 1983)

Schoumikhin, Andrey U., 'Soviet Perceptions of US Middle East Policy', *Middle East Journal*. 43:1 (Winter 1989)

Seale, Patrick, *Asad: The Struggle for the Middle East* (London: I. B. Tauris, 1988)

Sella, Amnon, *Soviet Political and Military Conduct in the Middle East* (New York: St Martin's Press, 1981)

Sestanovich, Stephen, 'Gorbachev's Foreign Policy: A Diplomacy of Decline', *Problems of Communism*, 37:1 (January–February 1988)

Shearman, Peter and Phil Williams (eds), *The Superpowers, Central America and the Middle East* (London: Brassey's Defence Publishers, 1988)

Shemesh, Moshe, *The Palestinian Entity, 1959–1974: Arab Politics and the PLO* (London: Frank Cass, 1988)

Simons, Thomas W., *The End of the Cold War?* (London: Macmillan, 1989)

Smolansky, Oles, *The Soviet Union and the Arab East under Khrushchev* (Lewisburg, N. Va.: Bucknell University Press, 1974)

Sneh, Moshe, 'The Soviet-Egyptian "Solution" to the "Israel Problem"', *International Problems*, 7:1–2 (May 1969)

Solmar, E. L., 'Document: Protocols of the Anti–Zionists', *Soviet Jewish Affairs*, 8:2 (1978)

Spechler, Dina Rome, *Domestic Influences on Soviet Foreign Policy* (Washington, DC: University Press of America, 1978)

——, 'The Politics of Intervention: The Soviet Union and the Crisis in Lebanon', *Studies in Comparative Communism*, 22:2 (Summer 1987)

'Special Document: The Soviet Attitude to the Palestine Problem: From the Records of the Syrian Communist Party, 1971–72', *Journal of Palestine Studies*, 2:1 (Autumn 1972)

Valkenier, Elizabeth, 'Revolutionary Change in the Third World: Recent Soviet Reassessments', *World Politics*, 38:3 (April 1986)

——, *The Soviet Union and the Third World: An Economic Bind* (New York: Praeger, 1983)

Wallach, John and Janet, *Arafat: In the Eyes of the Beholder* (London: Heinemann, 1991)

Whetten, Lawrence L., *The Canal War: Four Power Conflict in the Middle East* (Cambridge, Mass.: The MIT Press, 1974)

Yodfat, Aryeh, *Arab Politics in the Soviet Mirror* (Jerusalem: Israel Universities Press, 1973)

—— and Yuval Arnon-Ohanna, *PLO: Strategy and Tactics* (New York: St Martin's Press, 1981)

——, 'USSR Proposals to Regulate the Middle East Crisis', *International Problems*, 10:3–4 (December 1971)

Zak, Moshe, 'An International Conference on the Middle East', *Jerusalem Quarterly*, 37 (1986)

Index

216

Libya 131, 132, 133, 134, 143

Madrid Middle East Peace Conference
(1991) 167, 172, 173, 175
Malik, Iakob 59–60
Mao Tse-tung 37–8, 110
Maronite Christians 69–76, 78, 80, 85
Marxism 12, 13, 25–6, 109–10, 153,
154, 174
Al-Masri, Tahir 140
McGovern, George 102
Meir, Golda 19
Middle East
Britain's role in 3, 13, 16–17, 20
France's role in 13
Soviet Union role in 1, 3, 4, 8, 11,
25, 56, 114–15, 119, 135, 144–5,
167, 175–6
Tsarist Russia and 4, 7, 8–12, 21,
25, 174
Mirskii, Georgii 24, 41, 105
Monroe, Elizabeth 3
Mroz, John 112
Mubarak, Muhammad Hosni 155
Muhammed, Ali Nasir 121
Muhsin, Zuhayr 65, 97
Muliukov, Farid Seiful' 32
Murphy, Richard 140–1

Al-Najjab, Sulayman 150, 152
Nasir, Gamal Abd al- 22–3, 24, 30,
31–2, 34, 36, 39, 41, 42, 43, 44,
45, 67–8
National Alliance 137
Nazism 2, 14–15, 36
Netanyahu, Benjamin 172–3
'New Thinking' 1, 144–5, 153–7,
164–5, 167–8, 177
New Times 32
Nixon, Richard 41, 46, 50, 51, 56
Nkrumah, Kwame 34
North Atlantic Treaty Organization
(NATO) 21

Occupied Territories 41, 111, 120, 125,
145, 146, 171
October 1973 War 48, 49–55
Oman 155
Oslo Accords (1993) 2, 179
Ottoman Empire 7, 8–10, 13

Palestine
and Ottoman Empire 10–11
Britain and 10–11, 14, 15, 17, 18

conflict with Jordan (1970–1) 31,
43–7
Jews in 13–17
partition of 7, 16, 18, 24
Soviet Union and 7, 12, 13–16, 24,
28, 30, 31, 35–6, 48–9, 60–4, 78,
162–4
Tsarist Russia and 10–12
USA and 63–4, 92–3
see also specific Palestinian
organizations
Palestine Communist Party (PCP) 13–14,
17, 20, 110–11, 136–8, 140, 141,
147, 148, 150, 152
Palestine Liberation Army (PLA) 74,
75–6
Palestine Liberation Front (PLF) 136–7,
140, 169
Palestine Liberation Organization (PLO)
and China 33, 37–8
and Iraq 1, 2, 169–70
and Jordan 31, 41, 44–7, 70, 97,
110, 115, 122, 125–7, 129, 134,
138–40, 143, 145, 146, 157, 177
and Lebanon 69–70, 73–88, 114,
115–20, 127
and other PLO factions 148–52
and recognition of Israel 1, 52, 66,
67, 94–102, 106–7, 124, 145,
146–7, 152–3, 161–2, 164, 166,
176–7
Egypt and 30, 31–2, 41, 122
formation of 4, 7, 30, 31
Geneva Conference 50–5, 58, 62–3,
90, 93–104, 176
Rabat Summit 49, 59, 67, 68, 69
relationship with Israel 2, 172–3
relationship with Soviet Union 27,
30–1, 41–3, 48–9, 51–5, 57–63,
83–8, 90, 96–7, 99, 105–6, 110,
111–12, 116–17, 124–41, 146–8,
149, 151–2, 158, 159, 161–2,
165, 169, 177
relationship with Syria 70, 74–83,
86–8, 90, 108–9, 111, 114, 117,
127, 129–34, 137, 148–52, 157–8
relationship with USA 1, 89, 93,
94–5, 118, 121, 140–1, 143–4,
145–6, 164, 169, 177–8
Palestine National Council (PNC) 57–8,
65, 67, 96, 105, 110, 125, 126, 127,
137, 138–9, 144, 147, 148–9, 150–2,
156, 157, 158, 163, 164
Palestine National Front (PNF) 52, 111

THIRTY YEARS
WITH THE KGB

THIRTY YEARS
WITH THE KGB